Praise for *Leading Change*

"Jim O'Toole has written the essential work for organizations to survive and thrive in today's changing world. His intellectually penetrating thinking shows us how the sometimes conflicting problems we wrestle with—often in piecemeal fashion—fit together to form a complete picture, even as the picture itself continues to change. His message is so critical to the very existence of every organization that any leader who fails to heed his advice condemns his or her company to mediocrity and/or early death. It's that basic."

—Warren Bennis, professor and founding
chairman of the Leadership Institute at the
University of Southern California and author of
An Invented Life and *Why Leaders Can't Lead*

"*Leading Change* is inspiring from the start, giving us the keys to the future by helping us understand the discourse of the past. With great depth and clarity, Jim O'Toole reveals the essence and paradox of values-based leadership—that the leader's attitude toward people, philosophy, and process is more powerful than action."

—William F. Stasior, chairman and CEO,
Booz • Allen & Hamilton, Inc.

"The rigor of Mr. O'Toole's thinking, the broad spectrum from which he draws relevant cases, and the clarity and charm of his writing make this a must-read for those who accept responsibility for bringing their firms into the 21st century."

—*International Business*

"Intriguing reading, this book has something for anyone grappling with the challenges of leadership."

—*NAPRA ReVIEW*

"A thoughtful essay . . . O'Toole uses examples from art, history, philosophy, and . . . business to probe the answers to three questions: Why do organizations resist change? How can leaders effect change? What should the leadership philosophy be to most effectively (and morally) induce organizational change?"

—*Booklist*

James O'Toole

Leading Change

◆ ◆ ◆ ◆ ◆ ◆ ◆ ◆ ◆ ◆ ◆ ◆ ◆ ◆ ◆ ◆ ◆

The Argument for
Values-Based
Leadership

Ballantine Books • New York

• • • • • • •

http://www.randomhouse.com

Library of Congress Catalog Card Number: 95-96089

ISBN: 0-345-40254-5

Cover design by Kayley LeFaiver

Cover ii: Collection of the J. Paul Getty Museum, Malibu, California. James Ensor, *Christ's Entry into Brussels in 1889*, 1888. Oil on Canvas, 102½ × 169½ in.

Manufactured in the United States of America
First Ballantine Books Edition: April 1996
10 9 8 7 6 5 4 3 2

To Marilyn

Contents

Preface to the Paperback Edition

Practically on the same day the hardcover version of this book was published, the cartoon reproduced below appeared in Bill Watterson's syndicated comic strip, "Calvin and Hobbes." In three simple frames, Watterson succinctly captured the problem I had labored in dozens of pages to describe:

CALVIN AND HOBBES © 1995 Watterson. Dist. by UNIVERSAL PRESS SYNDICATE. Reprinted with permission. All rights reserved.

The problem identified by little Calvin confronts almost all of us who feel we've got the "right stuff" to lead change: *we have a great vision, but we fail to attract followers*. Seeking to overcome that rather formidable obstacle to the realization of our plans, we naturally search for some process, some guidelines, some sure-fire set of rules that will tell us how to get others to carry out our will. Indeed, countless scholars, consultants, and practitioners have anticipated our need for assistance on this score by preparing thoughtful recipes for "change management," including re-engineering, total quality, learning organizations, and the like. These varied methods and approaches are not only tried but true; that is, they are both tested and rational. The only difficulty with such cookbook procedures is that they do not address the most common underlying cause of the failure to bring about successful and meaningful change: ineffective leadership.

Transformation efforts seldom flounder because a would-be change agent has embraced a flawed set of procedures, or has been unfaithful in following the stages, steps, and rules experts prescribe for success. And the ineffectiveness of leaders seldom results from a lack of know-how or how-to, nor is it typically due to inadequate or rusty managerial skills.

Instead, when change fails to occur as planned, the cause is almost always to be found at a deeper level, rooted in the inappropriate behavior, beliefs, attitudes, and assumptions of would-be leaders. Simply put, effective change begins when leaders effectively begin to change themselves. Unfortunately, that truism is open to easy misinterpretation. When one starts to discuss "changing" leaders, psychologists reach immediately for their bag of handy instruments and seek to measure—and then change—leadership "styles." Such instruments are useful, maybe even necessary, but they are never sufficient. Creating leaders is not that simple.

Leadership, in the final analysis, is not about style but about ideas. Ultimately, it is ideas that motivate followers, and concepts powerful enough to energize people are typically broad, transcendent, even "philosophical" in nature. Such ideas are not learned by the mastery of technique, nor are they acquired through the application of psychological instruments (as useful as the best of these are in improving managerial and interpersonal skills). Lincoln never took a Myers-Briggs test; Gandhi never got "360° feedback." The ideas that are the currency of such great leaders are "idealized" images of a better tomorrow based on fundamental moral principles and universal values. It follows that, while there can be effective management absent ideas, there can be no true leadership. And that is why leadership is so hard to find, and why this book isn't an easy read!

In fact, history demonstrates that no social endeavor is more difficult than leadership. In the realms of both statecraft and organizational stewardship, effective leadership is as uncommon as it is essential. We have just begun to understand the essence and requisites of effective leadership: who leaders are, how they behave, what attitudes and ideas they possess. Thanks to a handful of scholars who recently have transformed leadership into a serious field of study, it is now better understood that the role of a leader is to create followers; the task of a leader is to bring about constructive and necessary change; the responsibility of a leader is to bring about that change in a way that is responsive to the true and long-term needs of all constituencies; and the greatest source of power available to a leader is the trust that derives from faithfully serving followers.

Learning to lead is thus not simply a matter of style, of how-to, of following some recipe, or even of mastering "the vision thing." Instead, leadership is about ideas and values. It is about understanding the differing and conflicting needs of followers. And it is about energizing followers to pursue a better end state (goal) than they had thought possible. It is about creating a values-based umbrella large enough to accommodate the various interests of followers, but focused enough to direct all their energies in pursuit of a common good. In practical business terms, it is about creating conditions under which all followers can perform independently and effectively toward a single objective.

Hence, the emphasis of this book is not where one might expect it to be. The central question addressed is: "Why do would-be leaders resist embracing the very ideas that would motivate followers?" We therefore do not ask, "Why do followers resist leaders?" but, rather, "Why do leaders fail to do the things necessary to overcome their followers' natural resistance to change?" In these pages we explore the paradox of why leaders fail to listen to their followers' true needs; why leaders fail to reframe issues in order to address those needs; and why leaders fail to set aside their own egos in order to energize followers to achieve the high objectives that are in the best interest of both leaders and followers. In exploring such questions, we get downright practical and factual, asking, for example, "Why did American executives resist for thirty years the sensible ideas advocated by such thought leaders as W. Edwards Deming and Peter Drucker—changes that were in the self-interest of corporate leaders to implement?"

In addressing such difficult questions, we examine leadership as a multidimensional phenomenon, in contrast with the prevalent unidimensional mode of assessing leaders on the singular measure of *effectiveness*. Leaders who effectively achieve their objectives are those who are typically called successful. After all, who could be called great leaders who failed to realize the ends they sought? But that necessary factor of effectiveness turns out to be insufficient. In the chapters that follow, we find that two other factors should be weighed in taking the measure of leaders. In addition to asking if leaders are effective, we must also ask, "Effective at *what?*" and "Effective *when?*" The values-based leadership advocated in these pages is different, therefore, from the prevailing modes in that its calculus includes the factors of *morality* (how change affects concerned parties) and *time* (why the desirability of any end must be measured over the long term). As we discover, those two added dimensions make all the difference in the world in solving Calvin's—and our own—problem of attracting followers.

In sum, the three frames from "Calvin and Hobbes" are extremely useful in illustrating the problem addressed in these pages. Yet, because solutions are more difficult to describe than problems, it might seem that we would need a museum full of drawings to illustrate the theme of this book: the argument for values-based leadership. Fortunately, a distinction between popular art and great art is the many (and deeper) levels of meaning to be found in the latter. In the introductory chapter, we find that some pictures are, indeed, worth a thousand words. I wish to thank Harold Williams of the J. Paul Getty Trust, and John Walsh of the Getty Museum, for generously granting permission to reproduce one such masterpiece on the inside cover.

I have revised Chapter Two for the paperback edition in order to clarify the difference between the higher-order task of values-based leadership and the lower-order activities associated with change management. In addition, at the end of Chapter Eight, I have added a summary of Peter Drucker's comments on the contents of that chapter. I am extremely grateful to him for taking the time to respond. Finally, I wish to thank the casts and crews at Ballantine Books and at Jossey-Bass Publishers for making it possible for this work to now reach a broader audience.

—James O'Toole
Aspen, Colorado,
November 1995

Preface to the Hardcover Edition

The genesis of this book was a recent decision by The Aspen Institute to create the Corporate Leaders Forum, a consortium of twenty corporations dedicated to preparing the next generation of executives to lead change. Not wanting to miss out on that exciting enterprise, I abandoned a well-cushioned university chair and headed for the mountains of Colorado. After twenty years of frustration with academia—where all change is resisted as a matter of principle—the commitment of the Forum executives to the difficult process of effectively and morally transforming their organizations energized me to write this book.

Nonetheless, I approached these topics with some trepidation. Leadership is too trendy a subject to inspire confidence in readers that one who writes about it is anything but a shameless gold-digger (and in an overworked vein, at that). Worse, *change* has become the mantra of the current era. In business organizations and government, we hear a constant murmur on the lips of executives of all stripes and persuasions about "the necessity of change," "the imperative of effecting major transformations."

I bother to write about these familiar themes because such popular talk is somewhat superficial and misleading. For starters, there is no shortage of change. Quite the opposite. As executives in the Aspen Institute Corporate Leaders Forum explain, leaders in the 1990s face all the change that they will ever need in the forms of disorder fueled by volatile economic conditions, rapid technological

obsolescence, turbulent international competition, market disloca-
tions, upstart institutional investors, and continually shifting political and social conditions. Of course, from time immemorial men
and women have complained of turmoil caused by unprecedented
changes; but there is reason to believe that in fact the depth of the
alterations experienced today is more profound than ever before.
Consider just one example of deep, unprecedented change in the
world of business—the imminent collapse of recognizable boundaries between nations, between firms, between business units, and
between functional disciplines. What precedent is there for managing amidst such chaos?

It is now increasingly recognized that the executive's challenge
is to pilot through these roiling seas in a purposeful and successful manner, to steer an appropriate organizational course in turbulent conditions. Hence, corporations must not simply change,
they must be transformed effectively. Executives say that nothing
could be harder.

In order to respond to the challenges of external chaos, the
management of change has become the prime occupation of those
who inhabit the executive suites of the world's leading enterprises.
Nearly everywhere, this requisite for change is being addressed
by one or more of a variety of powerful techniques: reengineering,
restructuring, downsizing, rightsizing, TQM, EVA, and the like.
Such techniques are designed to allow corporations to operate
more efficiently, usually by becoming smaller, leaner, and we hope,
smarter. It is increasingly clear to executives that while these techniques are absolutely necessary, they are not sufficient conditions for effective change. The fact is that such techniques, even
when they work, do not work well enough. For example, firms have
found that becoming smaller—even becoming markedly more efficient—does not equate with being effective and competitive.
Something is missing.

Executives increasingly believe that the missing element—the
necessary condition for long-term competitiveness—is *leadership*.

In particular, what is proving to be singularly effective is the emerging style of values-based leadership, both as motivation for constant innovation up and down all organization levels and as a source of unity and coherence across fragmented firm boundaries.

In sum, today's corporate executives believe they are struggling with an unprecedented leadership challenge *to create internal strategic unity within a chaotic external environment.* That is, they are convinced that today's leaders must create strong, shared corporate values to unite their increasingly decentralized operations, but they feel this is easier said than done in a world characterized by pluralism, diversity, and myriad other fragmenting forces. Moreover, some executives fear that the creation of shared values will lead to "group-think" and the accompanying loss of independent entrepreneurship and initiative that is needed more than ever throughout the ranks of their corporations.

Hence, that familiar imperative of contemporary leadership: organizations must decentralize, de-layer, and destroy bureaucracy in order to obtain the entrepreneurialism, autonomy, and innovation needed to serve customers effectively. Yet, in meeting that imperative, leaders must not lose the cooperation, synergy, economics-of-scale, and sense of community that are the central benefits of the corporate form of organization. In essence, the leadership challenge is to provide the "glue" to cohere independent units in a world characterized by forces of entropy and fragmentation. Only one element has been identified as powerful enough to overcome those centripetal forces, and that is trust. And recent experience shows that such trust emanates from leadership based on shared purpose, shared vision, and especially, shared values.

All of this is now familiar. Perhaps, it is too familiar. Indeed, most of today's executives agree with the above description of the challenges they face, as they agree with the general prescription for the kind of leadership they must provide. Yet, here's the rub—few leaders succeed at the task. Executives know what needs to be done and even how to do it. Nonetheless, they are unable to lead change effectively. Explaining the sources of this paradox and offering a practical way to resolve it are the purposes of this book.

While the problem I address is a familiar one, my approach is unorthodox. Instead of being the standard how-to manual (most of which are based on the narrow findings of academic social science research), the focus of this volume is broader, drawing insights from history, moral and political philosophy, and especially, the practical experiences of men and women in many different cultures and under diverse circumstances. I have been forced to this approach by necessity because *the how-to approach has proved impractical.* Admittedly, that conclusion is paradoxical, and therefore it presents the most formidable barrier to the acceptance of the unorthodox focus of this book. But, if decades of repetition of the orthodox, how-to approach has not helped leaders to become more effective, it stands to reason that the time has come to find a more efficacious tack.

Included in the pages that follow are distillations of lessons I have learned from over two decades of close observation of corporate leaders. My primary teachers have been men and women who have committed themselves to the long, tough slog of effecting meaningful change in their organizations. Thus, this is a practical book in that it is based on the successes and failures of the real leaders whose experiences I describe. Yet, that does not make this a how-to book, because the key lesson I have learned is that the primary determinant of a leader's success or failure is not a lack of know-how. Instead, the key variables are the leader's beliefs and attitudes. Hence, the somewhat unusual values orientation of this book.

Nor is this a "compleat guide to leadership." I start from the assumption that readers of this book have achieved a high level of competence in general business skills and are extremely knowledgable about their own industries. (It seems obvious that if a corporation is pursuing a flawed strategy, all the values-based leadership in the world won't save the day.) Hence, I address only the most difficult single question with regard to leadership: Why is it that competent leaders who seemingly do and say everything "right" may still be ineffective at leading change? Or to phrase the question as the most-common lament of the would-be leader: "If I'm offering the right strategy, why isn't anyone following me?"

Acknowledgments

It is the fashion today among authors of management books to pretend that what they offer has been generated whole cloth from their own fertile imaginations and rich experiences. I can't make that claim. Instead, I take my stand with the ever-generous Tom Peters (and a minority of like-minded authors) who gratefully acknowledge that what we have to offer is in fact a compendium not only of what others have practiced, but of what other writers have long preached. In my own case, I am proud to have been a "student" of several eminent "teachers," most notably Mortimer Adler, Warren Bennis, Peter Drucker, John Gardner, Max De Pree, and Robert Townsend—all of whom I have been fortunate to have had as mentors and friends. Moreover, I have been greatly influenced by the teaching of my former university colleagues, Betty Friedan, Edward E. Lawler, Barry Leskin, Morgan McCall, Ian Mitroff, Burt Nanus, and Kathleen Riordan. I am also lucky to have been in correspondence with W. Edwards Deming and have benefited (albeit too briefly) from his wisdom and insights in the two years prior to his death. While I never met him, I have built freely on the ground-breaking work of James McGregor Burns. My debt to each of these teachers is manifest on every page of this book.

I also wish to acknowledge the help and generosity of my colleagues at The Aspen Institute and the members of the Corporate Leaders Forum, with whom I first discussed the ideas presented here. In particular, I wish to thank the many partners of the distinguished consulting firm of Booz • Allen & Hamilton, who patiently and rigorously tested my assumptions in a series of challenging Aspen Institute seminars.

Finally, the shape of this book is the result of the advice and counsel of the fine team of editors at Jossey-Bass—rare publishers who practice the managerial state-of-the-art advocated in their fine publications.

My thanks to all these good and kind teachers whose wisdom and insights inform this book. And to them, my apologies if they should find I have not been a faithful disciple in these pages. The faults of wayward students should never be attributed to their teachers.

—James O' Toole
Aspen, Colorado
January 1995

The Author

. . . .

James O'Toole is vice president of The Aspen Institute where he heads all seminar programs, including the renowned Aspen Executive Seminar. His major responsibility at the Institute is as director of the Corporate Leaders Forum, a consortium of corporations dedicated to values-based leadership.

In 1994, O'Toole retired from the University of Southern California (USC) after a career of over twenty years on the faculty of the Graduate School of Business, where he held the University Associates' Chair of Management. At USC he had most recently been executive director of the Leadership Institute. For six years, he was editor of *New Management* magazine. Previous to that he was director of the Twenty-Year Forecast Project, where from 1973–1983 he interpreted social, political, and economic change for the top management of thirty of the fifty largest U.S. corporations.

O'Toole's research and writings have been in the areas of business and society, corporate culture, and leadership. He has addressed dozens of major corporations and professional organizations and has published over seventy articles. Among his twelve books, *Vanguard Management* was named one of the best business and economics books of 1985 by the editors of *Business Week*. His 1993 book, *The Executive's Compass*, which is a companion to this current volume, explores the philosophical origins of values-based leadership.

O'Toole received his doctorate in social anthropology from Oxford University, where he was a Rhodes Scholar. He has served as a special assistant to Secretary of Health, Education and Welfare, Elliot Richardson, and as chairman of Secretary Richardson's Task Force on Work in America. He has been a consultant with McKinsey and Company, has served as a Director of Field Investigations for the President's Commission on Campus Unrest and as director of The Aspen Institute Program on Education, Work and the Quality of Life.

In an American Council of Education survey, O'Toole was chosen among the "one hundred most respected emerging leaders in higher education." He has won a coveted Mitchell Prize for a paper on economic growth policy and was selected by his colleagues to receive USC's two highest academic awards, the Associates' prize for creative research and the Phi Kappa Phi award for the best faculty book. He has served on the prestigious Board of Editors of the *Encyclopædia Britannica* and was recently named editor of *The American Oxonian*.

"Christ Comes to Brussels"
An Introduction to Values-Based Leadership

The excruciating complexity of contemporary leadership was captured graphically in the influential nineteenth-century painting on the cover of this book. One's first glimpse of *Christ's Entry into Brussels in 1889* takes the breath away. The colors are garish, the multitude of faces depicted is surreal, and the daring theme is fittingly grand for the vast expanse of wall the painting occupies at the Getty Museum in Malibu, California. This 1888 work by the Belgian artist James Ensor is a marvel of form, color, and content— but a pretty picture it is not. Painted at the time when impressionists were producing their most beautiful baby-pink-and-powder-blue pictures, Ensor's masterpiece anticipated by some twenty years the gaudy, emotion-charged movement that would come to be known as expressionism.

The subject matter is a crowded street scene, the nineteenth-century equivalent of a New York ticker-tape parade to honor the return of a conquering hero. The celebrating crowd is frenzied, the myriad participants all joyously doing their own wild and crazed things. There is a band with a drummer in the foreground, but nobody is marching to his beat. This is a chaotic party—colorful, glorious, raucous, and, Ensor hints, decidedly democratic. Indeed, Ensor depicts the *demos* in all its self-interested diversity and variety; in this parade of the people, by the people, and for the people, there is no discernible beginning or end to the rowdy mass of humanity filling the streets of the Belgian capital.

Then it hits you: Where is Christ in all this confusion? You double-check the title to see if you read it correctly. Yes, you did; but shouldn't he be in the forefront, *leading* the parade? Shouldn't he be the visual focus of the painting? Studying this painting turns out to be a bit like playing "Where's Waldo?" After much searching, the Redeemer is finally located in the background, a little to the left of center, almost lost in a throng of revelers that threatens to engulf him.

This is unsettling to anyone, Christian or not, who has been raised on Western art. For nearly two millennia, all earlier depictions of Christ had placed him at the center of attention. Ensor reminds us of this tradition by portraying his modern Christ astride the onager on which he was said to have ridden into Jerusalem on Palm Sunday to the tumultuous welcome of the citizenry. In all previous versions of this familiar biblical scene, Christ is the subject. He isn't merely the largest figure in these paintings; he leads the parade. Whatever our religious beliefs—and it is essential to acknowledge that the primary theme of Ensor's painting is not religious—we are accustomed to seeing Christ depicted as king, at the head of every public manifestation, at the top of the hill even in death.

Ensor abandons this tradition. But his purpose is not to join the novelist Dostoyevsky in his cynical interpretation of the Second Coming. In a digression from the main narrative of *The Brothers Karamazov*, Dostoyevsky places his resurrected Christ in the middle of the Spanish Inquisition, where he is ingloriously rejected by a populace searching not for a leader to show them the hard path to freedom, but for a dictator who will tell them what to believe. Unlike Dostoyevsky, Ensor is no gloomy prisoner of Russian despotic darkness. The enemy of Ensor's Christ is neither Dostoyevsky's czar nor the New Testament's Caesar; instead, the Christ who visits Brussels must compete against the manifold distractions of modernity. In Ensor's painting, not a soul in the crowd pays a centime's worth of attention to the one who would be their savior.

And that condition turns out to be a pretty fair assessment of the starting place of all would-be agents of change in modern societies and organizations. The painting thus raises a question that has remained paramount to this day: Is leadership possible in modern, complex systems, or is "democratic leadership" simply an oxymoron?

Ensor understood that social chaos would soon arise from the secular democracy then aborning in Europe. A hundred years ago, he foresaw the seeds of the tradition-destroying trend that would eventually germinate and produce, among countless other cultural horrors, seventy-six channels of cable television. The painting forces the viewer to think about the unprecedented obstacles to effective leadership in a world that has grown, in the subsequent century, even more turbulent than Ensor's frenetic Brussels street scene. As chaotic as it may appear in the painting, that epoch was far simpler than ours: the relevant theater of operation was the local community and not the greater world, cross-oceanic communications entailed weeks and not split seconds, and no one had ever heard of environmentalism, microchips, or cultural diversity. Of course, leadership wasn't easy in late-nineteenth-century Europe— for that matter, it hadn't been a piece of cake in A.D. 33 either. Nonetheless, the radically altered scope, scale, and speed of modern life has complicated the challenge immensely. In particular, the sources of resistance to leadership are more varied and more numerous in our modern, pluralistic democracies. On this score, Ensor saw that henceforth leaders would face the challenge of having to lead without the traditional powers of station, sanction, or threat of suppression. Instead, like Christ, leaders would have to appeal to the minds and hearts of their followers.

Ensor causes us to wonder how *anyone* could lead from the middle of an inattentive crowd of individualists, each a political and social equal, and every last one bent on demonstrating that fact. Though people have always resisted efforts to bring about changes, even those in their own self-interest, Ensor suggests that modern times would be characterized by widespread resistance to being led at all.

I am confident that Ensor's painting is about these complexities of leadership in modern society; yet I also recognize that we are each a prisoner of our own discipline (hence a dentist sees the Mona Lisa as a warning about the perils of neglecting to floss, and the animal rights activist regards Picasso's *Guernica* as a protest against inhumane treatment of horses). Still, if we choose to view *Christ's Entry into Brussels in 1889* as a comment on the dilemmas of modern leadership, we may profitably employ the painting to focus our attention on an extremely practical question: How can any leader overcome the powerful forces of resistance to change?

Presumably, Christ has come to fin-de-siècle Brussels not simply to enunciate his central teaching to "love thy neighbor as thyself" but also to win actual converts to that cause. We may assume that his leadership goal is to change the beliefs and behavior of all the world, starting with as many Belgians as he can convert. But he finds himself alone, powerless, confronting a multiplicity of self-interested agendas in an amorphous crowd lacking any sense of followership. Where and how can he begin?

Traditionally, three generic answers have been given to such a question: to effect change, a leader can command, manipulate, or paternalize. Let us examine each alternative in turn.

1. Can change be commanded? Realistically, what would be the effect of Christ's picking up a bullhorn and barking the order, "Listen up, all you Belgians. From now on you have to love your neighbors!" Such an effort would be as predictably futile as a family member ordering a loved one to stop smoking. For even when it is clearly in our own self-interest to obey a command, we all bristle when we are told what to do. Save questions of obeying the law, in modern Western society no one is seen as having a right to impose his or her will on another adult. To do so is widely considered the ultimate act of

disrespect for the rights and integrity of the individual. In fact, when anyone attempts to impose his or her will on that of another, the predictable effect is to heighten the resistance to change.

With precious few exceptions, the era of the dictator, the czar, the general—even the traditional boss—has passed in Western society. Today we all feel entitled to a say in dealing with the problems that affect us all. We, all of us, will rule ourselves. It is ironic, however, that our cultural images of leadership remain rooted in the quite different past of czarist Russia and Inquisition-era Spain. When I ask even young undergraduates raised on the anarchistic milk of MTV, "Who comes to mind when you hear the word *leader?*" the names of generals, dictators, and tyrannical football coaches will be proposed. When I ask the same question of business managers, the contemporary figure most often cited is Singapore's velvet despot, Lee Kwan Yew. Paradoxically, then, to some degree we still long for the "strong leader," even as we rebel against anyone who dares to tell us what to do.

2. Can leaders achieve change by manipulating followers? The most enduringly popular treatise on leadership is Niccolò Machiavelli's sixteenth-century masterpiece, *The Prince*, in which the following advice is proffered: "It is necessary for a prince, who wishes to maintain himself, to learn how not to be good, and to use this knowledge and not use it according to the necessity of the case." Machiavelli thus advocated expediency as the only inviolable rule of leadership. To achieve his goal of power, any "prince" must manipulate his followers, using them as means to his personal end.

Can Ensor's Christ succeed in manipulating the masses into behaving according to his will? Though history shows that Machiavellian leadership often succeeds in the short term, it almost always fails ultimately because expediency cannot be concealed forever. Would the people of Brussels ever again trust Christ once they learned that he had lied to them? Still, many of the corporate heroes whose praises are currently sung in the press are those who transformed their organizations using expedient means that may have compromised the welfare of their followers. Again a paradox: as a society we celebrate leaders who in a corporate setting betray the very values that we espouse in our churches, homes, and communities.

3. Can change be shepherded? The central Christian metaphor of the leader is the Good Shepherd, the paterfamilias whose "children" are likened to a flock of sheep. The Good Shepherd differs from the Machiavellian leader in that he acts selflessly for the benefit of his followers. But Ensor tells us that this philosophy, too, has become anachronistic. In modern society, paternalism is preferred to tyranny; just don't expect it to work. How far would a materfamilias in business get today acting on the assumption that her employees are a flock to be herded by the organizational equivalent of the yank of a crook or the nipping of a sheepdog at their heels? The old line "I'm making you take this medicine for your own good" is likely to be welcomed only slightly more eagerly than the self-interested crack of a whip. Ensor's painting suggests that leaders today can no more be thought of as shepherds than their followers can be thought of as sheep. Indeed, over the past few years, leadership has been likened more often to herding cats than sheep. Although the concept of the Good Shepherd has its lingering attraction, its shortcoming is that today few people tolerate being paternalized.

While these three alternative models are quite distinct, they have in common an all-knowing leader who is wiser than the collective followers. Hence the observed tension between the long-standing cultural belief in, on the one hand, the necessity of a stern father as leader and, on the other, the more modern, individualistic values, which reached full flower in this democratic century.

So Ensor got the question right: If Christ were to visit Brussels today, how would he be able to lead from the middle of a distracted crowd imbued with the democratic ethos? Make the question more immediate: How can the manifestly un-Christ-like CEO of a publicly held corporation overcome resistance to change when the CEO's power is constrained by the diverse and conflicting interests of investors, board members, union chiefs, environmentalists, government regulators, and careerist fellow managers, all intent on marching to the beat of their own drummers? Indeed, how can any leader effectively transform an organization in the midst of competitive, technological, social, and political chaos?

The "Answer": *It All Depends*

Where can we turn for an answer to this question? We are told that we need only visit the groves of Academe to reap the benefits of science. In recent years, a near consensus has developed on the subject of leadership, a state of harmony quite unusual in the normally fractious scholarly community. There is currently a deep, widespread, and unquestioning academic commitment to contingency theory, which is the belief that to implement change, effective leaders do whatever the circumstances require. Hence, to whatever practical question that arises concerning how to lead, scholars now respond, "It all depends." The intellectual attraction of this concept is that it appears to be nonprescriptive, nonjudgmental, and nondeterministic.

Moreover, on the surface it appears responsive to the challenge depicted by Ensor. The theory seems to say that if the world has changed, the style of leadership must change to meet the altered conditions. Scarcely a soul alive who is influential in academia questions this received wisdom. Significantly, this now-conventional wisdom has also been embraced by most current corporate leaders. Yet evidence mounts that contingency, or situational, leadership is ineffective. All around we see the signs of failure: the depressing social and organizational indicators that point to the inability of leaders to bring about constructive change. Witness executives, the most up-to-date on the latest managerial techniques, who nonetheless admit that they, too, have trouble overcoming the resistance to change.

Why? Could it be precisely *because* they practice contingency leadership? It is common sense, after all, for leaders to assume that the contingency of chaos requires toughness. Thus whenever the pressure to perform builds, whenever the challenges of leadership seem overwhelming—as they almost always do in this chaotic era—the leader's temptation is to conclude that "this is one of those times when I've got to be tough." The problem with the belief that "it all depends," then, is that it confirms the cultural predisposition to seek out the wisdom of a stern father. Hence the puzzling phenomenon of reasonable men and women turning tyrannical upon assuming positions of leadership is explained, as is the continuing fascination with "men on white horses" who promise to bring order out of chaos. Paradoxically, then, contingency theory ends up being prescriptive, judgmental, and deterministic—exactly the opposite of what are claimed to be its greatest virtues. It is also ineffective in the long term: a contingent leader who acts tough even once will be seen as inconsistent, thereby destroying the trust that is essential to win people over to change.

A Values-Based Alternative to Contingency Leadership

There is cause, then, to challenge the conventional wisdom: Is effective leadership in fact a morally and behaviorally relativistic act? Is leadership, as claimed, really situational? Does it actually just "all depend," or are there some basic moral guidelines that are constant and noncontingent? In thinking about these questions, let us look again at Ensor's painting. If Christ wishes to overcome resistance to change, what choice does he have? What strategic and philosophical courses are open to him that are both practical and moral? If the three traditional courses of command, manipulation, and paternalism fail either or both the tests of morality and practicality, are there other viable choices, other contingencies, that we might consider?

I can imagine only one course that will be effective in winning converts to Christ's message of brotherly love. Christ must begin with the people closest to him in the crowd. First, he must get their attention. Anyone who has ever tried to engage strangers in conversation knows that there is only one certain way to do this: ask them questions about themselves. The opposite clearly won't work: if a would-be leader starts off by talking about personal concerns—personal values, beliefs, or ambitions—people will simply pay no attention. However, if the leader listens carefully to what the potential followers say they need and want and responds thoughtfully, they will become engaged in the process because they will have been given what they all crave: respect.

It may be objected that in following this strategy of listening, Christ would be behaving as manipulatively as any Machiavellian. Nothing could be further from the truth. Moral and effective leaders listen to their followers *because* they respect them and *because* they honestly believe that the welfare of followers is the end of leadership (and not that followers are the means to the leader's goals). President Dwight Eisenhower was confused slightly on this issue when he defined leadership as "the art of getting someone else to do something you want done because he wants to do it." While that is certainly a part of the art of leadership, it falls short on the essential moral dimensions of purpose and motivation. What creates trust, in the end, is the leader's manifest respect for the followers. That requires putting them first, as James MacGregor Burns explains: "Moral leadership emerges from, and always returns to, the fundamental wants and needs, aspirations and values, of the followers. I mean the kind of leadership that can produce social change that will satisfy followers' authentic needs. I mean less the Ten Commandments than the Golden Rule. But even the Golden Rule is inadequate, for it measures the wants and needs of others simply by our own."

Such leadership is not to be confused with the too common political practice of pandering to the base wishes of the lowest common denominator—promising whatever the masses think they want, even if that may be inherently evil. With regard to the base desires often expressed by the masses, President James Madison argued that, although leaders must listen intently to the stated aspirations of followers, they must not become prisoners to these literal demands. Instead, leaders must "discern the true interests" of the public from their stated desires and learn to address the underlying needs that the people as a body are unable to articulate. Madison wrote that the effective democratic leader must "refine the public views" in a way that transcends the surface noise of pettiness, contradiction, and self-interest.

Again, the cynic might say that that is precisely what the greatest Machiavellians—Hitler, Mussolini, and Stalin—did. To understand the difference, consider again the Christian myth. Christ offered a vision that transcended immediate wants, yet at the same time he encompassed these in a higher-order view of the common good. All moral and effective leaders so illuminate their followers' better sides, revealing what is good in them and thus ultimately giving them hope. This hope, this transcendent vision of a New Jerusalem, encompasses the followers' needs and aspirations—yet it is a better place than they could imagine on their own.

In the end, the leader's vision becomes *their* vision because it is built on the foundation of their needs and aspirations. They see in the vision what they desire, and they embrace it as their own. Christ's cause becomes their cause. Leadership becomes not a matter of Christ telling people to love their neighbors; instead, people come to want to love their neighbors of their own volition. There are no contingencies here; the only course for the leader is to build a vision that followers are able to adopt as their own *because it is their own.*

The logical test of a proposition is to see if its opposite is reasonable: Can we imagine a situation in which Christ would be successful in winning over the crowd by being tough, abusive, and unconcerned with their needs? How far would he get by commanding them to love their neighbors? Clearly, the leadership of change does not depend on circumstances: it depends on the attitudes, values, and actions of leaders.

Relatedly, the leader has no options when it comes to the practical issue of spreading the gospel. Can we imagine any way whereby Christ, acting alone, could convey his message to everyone in the crowd? No, it is clear that he must create disciples. He has no choice but to inspire others to lead the transformation as well. To be an effective leader, no one can remain a solo operator (even with the aid of television). Instead, one must become a *leader of leaders*. Christianity did not depend on Christ personally; it did not depend on the force of his personality, his charm, or, for that matter, his "media persona" (if one naively insists that technology can solve the human problem of leadership). The ultimate measure of Christ's leadership is that the movement he founded continued to spread after his death. In fact, from the moment of his first conversions, Christianity belonged not to Christ but to the Christians.

Even to people who, like myself, are not practicing Christians, Ensor's painting communicates a few absolute requisites for leading change. In complex, democratic settings, effective leadership will entail the factors and dimensions of vision, trust, listening, authenticity, integrity, hope, and, especially, addressing the true needs of followers. Without these factors, the likelihood of overcoming the ever-present resistance to change is all but nil. If this is correct, what is required to guide effective change is not contingency theory but, rather, a new philosophy of leadership that is always and at all times focused on enlisting the hearts and minds of followers through inclusion and participation. Such a philosophy must be rooted in the most fundamental of moral principles: respect for people. In this realm of morality, there are no contingencies.

In sum, to be effective, leaders must begin by setting aside that culturally conditioned "natural" instinct to lead by push, particularly when times are tough. Leaders must instead adopt the unnatural behavior of *always* leading by the pull of inspiring values. The difficulty lies in that imperative *always*. To be effective, leaders must change their attitude about followers forever and under all conditions. Moral leadership, by definition, cannot be situational or contingent. The reason is simple: if ever leaders revert to paternalistic behavior (which, as we shall see, many experts claim is appropriate in some situations), in doing so they will break trust with followers. The ultimate in disrespect of individuals is to attempt to impose one's will on them without regard for what they want or need and without consulting them. To behave paternalistically toward followers—even for their own good—is to deny them the basic right of individual dignity. Thus treating people with respect is what moral leadership is about, and nothing could be harder. But when there is organizational or social necessity for change, nothing is more practical.

Organization of the Book

In light of the foregoing, this book addresses three related questions:

- What are the causes of resistance to change?

- How can leaders effectively and morally overcome that resistance?

- Why is the dominant philosophy of leadership, based on contingency theory, neither an effective nor a moral guide for people who wish to lead change?

The approach to these topics differs from that found in many excellent books published over the past decade on the theme of leading change. Almost all of those were written from the perspective of corporate CEOs struggling to get their troops to accept a new corporate culture, a new ethic of customer service, or a new program such as reengineering. My focus is somewhat different. I am concerned with two levels of resistance to change. The first is that same important issue addressed by other authors: how a leader can motivate an organization to embrace a needed transformation. But, in addition, I am concerned with the chronic resistance to change among corporate leaders *themselves*. It is ironic that many of the executives who complain today that their subordinates resist change were the most vocal in rejecting decades ago the initial calls for planned organizational transformation by the likes of W. Edwards Deming and Peter Drucker. Indeed, the current need to act in a crisis mode might not have been necessary had business leaders embraced the ideas of such pioneering change agents.

In hindsight, of course, it was perfectly understandable that business leaders would reject such calls for change. *Everybody* resists change—particularly the people who have to do the most changing. We are not concerned here with pointing a finger at those—all of us, in fact—who have resisted necessary change. Instead, we address the most common error made by would-be agents of change. Potential leaders too frequently assume that others will recognize the potential benefits of their recommended changes and hence willingly adopt them by simple virtue of the fact that it's the right thing to do. That common mistake can confound the leadership efforts of otherwise perceptive individuals. Assuming that people will follow you because you are right is an error that trips up most potential leaders before they ever get out of the starting blocks. (Importantly, our focus is on the resistance to changes that are in the best interests of the followers; we are not concerned with rational resistance to would-be leaders with ignoble goals.)

The organization of the book is simple. Like a football game, it has two halves. The first half deals with followers' resistance to change, the second with the resistance of leaders themselves.

In the first half of the book, we explore the "unnatural" attitude of values-based leadership. We examine the experiences of leaders—in government, business, and elsewhere—who have brought about effective change in modern, complex settings. In today's advanced democracies, we see that contingency commanders may enjoy short-term success but values-based teachers are most effective at leading change over the long term. Reviewing the experiences of individuals who have inspired others to abandon the tyranny of custom, we conclude that the seeker of change is not engaged in a quixotic quest. Evidence indicates that people who understand why change is resisted—and are willing to make the personal investment required to overcome that resistance—are likely to achieve the goal they seek. Leaders overcome this chronic and inevitable pattern of resistance in only one way: by building an alternative system of belief and allowing others to adopt it as their own. That is the essence of values-based leadership. Moreover, to effect true change, one must become a *leader of leaders*, one who inspires *others* to lead the transformation. Such leadership is difficult to achieve because no formula, no documentable technique, and no replicable skill is involved. Instead, values-based leadership is an attitude about people, philosophy, and process. To overcome the resistance to change, one must be willing, for starters, to change oneself. In essence, then, values-based leadership is "unnatural."

These themes—the tyranny of custom, the natural resistance to change, the unnatural nature of values-based leadership, the requirement of enrolling others in the process of transformation, and the essential attitudes required of leaders—recur throughout this book. Indeed, these themes are repeated, in the words of John Kenneth Galbraith, with the predictable frequency of "the military symbolism of marching and combat in Protestant hymns and intercollegiate athletics."

The repetition is necessary for, as we shall see, most leaders in their guts are uncomfortable with the best alternative to situational leadership: the values-based philosophy described in the chapters that follow. We must recognize that in a world dominated by the realpolitik of contingency thinking, nothing appears more naive than leadership based on morality. Worse, to claim that contingency theory is wrong flies in the face of nearly everything that is taught in universities, runs against the grain of conventional wisdom, and frightens the timid because to so argue lends itself to a kind of unfashionable absolutism (in this relativistic era, nothing gets backs up like an argument that uses the word *always*). The purpose of the chapters to come is to counter that powerful opposition and to show why, if the goal is to bring about constructive change, values-based leadership is, yes, always more effective. We shall discover that this philosophy is both moral and practical. We begin this inquiry in Chapter One with a brief review of the careers of four familiar politicians, each a flawed, un-Christ-like individual in his private life who was, nonetheless, an effective leader of change because of the moral bond created with followers.

The second part of the book grows out of Drucker's observation that there is only one characteristic common to all leaders: *followers*. We therefore focus on how leaders go about creating followers. Our analysis includes a lengthy exploration of why people resist change—why we refuse to become followers. As this book is not a whodunit, there is no harm in revealing my conclusions: the major source of resistance to change is the all-too-human objection to having the will of others imposed on us. We look at a few sobering examples of individuals who, long before disaster struck, unsuccessfully attempted to convince others to change proactively in their own self-interest. From these examples we discover why for nearly five decades American industry was able to resist the ideas of such eminent thinkers as Drucker and Deming—ideas that, had they been embraced, would in all likelihood have spared the nation its competitive disasters of the 1980s.

In this review, we learn that all successful organizations become prisoners of comforting ideologies that eventually lead to their downfall. We see that the ability to ignore the warnings of people who know how to save us from ourselves is widespread in organizations, and we review the somewhat depressing evidence that there is a natural conservatism in all human societies that typically delays the acceptance of requisite change until it is too late. We learn that resistance to change is as prevalent among organization heads as it is among followers, and we see why would-be leaders who were "right" failed to attract followers. We also see that there is a marked pattern to resistance, a predictable enough pattern that allows us to formulate a theory of leadership with more substance to it than "It all depends."

Postscript. James Ensor, who painted *Christ's Entry into Brussels in 1889* at the time when Vincent van Gogh was doing his best work in the 1880s, died in Belgium in 1949. Having produced little of note during the last five decades of his long life, Ensor spent those years embittered by the fact that few people had recognized his early genius, and that few later gave him credit for having been the first to be right about the direction that art would take in the twentieth century. Others would get that credit and become known as the leaders of expressionism. Ensor came to identify with Christ as a leader who had been wrongly rejected. Ensor saw himself as a deserving leader who had failed to attract followers, and he blamed *them* for their lack of understanding.

Part One

. . . .

Leaders Leading Change

The Rushmoreans

An Indelible Lesson in Values-Based Leadership

When threatened by a proposed change—particularly when unable to refute the proposal logically and panic starts to set in—we unconsciously revert to the lowest level of defense: challenging the validity of the examples used to illustrate the general proposition. When Mother served us salad and admonished us to eat our vegetables, by adolescence we had learned to reply, "Iceberg lettuce is a terrible source of vitamins." Similarly, had I introduced values-based leadership with reference to a contemporary corporate leader, the general points would have been lost in the clatter of objections to this or that aspect of the leadership of whoever was offered as exemplifying the philosophy. (Peters and Waterman suffered this fate with *In Search of Excellence*: readers who resisted the changes advocated in the book did so not by arguing the merits of the authors' proposals but rather by gleefully proclaiming that many of the companies cited as examples lost money shortly after publication of the book.) That is why, in the Introduction, the example of Christ was the sole illustration: I did not want to give cynics an easy way out.

Yet there are problems with that choice—not the least of which is the difficulty for nearly everyone (James Ensor excepted) of identifying with the example: none of us is Christ-like; we are flawed and all too human. Hence the example may let us off the hook after all. Yet paradoxically, another unconscious manifestation of the resistance to change is to reject any example that isn't perfect. If

Mother used broccoli to illustrate her call for the consumption of more vegetables, we replied, "Broccoli may have lots of vitamins B and C, but it doesn't have any E!" Thus people who object to the policy consequences of Thomas Jefferson's declaration of human equality use the same diversionary tactic: "But he kept slaves!"

We will never be able to find the perfect leader. All are flawed because all are like us. Individuals long dead whom we have come to think of as heroes were, during their lives, ordinary human beings. That holds even for the famous heroes depicted on Mount Rushmore.

Mount Rushmore has never ranked high on critics' lists of great artworks; among the cognoscenti, the whole idea of those sixty-foot-high slabs of presidential granite is ridiculous. Even people who aren't jaded supersophisticates find humor in parodies of the famous profiles of the four presidents (a memorable cover of *Mad* magazine depicted Alfred E. Newman up there in Teddy Roosevelt's niche, between Jefferson and Lincoln). More seriously, the monument has been criticized for lacking democratic virtues. Although it was carved during the respectably bourgeois Coolidge administration, it looks more like a grandiose product of Stalinist realism, or the remnant of some long-lost Dakotan cult of personality.

Let the critics carp; I like the monument. What impresses me most is that somehow the right foursome was chosen. A case can be made for having included Madison (his administration was not a great success, but he deserves enormous credit for the Constitution, the Bill of Rights, and such nifty ideas as federalism and pluralism). Thanks to David McCullough's recent biography, Harry Truman would garner consideration if a modern annex were to be sculpted. Still, I'll stick with the existing Gang of Four—even if I am a bit uneasy about the official reason given for their choice. They were said to have been chosen because they each represent one of four major themes of American history: the founding (Washington), political philosophy (Jefferson), preservation of the Union (Lincoln), and expansion and conservation (TR). There's nothing much wrong with that logic, I suppose, but I much prefer to think of the four as the best representatives of a school of values-based leadership dedicated to democratic change. Let's now give a name to this philosophy—and to the great presidents who practiced it—and call it the Rushmorean school.

To shake nitpicking historians off our backs, we are not out to rewrite history here. Each of these presidents has been made the subject of searing revisionism by politically correct scholars bent on judging the past by present standards. We are accepting the lives and careers of the four presidents much as they have been told and retold by mainstream historians because our intent is simply to use Mount Rushmore as a mnemonic, a reminder of what great leadership is and can be, and the traits of the presidents as a convenient checklist for would-be leaders.

Nonetheless, we should acknowledge at the outset that each of the four Rushmoreans was quite different from the others in terms of social origin, educational and professional background, and personal interests and style; moreover, as presidents, they each faced quite different challenges, and their respective administrations achieved varying levels of success. Washington, in particular, stands apart from the other three in that he was not a deep thinker or a brilliant writer and lacked a coherent political philosophy. Moreover, there is an explicit philosophical link among the other three: Lincoln identified himself as a Jeffersonian, and TR associated his ideas with Lincoln's. But these and other important differences notwithstanding, the Rushmoreans were remarkably similar as leaders.

One is struck by these similarities on even a casual reading of the lives of the four presidents. Their many biographers use the same vocabulary in describing their leadership characteristics: courage, authenticity, integrity, vision, passion, conviction, and persistence. The ways in which each led are said to be similar: to varying degrees, they listened to others, encouraged dissenting opinion among their closest advisers, granted ample authority to their subordinates, and led by example rather than by power, manipulation, or coercion. They were all recognized as masterful teachers. In essence, all four were said to have inspired trust and hope in their followers, who in turn became encouraged to serve, to sacrifice, to persevere, and to lead change.

Courage is perhaps the most misleading of the virtues all four were said to possess. Although GW and TR loved the sound of bullets whistling past their ears, too much physical courage is foolhardiness, and even the devil-may-care TR knew when it was prudent to cut a retreat. The most significant manifestations of their courage did not occur in battle; their real courage was moral. It surfaced when they refused to become discouraged when their ideas, principles, visions—even their very selves—were publicly rejected, attacked, and vilified. That language is strong, but the Rushmoreans were not as universally loved during their lives as they have become since their deaths; in fact, it is not an exaggeration to say that during significant parts of their respective careers, they were each savaged by their opponents, the press, and even a few purported friends or allies. All four were repeatedly—and wrongly—accused of harboring despotic designs. Mark Twain called Roosevelt a clown; the socialist Eugene V. Debs called him worse: "This political pet of the plutocrats, this bogus reformer, this shrieking charlatan, this raving mountebank, this crazy-horse of Oyster Bay Ranch, this blood and thunder prophet, this opéra bouffe ghost-dancer, this blatant quack hero, this freak of froth and foam and buncombe, this nauseating moralizer, this dysenteric scold, this cattering midwife and meddler and all-around nuisance. . . ."

Doubtless there was more than a grain of truth to even such intemperate outbursts against the Rushmoreans. They were not gods. Each experienced a lengthy period in which he was out of power, out of favor, and out of the public eye. And they each responded to these hard times in the most human of ways: they became depressed. They were not even saints. The manifest flaws of each break the hearts of all who seek heroic perfectionism in their leaders. If only Washington had read more and had pursued a more progressive agenda; if only Jefferson had not owned slaves; if only Lincoln had not entertained doubts about the inherent equality of the races; if only TR had talked less and not carried such a "big stick" in international affairs. But saints are worthless as role models, at least to those of us who are aware of our own shortcomings and weaknesses. That is why the Rushmoreans are such engaging subjects for study: they were reassuringly human in their behavior and emotions, with weaknesses, foibles, vulnerable egos— and embarrassing incidents in their pasts that they tried to get the world to forget. But their rivals and especially the press would not let them bury their past mistakes or current problems: Jefferson was constantly reminded of the occasions when he had been a fool at love; TR's attempts to play the cowboy, soldier, and boxer were portrayed as silly in a grown man and dangerous in a president; Lincoln's marriage was scrutinized in embarrassing detail, and he was caricatured as an incompetent ape. It could happen to any of us; but when it happened to them, they didn't crack or quit.

During most of the Revolutionary War, it appeared that the British would win, and many Americans blamed Washington personally for the many losses his troops endured. Much of the criticism was fair; even his steadfast admirer, Jefferson, admitted that Washington was not always a brilliant tactician and, as a consequence, he often "failed in the field." During the Civil War, Lincoln went through commanding generals the way allergy sufferers go through Kleenex. The war was won by the skin of his teeth, and during the long ordeal he was called to personal account for the repeated failures of the Union forces.

Integrity

But it was for their ideas that they were most reviled. Jefferson and Lincoln both paid a heavy political price for their opposition to slavery. Although the vigor of their opposition seems insufficient by contemporary standards, during their lives they were portrayed as dangerous extremists on the issue. By pledging to make good on Jefferson's "unalienable" right to the "pursuit of happiness," TR was denounced as a communist by members of his own party, which rejected his bid for their nomination *after* he had served successfully as one of the most popular presidents in U.S. history. Facing such obstacles, they each changed tactics and pragmatically cut and trimmed their programs and proposals. But they never lost sight of their goals or compromised their principles. They were simultaneously principled *and* pragmatic. Attacked by cynics for being the former and by idealists for being the latter, they succeeded as leaders because they were able to be both at once.

How can such pragmatism be labeled "integrity"? The Rushmoreans' integrity is evident from the fact that the long-term courses they adopted were based on what was morally right. For all their tactical backsliding and sidestepping on the issue of emancipation, there is not a word in the writings of either Lincoln or Jefferson to indicate that either ever wavered for a moment in his convictions about the immorality of slavery. The institution was wrong, and they never lost sight of that overriding moral principle. But as pragmatic politicians, they understood that rigid abolitionists neither won elections nor had influence with slaveholders and the majority of Americans who sat on the fence. More important, Lincoln and Jefferson both understood that they were not authoritarian rulers with the power simply to abolish the evil practice with a wave of the hand. Among his fellow Virginian planters, Jefferson was one of only a tiny minority who opposed slavery. The powerful majority viewed abolitionists about as positively as capitalists were viewed in Maoist China—and they had about the same influence. Jefferson was a reformer and not a radical revolutionary. He can be faulted legitimately for that, but he chose to attempt to change the hearts and minds of people who did not share his discomfort with the status quo rather than to castigate and alienate them. Of course, the fact remains that he did not succeed in winning them over on the issue of slavery, as he did not succeed on the issue to which he devoted most of his life after the presidency, universal public education. But he never gave up trying on either issue, and ultimately, his successors won the day on both.

Jefferson, Lincoln, and TR each understood that the ultimate goal was not emancipation, enfranchisement, or any other single act no matter how necessary or worthwhile; they focused, instead, on securing the long-term and general goal of equality of opportunity for all men and women. They focused not on ephemeral details but on fundamental values, the importance of which they were able to articulate and communicate clearly. They were willing to lose on this or that immediate issue because they would not be distracted from the ultimate objective. Radicals such as the abolitionist William Lloyd Garrison castigated the likes of Jefferson and Lincoln because of their pragmatic compromises on slavery: "I will be harsh as truth, and as uncompromising as justice. . . . I will not equivocate—I will not excuse—I will not retreat a single inch." Garrison said he would tear up the Constitution, let the South secede, and do whatever it took to abolish slavery (leading James Russell Lowell to observe of the abolitionists that "they treat ideas as ignorant persons do cherries; they think them unwholesome unless they are swallowed stone and all"). James MacGregor Burns reminds us that once the slaves were emancipated, Garrison packed up and went home, satisfied that justice had been fully served. Unlike the "compromisers," he refused to participate in the efforts then to make good on the American dream for African-Americans. In contrast, for all their willingness to backtrack temporarily on the issue of abolition, in everything they wrote and did Jefferson and Lincoln focused on the ultimate question of how to secure equality in the long term. Successful completion of one's short-term mission is not the clearest sign of effective leadership, but lifelong consistency of high moral purpose is.

One of the clearest written manifestations of values-based leadership is the second paragraph of the Declaration of Independence, a document that today would probably be called a vision statement.

In the Declaration, Jefferson set out the long-term aspirations of the new nation, the highest of which would be to realize the values of "life, liberty, and the pursuit of happiness." In asserting a "natural right" to pursue happiness, Jefferson meant that all individuals are entitled to make all they can of their lives. In the Enlightenment scheme of values, borrowed from Aristotle, all people have the right to self-development by virtue of their humanity. This statement of the value of equality of opportunity has stood as an inspiration to Americans in the political arena for over two centuries. Significantly, as we shall find in subsequent chapters, Jefferson's concept has found its way into the value statements of the leaders of many eminent contemporary corporations.

Lincoln himself noted that Jefferson's words in the Declaration were aspirations for what someday might be achieved in the new nation. Jefferson and his like-minded confrères lacked the power to deliver on their vision of equality of opportunity, but they included the notion in the Declaration as a goal to which the nation must continually aspire, a goal to be realized bit by bit over time as changing conditions warranted. By 1865, Lincoln argued that the time had come to make good on part of that promise by emancipating the slaves. In 1910, citing both Jefferson and Lincoln, TR said that the time had come to extend the Jeffersonian promise to all men and women of all colors and classes. But he, too, lacked the power to realize that vision, which to this day remains unfulfilled.

Even though Jefferson, Lincoln, and TR each failed to provide the wherewithal needed for all to pursue the American dream, they succeeded in giving the citizenry the basic requirement for change: hope. They encouraged their followers to believe that it is possible to create a better society. They were able to mobilize large numbers of previously hopeless and passive people to believe that better conditions could be created and that there was a role for all citizens to play in that process of change. People who do not think well of themselves do not act to change their condition; that is why the Rushmoreans continually reminded the citizenry of all that was good in them, and of the tremendous power latent in government of the people, by the people, and for the people. Although these leaders did not achieve their overarching visions, they did bring about bits and pieces of positive, ameliorative change—which is all that is possible in a large, democratic society. (Obviously, leaders can achieve much more in less time in business organizations, which are smaller and more focused.)

Trust

The obverse of hope is trust, and it was Washington's lasting contribution to have established the legitimacy of the presidency—and, by extension, of the Union—by securing the trust of the people. Since about 400 B.C., no leader until Washington who had assumed such vast power had ever relinquished it voluntarily. Many Americans—and most of the world watching in the wings—had assumed that Washington would follow in the time-honored tradition of the "champions of the people" who had made themselves kings. Indeed, Washington's personality and style led many to conclude that he would be the American Julius Caesar. GW had an observed weakness for pomp, high living, and all the little pleasures and luxuries of aristocratic life ("It's good to be the king," as Mel Brooks, in the guise of Louis XIV, once said). But Washington did not succumb to the temptations that would soon ensnare Napoleon in France (Bonaparte declared himself first consul two years after Washington left office). It came as a surprise to the world that Washington had a different Roman model in mind than Caesar—namely, Cincinnatus, the citizen soldier who, legend has it, saved Rome but would not accept the spoils of victory when the crown was proffered. Like Cincinnatus, Washington would release the reins of state and return to his farm as a common citizen.

Washington thus established the democratic ideal of the leader as servant. To him, leadership meant responsibilities, not privileges. With the exception of Cincinnatus, Pericles, and a handful of others, leaders had always ruled to meet their own needs; Washington led to achieve the ends of the people. His ability to diffuse his courage and optimism among his troops—and, later, among the American public—was a by-product of the trust he had earned by serving them. He had not promised the people he led much in terms of victory, glory, or abundance; he won their loyalty instead through deeds and by example. He asked no one to make a sacrifice that he himself was unwilling to make; he sought no financial reward for his service. The public's trust in him grew out of his manifest integrity; his ability to lead emanated from his willingness to serve. He imposed no doctrine on his people; instead, he came to symbolize their aspirations and their needs. In these important respects he was much like Kemal Atatürk, Gandhi, de Gaulle, Martin Luther King Jr., and others who would follow as either "fathers" of their nations or as the first to serve where no one had previously dared.

All of the Rushmoreans understood that, paradoxically, they would succeed in bringing about the changes they sought to the extent that they were seen as reflecting the values and aspirations of their followers. During their long careers, each of the four presidents had, on occasion, stepped out too far ahead of public sentiment, and each had experienced a severe backlash (Jefferson's call for the abolition of slavery in the Declaration was unceremoniously excised by the drafting committee of the Continental Congress). Yet, equally important, they constantly tested those limits, attempting to expand the range of public tolerance for change. For instance, in 1862, observing that "the dogmas of the quiet past are inadequate to the stormy present" of the Civil War, Lincoln put forward an imaginative proposal for the gradual emancipation of the slaves over a period of thirty-eight years, during which time slaveholders would be compensated for the loss of their human chattel. When this bold initiative was attacked by slaveholders and abolitionists alike, he countered that "as our cause is new, so must we think anew." He challenged the prevailing ideology of comfort ("We must disenthrall ourselves") and called on citizens to think in terms of their long-term self-interest ("It is easier to pay a large sum [now] than it is to pay a larger one [later]"). Historian David M. Kennedy points out that "Lincoln's proposal was at once too bold and too modest—and too late." But it helped establish Lincoln's credibility with the wavering majority who were not extremists and whose support he would ultimately need when he issued the Emancipation Proclamation.

Listening

The Rushmoreans listened to the people they served, but they were not prisoners of public opinion. Madison argued that the role of leadership in a democracy is "to refine and enlarge the public views," and in so doing, "it may well happen that the public voice, pronounced by the representatives of the people, will be more consonant to the public good than if pronounced by the people themselves." During their careers, the Rushmoreans would elevate base and selfish interests to high moral values that all could embrace as being in the public interest.

Their means and methods were listening to their followers and encouraging dissenting opinion among their advisers. Save Coolidge, Washington was the most silent of the presidents. During the four months he chaired the Constitutional Convention, he spoke publicly on only one occasion—yet all in attendance credited the successful outcome of the convention to his strong leadership (often exercised out of the public limelight). Lincoln, too, was an avid listener, to the consternation of his wife, staff, and cabinet. He received scores of common citizens, listening patiently by the hour to their petitions, complaints, grievances, and ideas. In this way, he kept his finger on the pulse of the public in an era before the advent of survey research.

All four Rushmoreans used their cabinets to test ideas, explore all sides of issues, and air the full range of opinion. They did not hire yes-men. Washington's greatest strength was the supreme self-confidence that allowed him to assemble—and heed the advice of—a team of men who were each far more brilliant than the president they loyally served. His vice president, John Adams, wrote that Washington's cabinet members Hamilton and Jefferson quarreled "like cats and dogs." Yet these two feuding geniuses could agree on one important thing: their respect for Washington. He won that respect by showing his respect for them both, by encouraging each to speak his mind, and by keeping an open mind himself about the opposed positions they advanced. Frequently, in the heat of battle, they had attempted to offer their resignations, which GW refused to accept (when Jefferson finally did resign, he left on good terms with the president and never once spoke negatively about Washington's leadership).

Washington's style was similar to that of two modern presidents who were also great leaders but not great intellects: FDR and JFK. Had any of these three presidents lacked self-confidence and hired worshiping sycophants who posed no threat to them intellectually, their administrations would have been mediocre. That the contrary occurred is due to the fact that these leaders were able to capture the brilliance of their advisers and raise the level of competence of their respective administrations to remarkable heights. In contrast, the feeblest administrations were those headed by presidents who were comfortable when surrounded by mediocrities who posed no threat to their egos or authority (Harding and Grant come to mind).

But even the few presidents so competent as to make it impossible to find people more capable than themselves—Jefferson, Lincoln, and TR—went out of their way to assemble brilliant cabinets and staffs. Like Washington, Lincoln benefited from the strong and antagonistic views of two key members of his cabinet, Salmon Chase and William Seward. Jefferson listened to, and relied heavily on, the advice of his secretary of state, James Madison, and his treasury secretary, Albert Gallatin, much as the first president had used the talents of Jefferson and Hamilton in the same posts. According to Alf Mapp (a recent Jefferson biographer), Madison and Gallatin "were never 'yes men' behind the closed doors of the conference room.

The effectiveness of the cabinet was due as much to Jefferson's facility for tact as to his wisdom in selecting co-workers." Jefferson's grandson wrote that he learned leadership skills in business from the way the president ran his cabinet meetings: "He inquiringly followed out adverse opinions to their results, leaving it to their [advocates] to note the error into which it led them, taking up their doubts as important suggestions, never permitting a person to place himself upon the defensive, or if he did [so place himself], changing the subject so as not to fix him in a wrong opinion by controverting it." Hence arguably the brightest leader this nation has known found it prudent, if not necessary, to listen to his subordinates and to encourage their contrary opinions. TR was the weakest of the Rushmoreans on the listening index, but even he—who seemed never to be silent—deferred to his great secretary of state, John Hay, and made good use of the talents of such fine staffers as James Garfield and Gifford Pinchot. And TR apparently remained silent long enough to garner sound advice on conservation matters from his friend John Muir. In theory, at least, Roosevelt had it right when he said, "The best leader is the one who has sense enough to pick good men to do what he wants done, and the self-restraint to keep from meddling with them while they do it."

Respect for Followers

If there were ever a man fit to be a benevolent despot—a philosopher king—it was Jefferson; yet of all of the presidents, he was the most articulate and the most adamant on the point that no man is fit to be king. In contrast to Jefferson's messy and raucous democracy, Pierre S. Du Pont de Nemours argued in favor of the benign despotism of Platonic paternalism. Jefferson offered the following retort to the father of the founder of the industrial empire that still bears his name: "I acknowledge myself strong in affection to our own form, yet both of us act and think from the same motive; we both consider the people as our children, and love them with parental affection.

But you love them as infants whom you are afraid to trust without nurses, and I as adults whom I freely leave to self-government."

Jefferson understood that in a democracy, there could be no such thing as *the* leader; instead, there must be a *leader of leaders* (a topic of subsequent chapters). Indeed, all four Rushmoreans, each recognized widely as a great leader, were suspicious of leadership as it is commonly defined. In their writings they expressed the concern that too much leadership—particularly of the wrong kind—is tyranny.

As Jefferson's note to Du Pont implies, the right kind of leadership is more like teaching than commanding. That is why TR likened the presidency to a "bully pulpit" and not to a throne. John Stuart Mill, perhaps the finest explicator of representative government, defined democratic leadership as "a rostra or teacher's chair for instructing and impelling the public mind." Such teaching is what Madison no doubt had in mind when he said that the role of the democratic leader is "to refine and enlarge the public views."

Never has a politician been a finer teacher than Lincoln; his Gettysburg Address is the ultimate review lesson on Jeffersonian democracy. The essence of great teaching is the ability to reach students, to put the lesson in language that students can not only understand but also make their own. Lincoln, perhaps because of his humble origins, spoke in words that all could understand and imparted lessons that all could internalize. The aristocratic TR was almost as masterful in communicating with the masses. Far from being as poetic as Lincoln, Roosevelt employed what has been recently called the "rhetoric of militant decency." Part of his secret was his manifest passion, a passion so intense that people who had been in a room with him would later report that something akin to an electric current had spread through the audience (yet recordings reveal that he did not have an impressive speaking voice). Even the cerebral and publicly shy Jefferson has been described as the "passionate Pilgrim." All four Rushmoreans, albeit pragmatists to their cores, believed passionately in what they said and did. Unlike sexual passion, the passion for ideas cannot be faked.

Teachers must have ideas. Great teaching is about something, and what the Rushmoreans were about was the creation of the good society through the process of democratic change. The ideas of liberty, equality, and natural rights enunciated in the second paragraph of the Declaration of Independence recur throughout the public statements and private writings of all four Rushmoreans. Lincoln said that he "never had an idea that didn't stem from the Declaration." Leaders without ideas are about power; the Rushmoreans were about the empowerment of the people through democracy.

A useful summary of the central aspects of the Rushmorean school of leadership may be found in a remarkable address, "The New Nationalism," delivered in a Kansas cornfield by Theodore Roosevelt in 1910. If nothing else, this speech stands as an eloquent refutation of Henry Kissinger's mistaken labeling of TR as an amoral leader. Perhaps TR practiced realpolitik in international affairs, but on domestic issues, where he spent the most of his energies, he was a moralist.

Speaking in plain language to aged Civil War veterans, TR described the need for moral symmetry in the creation of public policy. He elevated the humdrum concerns of the time to the level of the moral principles earlier enunciated in the Declaration and in the Gettysburg Address. Roosevelt displayed great passion in calling for the simultaneous pursuit of liberty, equality, economic efficiency, and community in national life. He called for change in the name of the enduring values of Washington, Jefferson, and Lincoln—all three of whom he cited in the first two minutes of the talk. He displayed vision, integrity, and courage, considering that his message of change was unpopular in that self-satisfied era. Then, as now, there was great resistance to change. The people who feared the changes he advocated did not join the debate on the issues that Roosevelt raised. Instead, they attacked him personally—he was egotistical and crazy for power, they said—and he lost his bid to regain the White House. Was he, then, a failure as a leader? Significantly, all of the nearly two dozen reforms that he called for that day in Kansas would be enacted over the next quarter century.

Contemporary critics accused each of the four presidents of being calculatingly ambitious—and the critics were probably not far off the mark. No one becomes president of the United States (or leader of much of anything) without ambition. Even the saintlike Gandhi, when asked why he had gone to England, would answer, "Ambition!" That thoughtful scholar of presidential leadership, James MacGregor Burns, reminds us that the real question is, "Ambition for what?" In the case of the Rushmoreans, it was ambition in the cause of idealism. That may sound like a contradiction in terms, but it is not. Burns's book, *Leadership,* is replete with such paradoxes, and the proof that idealism and ambition can beat in the same heart is found in the lives of these four presidents. They brought about change by pursuing moral ends that their followers would ultimately adopt as their own, ends that derived from the real needs of their followers.

Must Leaders Be Saintlike?

Effective leadership of change almost always begins with commitment by leaders to the moral principle of respect for followers. Granted, to predicate a theory of leadership on a moral foundation is to risk confusion with the current, trendy concern with individual "virtue" or "character." Without question, the leader's relationship with followers must be a moral one, but that does not mean that only leaders who are Christ-like in their private lives can be effective. In fact, a review of any list of great leaders will reveal that almost all were flawed human beings with notable private failings. The practical problem with the current wisdom that "private behavior predicts public behavior" is the simple fact that in the lives of most men and women there is at least one act that if made public would disqualify them from positions of leadership. If we insist on perfection of character, we are unlikely to find many exemplary leaders, and our analysis will end in despair.

In the late nineteenth century, the people of Ireland made the terrible mistake of confusing private with public morality. In 1889,

Charles Stewart Parnell, arguably his country's greatest leader, had succeeded in the British parliament to create the conditions necessary to win Home Rule for Ireland. As his country stood on the brink of freedom from British domination, it was revealed that Parnell was involved in an adulterous relationship with the woman he would subsequently marry. The Irish responded to the news by rejecting totally the legitimacy of Parnell's leadership. By thus insisting that their leaders be saintlike in their private lives, the Irish lost the opportunity for freedom, an opportunity that did not arise again until the next century.

Leaders must always keep faith with their people: they must never lie to their followers or break the laws they are charged with upholding. In all dimensions, their public lives must meet the strictest standards of morality. But distinctions need to be made: a great senator is no less great as a leader if he is occasionally drunk at home over dinner, for that is a *private* matter; a senator who takes the smallest bribe is an unworthy leader regardless of anything else, because that is a *public* matter. Franklin and Eleanor Roosevelt were great leaders because they were true to the citizens of America—even though they were unfaithful to each other. In contrast, Richard Nixon failed the test of leadership because he was unfaithful to his oath of office and lied to the citizenry. His failures as a leader are in no way mitigated by the doubtlessly reliable accounts that he was faithful to Pat, his wife.

Jimmy Carter was perhaps the most moral of presidents in both private and public life, yet he was not a great president. Although he was as committed as Jefferson and Lincoln to securing the natural rights of all humankind, unlike the Rushmoreans he was ineffective in his pursuit of that end. In short, while morality is a necessary ingredient of leadership, it is not sufficient.

The Rushmorean standard of excellence is the two-fold ability to lead change both morally and effectively. And the gauge of the greatness of leaders is their public record measured over their entire lifetimes. By the absolutist moral standards applied today, the private lives of the four Rushmoreans, if given a thorough airing in the media, would probably not appear sufficiently clean to allow them to hold office. Yet, by standards of public morality, the lives of all four presidents were exemplary. The morality of their leadership was rooted in the goals they pursued and the nature of their relationship with those they served. The Rushmoreans served not to aggrandize their personal power but instead to realize the needs and aspirations of their followers.

What the four Rushmoreans had in common was the practice of values-based leadership. We find evidence of this in Washington's Second Inaugural Address, in Jefferson's Declaration, in Lincoln's speech at Gettysburg, and in TR's cornfield oration. Each of these addresses contains valuable clues to the mystery of how flawed humans are able to turn themselves into great leaders. By calling attention to higher-order values, these leaders offered visions of a better world that transcended the petty differences of their followers.

Jefferson believed that it was the duty of the president "to inform . . . the legislative judgement." He sought to mold public opinion by elevating the debates of the day above the petty concerns that divided the Congress. In a State of the Union address, he sought to unite the people's elected representatives around a vision of the common good, telling them that "[t]he prudence and temperance of your discussions will promote, within your own walls, that conciliation which so much befriends national conclusion; and by its example will encourage among our constituents that progress of opinion which is tending to unite them in object and in will." That is values-based leadership. And that is why business leaders could do worse than to study the careers of the Rushmoreans.

The Corporate Rushmoreans

How to Lead Change Effectively and Morally

What can business leaders learn from the Rushmoreans? Can they discover a surefire process or blueprint for leading change? No. Success does not hinge on which of the many available change methods, programs, and processes is employed. Why? Because leadership effectiveness has little to do with matters of what to do or how to do it.

Contrary to received wisdom, when leaders fail to bring about change, the fault seldom lies in a mistaken choice of how-to manuals. Our review of the Rushmorean approach to leadership prepares us for a different conclusion: leaders fail when they have an inappropriate attitude and philosophy about the relationship between themselves and their followers. Those who do not respect and trust their followers cannot lead them. Conversely, those who succeed at bringing about effective and moral change believe in and act on the inherent dignity of those they lead—in particular, in their natural, human capacity to reason. In bringing about change, these leaders of leaders always include the people affected in the change process. Hence wherever successful leaders may start the process, whatever particular program they may adopt, and however they may choose to proceed along the way, they always practice the art of inclusion.

That *always* may still stick in the craw of people attracted to the moral relativism of contingency thinking. Indeed, there are exceptions to the rule: Rushmorean leadership does not exist in traditional (often called primitive) societies. And even in advanced, modern societies, the paternalist, the authoritarian, the strong man or woman may for a time get away with exclusionary leadership. In fact, for a period of time such individuals may be praised for their boldness, their brilliance, their strength, and their capacity to enforce their will on others. But in the final analysis, most such leaders will join the ranks of yesterday's heroes.

Consider the case of American Airlines's CEO, Robert Crandall. As the 1980s drew to a close, Crandall was widely acclaimed as America's toughest boss, the paradigm of the successful, forceful, no-nonsense leader. There were two reasons for his high standing in the media and academia: his company was a financial winner in an industry characterized by losers, and he was unashamedly as tough as they came. On the latter score, the *New York Times* called Crandall "the bully of the skies." Reporter Stephen Solomon wrote that "Crandall retains a volcanic temper and frequently erupts with a range of expletives that would stand out on the docks of New York." By admirers and critics alike, Crandall was called autocratic, hard on people, even abusive. Then, in 1993, after a spell of steadily declining profits, American was hit by one of the costliest strikes in airline history. That's when the employees whom Crandall had been bullying for a decade got their revenge: they refused to compromise on the terms of a new contract. Not only was the strike settled on the employees' terms, but the bully of the skies was forced to eat crow on prime-time news. Crandall, who had not shown great interest in the welfare of those who worked for him, thus found the attitude returned at the first opportunity. But he didn't get the connection. After the settlement, he told Solomon, "I work like hell all year and at the end of the year we have a big loss. That makes me a loser." Note carefully his choice of pronouns: *I* work, but *we* have a big loss.

Frances Hesselbein

Unlike Crandall, Frances Hesselbein doesn't use the pronoun *I* in the organizational context; she makes change a matter of *we*. On

July 4, 1976, Hesselbein assumed the leadership of the Girl Scouts
of the United States of America. The organization was a big one,
with some three million members, a largely volunteer workforce of
650,000, a headquarters budget of $26 million, and cookie sales
grossing a third of a billion dollars annually. But the Girl Scouts had
lost its way. Because of enormous social changes that had occurred
over the previous decades, the world's largest and most venerable
organization of girls and women no longer knew what business it
was in. Before Hesselbein acted, she met with her board and management team for six months to study and debate the purpose and
mission of the scouts. She encouraged everyone in the organization
with whom she consulted to "question everything—every assumption, policy, practice, detail."

Eventually they distilled the purpose of the organization into
nine words: "To help each girl reach her own highest potential."
Probably unconsciously, the Girl Scouts had thus restated the most
basic natural right of each human being, in effect dedicating itself
to making good on Jefferson's promise of the pursuit of happiness
for all girls in America. It was immediately clear to the leaders of
the scouts that this promise included nonwhites as well as whites.
But the facts belied the promise: the Girl Scouts was largely a white
club. The leaders then dedicated themselves to tripling their minority membership. But how to achieve this enormous change? "We
could sit in New York and say, 'Let there be diversity,'" Hesselbein
now explains, "but the neighborhood leaders in Altoona had to
really believe in this [new] vision of why we were in business, and
in our passionate belief in equal access."

She could not command the change because her position had
little inherent power. But she had a clear philosophy of leadership:
"The more power you give away, the more you have." She started
by throwing out the organization chart ("Boxes make you feel boxed
in") and introduced a "bubble chart" with sets of concentric rings
to represent "participatory leadership, sharing leadership, to the out-
ermost edges of the circles." Following that philosophy, her authority grew as she practiced the art of including dissenters and resisters

in the process of change. Two examples will make this clear. First, when the national organization voted to replace the traditional 1912 Girl Scout eagle pin with one that contained multiracial profiles of three girls "facing the future," the reaction on many fronts was, "You can't take my eagle away from me." So Hesselbein didn't. Treating the dissenters with respect, she promised them that "as long as one person in this organization wants to wear the traditional pin, we will manufacture it." The upshot? Resistance melted.

Second, the national leadership sought to include in membership children as young as five, little girls from single-parent households who had come out of the Head Start program. The initiative met with predictable resistance from some mothers in the field who balked at becoming "baby-sitters" for five-year olds. In fact, the vast majority of the organization's 335 national councils did not favor the plan. Instead of forcing the issue, Hesselbein began work immediately with the seventy-eight councils that were "ready to move." A year later, 225 councils were on board. Why? Hesselbein explains: "Paradoxically, I think the respect for differing opinions helped build cohesion within the organization rather than splinter it."

When she retired in 1990, not only had the Girl Scouts been reinvigorated and its diversity goals been met, but the organization was united in a way that it never had been in its seventy-eight-year history. Hesselbein says that the key was values-based leadership: "This could not have happened if we had not begun with the mission and had not emphasized the values undergirding everything we did to achieve it." The values she practiced—service, community, self-worth, friendship, fair and equitable treatment—became an umbrella broad enough for members from a variety of backgrounds to cluster under comfortably. She says that such "leadership is basically a matter of how to be, not how to do it. Leaders need to lead by example, with clear, consistent messages, with values that are 'moral compasses,' and a sense of ethics that works full time."

In a 1990 *Business Week* cover story, Peter Drucker concluded, "If I had to put somebody in to take Roger Smith's place in General

Motors, I would pick Frances Hesselbein . . . because the basic problem is in turning around a huge bureaucracy, and that is her specialty." To skeptics, Drucker's conclusion may seem naive: the challenge of leading change in the Girl Scouts is surely different from leading a for-profit corporation. But is it? The facts speak otherwise. With just a little searching, we can find corporate examples of values-based leaders of leaders in the mold of Frances Hesselbein.

Corporate Rushmoreans

If I were a sculptor, I'd chisel a Mount Rushmore frieze of corporate leaders. Choosing the quartet to portray would be harder than choosing America's four greatest presidents, so I'd make the task easier for myself by arbitrarily limiting the candidates to living CEOs of large, publicly held corporations. That would free me from having to choose among such legendary entrepreneurs, managers, and financiers as Andrew Carnegie, Henry Ford, Alfred Sloan, J. C. Penney, Pierre Du Pont, Lincoln Electric's James Lincoln, Polaroid's Edwin Land, Wal-Mart's Sam Walton, AT&T's Theodore Vail, Johnson & Johnson's Robert Wood Johnson, Atlantic Richfield's Thornton Bradshaw, and Sears's Robert Wood. And if I had more than four votes to cast among the living, I'd want to include profiles of John Deere's William Hewitt, Levi Strauss's Robert Haas, Sony's Akio Morita, Avis's Robert Townsend, Ford's Donald Petersen, Dayton Hudson's Kenneth Macke, Cummins's J. Irwin Miller, Chapparal's Gordon Forward, Saturn's Skip Le Fauve, Phillips–Van Heusen's Larry Phillips, Ben & Jerry's Ben Cohen, Body Shop's Anita Roddick . . . and how could I leave out Disney's Michael Eisner if transformation were a main criterion of inclusion? Hey, who set the rules for this silly game anyway?

I'll discuss some of those leaders later, but here I'll play my own game and carve out brief portraits for my personal Mount Rushmore as exemplified by just four well-known CEOs: Herman Miller's Max De Pree, Corning's James Houghton, Motorola's Robert Galvin, and Scandinavian Airlines's Jan Carlzon.

Like the four famous U.S. presidents, these corporate Rushmoreans are more unlike each other than they are similar; they are imperfect human beings who have made mistakes (some of them serious) during their careers, and they all have suffered the slings and arrows of outrageous criticism from rivals, the press, the financial community, and cloistered academics. Moreover, they are not comfortable on white horses and hence will never be mistaken for the leaders at the heart of my next project: a military Rushmore of Alexander the Great, Napoleon, General Patton, and Charles de Gaulle! In fact, I have chosen my Corporate Rushmoreans not because they are exemplary leaders in the military sense but because they are exemplars of outstanding leadership in the moral sense. This is a significant distinction. These four corporate CEOs have in common the practice of inclusionary leadership. In their respective companies, they created conditions under which many others also led. They created systems in which the talents of the many more than compensated for whatever strengths they themselves may have lacked. The famed ad man David Ogilvy almost had it right when he described the benefits of such leadership in the following way: "It does an organization no good when its leader refuses to share his leadership function with his lieutenants. The more centers of leadership you find in a company, the stronger it will become."

That would be it in a nutshell, except at Herman Miller, Corning, Motorola, and SAS, people do not think of themselves as anybody's "lieutenant." All the employees of these companies act "as if they own the place," in the words of Max De Pree. In Max's marvelous little book *Leadership Is an Art* he describes in loving detail the policies, programs, and practices at Herman Miller that caused employees at all levels to feel that the company was every bit as much theirs as it was Max's. When Max retired a few years back, he left behind a system under which all employees could be leaders, were encouraged to be leaders, and were rewarded for exerting leadership, but were free not to be leaders if, for whatever reason, leadership was not what they wanted to (or could) contribute to the firm. Yet most significant about the environment at Herman Miller, Corning, Motorola, and SAS is that when given the opportunity, the vast majority of employees at all levels opt to exert leadership. Let us see how De Pree, Houghton, Galvin, and Carlzon became leaders of leaders.

Max De Pree

The first person I'd portray on my corporate Mount Rushmore would be De Pree, former CEO of Herman Miller, one of the country's largest producers of office furniture. The company was founded in 1923 by D. J. De Pree, Max's dad, and it has generated ripples of distinction—and waves of innovation—since the 1930s. For years, Herman Miller has been respected internationally for the quality of its products and especially for its contribution to design (its Eames chair is in the permanent collection of both New York's Museum of Modern Art and the Louvre's Musée des Arts Décoratifs). The open office, the wall-attached desk, stackable chairs—these are among the many Herman Miller innovations.

How, you might ask, could such radical design ideas come from a company headquartered in Zeeland, Michigan, a frosty town with no trendy watering holes and no theaters? Don't all top designers live in New York, Paris, or Rome? They came to Zeeland, Max says, because D. J. "had the strength to abandon himself to the wild ideas of others." D. J. talked some of the greatest designers of the century—Gilbert Rhode, Charles Eames, and Robert Propst—into visiting Zeeland, where he promised them a free hand in designing what Eames called "good goods." D. J. had decided that there was a market for good design and that great designers needed freedom to try out their wild ideas. In short, D. J. concluded a long time ago that Herman Miller would be a leader, not a follower. His son followed suit.

Max De Pree, like his dad, believed in the rule of "abandoning oneself to the strengths of others." Not just expert others—that is, not just world-class designers and people with university degrees—but trusting the strengths of all Herman Miller employees. For example, through the company's Scanlon plan, workers make suggestions to management for ways to improve such things as customer service, quality, and productivity. The Scanlon plan has been the modus operandi at Herman Miller since the early 1950s. The Scanlon idea is simple: when workers suggest ways to improve productivity, they are cut into the financial gains that result from their contributions. One day a month, top managers report to workers on the company's productivity and profits—the kind of information that is normally hoarded in most big U.S. firms—and the managers also report on the status of all employee suggestions. This wasn't unbridled fun for Max and his top management team. Imagine being the CEO of a *Fortune* 500 firm facing a monthly interrogation on your performance by shop floor workers: "Max, why didn't you do what we told you last month?" "Why hasn't top management purchased that new equipment we told you about?" "Why does it take so long to change procedures that keep us from responding directly to customers?" "Our profits would be higher if you guys would respond faster to what we tell you to do."

Why did Max put up with this? Wasn't it hard work? Wasn't it threatening for a boss to be grilled by subordinates? Didn't Max abandon power by abandoning himself to the ideas of others? Listen to what Max says about leadership, and remember that he practiced what he preached:

- The first responsibility of the leader is to define reality. The last is to say thank you. In between, the leader is a servant.
- The signs of leadership are among the followers. Are they reaching their potential? Are they learning? Are they achieving the desired results? Are they serving? Do they manage change gracefully, and do they manage conflict?
- Leaders don't inflict pain, they bear it.
- Leaders respect people. Leadership is about relationships. Relationships count more than structure.
- Good communication means a respect for individuals. Good communication is an ethical question.

- The best communication forces you to listen. Information
is power, but it is pointless if hoarded. Power must be shared
for an organization or a relationship to work.

The problem in most organizations, according to Max, is that
CEOs limit the capacity of their firms to their own level of competence. That is, they surround themselves with loyal "lieutenants"
who are nonthreatening. Unlike many of his peers, Max was willing to admit that he couldn't do most of the jobs in the company
nearly as well as the people who held them. He wanted people who
were more qualified than himself to do every job in the organization. He also knew that he couldn't be everywhere in the company
at all times, nor could he invent rules to ensure that everyone
always did the "right thing." All he could do was to make it possible for all Herman Miller employees to take responsibility for meeting whatever situation might arise—that is, to act as Max or his top
management team would have done had they been there themselves. Again, as Max always said, "around here the employees act
as if they own the place." And isn't that the goal of organizational
leadership? Isn't that the employee attitude that every CEO would
nurture if it weren't so threatening "to abandon oneself to the
strengths of others"? What Max did was institutionalize responsibility and continuing change. How could there be resistance to
change if the source of innovation was the followers themselves?

I have often been asked to describe Max's leadership "style,"
and after many unsatisfactory attempts to do so, I came to realize
that my difficulties stemmed from a false premise inherent in the
question. Indeed, most of us wrongly assume that leadership has
something to do with style. The error is perpetuated in management books in which leaders are portrayed, variously, as charis-
matic personalities, showmen, cheerleaders, con artists, visionaries,
autocrats, and circus stuntmen. They bark orders and run around
doing everybody else's work for them. How preposterous that this
could work in a company of a thousand (let alone a hundred thousand) employees!

Max's idea of leadership is different. He knows from experience that it is not a leader's strong voice, the snap of a whip, or a trendy TV persona that motivates employees. The art of leadership, as Max says, is "liberating people to do what is required of them in the most effective and humane way possible." Thus the leader is the "servant" of the followers in that the leader removes the obstacles that prevent them from doing their jobs. In short, the true leader enables followers to realize their full potential. That is not a matter of style.

To lead effectively is a matter of clear thinking on the part of the leader. Leaders must be clear about their own beliefs: they must have thought through their assumptions about human nature, the role of the organization, the measurement of performance, and so on. Max De Pree leads by asking questions. Because he has carefully considered his questions in advance, he has the self-confidence "to encourage contrary opinions" and "to abandon himself to the strengths of others." In short, Max is a listener. He listens to the needs, ideas, and aspirations of his followers; then, within the context of his own well-developed systems of belief, he responds to these in an appropriate fashion. That is why leaders must know their own minds. That is why leadership requires ideas.

And that is why leadership requires integrity. Integrity has at least two meanings relevant to a discussion of leadership. It is synonymous with truth-telling, honesty, and moral behavior. It goes without saying that a true leader must behave with integrity in this sense by being an honest and ethical individual, someone whose every word and deed is consistent. That describes Max to a T. But such morality, though necessary, is insufficient. In addition, the leader needs that related type of integrity that has to do with "selfness," with the integration of one's personality (to use the language of psychologists). Integrity in this sense refers to the much-admired trait of wholeness or completeness that is achieved by people who are said to have healthy self-confidence and self-esteem. People with integrity "know who they are." Their self-esteem allows them to esteem and respect others. Such leaders' ease with themselves allows others to esteem and respect them. Max De Pree is one of those people who is so comfortable with himself that he makes other people comfortable with themselves. Without Max's trying, people follow him.

But they wouldn't follow him willingly if he were so wishy-washy as to agree with the last person to visit his office or so rigid that he couldn't listen and respond to ideas different from his own. Both of those familiar types lack integrity. According to Warren Bennis, all successful leaders must know "what they want, why they want it, how to communicate that to others to gain their support to get it." You don't have to become someone else to be a leader, Bennis says; "you have to become yourself." *That's* integrity.

But how does one know what one wants? The key, as the poet writes, is to "know thyself." That requires listening carefully to Ralph Waldo Emerson's "inner voice" and heeding that voice "all others to the contrary." In short, the only way one can be a leader is to be true to oneself, and that is hard to do. The world may say that it prizes originality and individuality—but then it goes and punishes their expression. That is where moral courage comes in. We all know what is right. But it is the leaders among us who behave in the right way no matter what others may say. Thus Bennis observes that "conformity is the enemy of leadership. We let others define ourselves." But aren't leaders also supposed to listen to their followers? Leadership requires listening to followers but not becoming prisoners to their low expectations. Fortunately, as Bennis writes, "we can have unity without conformity." And in that seeming paradox is the escape from the terrible organizational dilemma that bedevils would-be leaders of change: a "paradox of values" in which leaders must create a culture with strong strategic unity while at the same time fostering sufficient internal openness to encourage freedom of action and entrepreneurial initiative.

The resolution of that paradox does not rest on a technique, a skill, or a style of leadership. Such leadership is an attitude, as Frances Hesselbein puts it, an attitude that rests on the most important value practiced by Max De Pree: respect for people. Above all else, Max created an organization in which the different abilities and contributions of all people were respected and rewarded. Everything the company did, all its goals and objectives, were subsumed under that master value.

Respect for people leads to the right of all employees to participate in the decisions that affect their own work and the right to share in the fruits of their labor (through the Scanlon plan and through stock ownership). Among employees with over a year of service, 100 percent are stockholders by way of a profit-sharing plan. While executives in other companies were busy "taking care of number one" by arranging golden parachutes for themselves, in 1986 Herman Miller introduced "silver parachutes" for all its employees with more than two years of service. In case of an unfriendly takeover of Herman Miller that led to termination of employment, the silver parachute plan would offer a soft landing for the people in the ranks of the organization whose welfare is ignored in most acquisitions. But then, Herman Miller wasn't like most other business organizations. For example, company policy limited the CEO's salary and bonus to no more than twenty times the average paycheck (in 1991, when most CEOs of *Fortune* 500 firms were drawing seven figures, Herman Miller's highest-paid executive made $490,000 and the company's average employee made $28,000). That's respect for people.

Yet some executives have told me that Max cannot stand as a practical model of leadership because he is "too good," that is, because his character is almost saintly. It is true that Max is an extremely moral man in his *private* life, but I do not believe that goodness is what made him a successful leader. He inspired followers because he was trustworthy in his *public* leadership role. He showed his respect for employees in sound, practical business ways, such as involving them in decision making and profit sharing. Had Max been a saint off the job, yet failed to respect his associates at Herman Miller, he would not have attracted followers.

One question remains: Does it work? Is such moral leadership effective? During Max's eight-year term as CEO, the company was seventh on the *Fortune* 500 in total return to investors. A hundred dollars invested in Herman Miller stock in 1975 had grown in value to about $5,000 in 1986. Was the success of Herman Miller related to Max's leadership? The answer is an unqualified yes. Bear in mind that the affirmative comes from a skeptic who has learned (painfully) that there is almost always a gap between what a CEO *claims* his philosophy to be and what he actually does on the job. For a time I had treated what Max De Pree said about leadership as mere theory, until I could put it to the ultimate test of asking his followers what *they* thought of Herman Miller's top management.

Then I got my first chance to visit a Herman Miller factory. I was given carte blanche to go anywhere and talk to anyone, managers and workers alike. The only problem was that I couldn't tell one from the other. People who seemed to be production workers were engaged in solving the "managerial" problems of improving productivity and quality. People who seemed to be managers had their sleeves rolled up and were working side by side with everybody else in an all-out effort to produce the best products in the most effective way. As Max says, "The signs of outstanding leadership are found among the followers." I found that Max was a leader of leaders.

And I found that Max's excellence as a leader was manifested in the spirit of *self-management* that I found in every Herman Miller employee with whom I spoke. Among the dozens of corporations I had previously visited, I'd never seen anything like it. I discovered that not only did Max practice what he preached, but so did the people who worked for him, the people Max *served*. These people were dedicated to the beliefs and ideas that Max espoused; they even sounded like Max when talking about the company's values, but were all rugged individualists with their own ideas about how to realize those values and how to live their own lives. As Warren Bennis says, "We can have unity without conformity."

Having sketched this glowing portrait, I hasten to add that there is no such thing as the perfect company or the ideal leader. Max lost his deft touch while establishing a process for choosing his successor, who lasted in the CEO's job just long enough to discover that he did not want to be a CEO. As he came to this realization, the competitive environment in the furniture industry changed, and customer responsiveness became as important for success as product quality. Recognizing that the CEO was not coping with this change, the board resolved to look for a new change-oriented leader who, at the same time, was committed to preserving the company's values.

With Max's active participation, the board identified an individual from outside the company who appeared to have the requisite qualities. However, after a couple of years during which it became clear he too was unable to bring about needed transformation of the company's strategy and product line, the new CEO did what many leaders do when faced with a crisis: he got tough. He resorted to classic situational leadership. Failing to understand that, while leadership requires constant changes of strategy and tactics, it equally requires steadfast adherence to basic principles, he fired nearly the entire top management of a company in which firing had occurred only in rare instances of misconduct. Worse was the abusive manner in which the deed was done: a stranger to the Herman Miller community assembled those who had been chosen for termination—most of whom had no inkling of what was about to transpire—and summarily announced that they had been dismissed.

In one blow, five decades of goodwill that had been accumulated under three De Prees—D.J., Hugh (Max's brother, who had been CEO for seventeen years), and Max himself—was squandered in one gratuitous act of "get tough" leadership. The essential glue of trust that had held the company together was suddenly dissolved. Max had just retired from the board, but the shocked directors immediately understood what had happened and removed the CEO before he could do more damage.

There is a chance that Herman Miller might still recover but, for now, the company stands as a cautionary tale of how easily the trust that undergirds values-based leadership can be lost. And Max, for all his skill, reminds us that the most difficult of all leadership tasks is, perhaps, developing worthy successors. Yet, because he so brilliantly fulfilled the other tasks of leadership, I unhesitatingly put him on my Mount Rushmore. As we shall see, no mortal is a perfect leader.

James Houghton

The second leader I would profile on my Corporate Rushmore is Corning's James R. Houghton, who in the 1980s revitalized the $3 billion glassworks that had been founded by his great-great-grandfather in upstate New York over a century and a quarter before "Jamie" became CEO. In 1983, facing the prospect of his family's legacy gradually withering as the result of new technologies and global competition, Houghton called together his top management team to discuss how to resuscitate the firm. They decided that the key was quality. Among the first American executives to hear W. Edwards Deming's message, Houghton's team committed the company to the earliest of the "total quality" programs that would soon take American industry by storm.

But Corning differed from most of these companies that would follow in that Houghton recognized almost immediately that the issue wasn't just quality but the total transformation of the culture of the old-line firm. Just prior to his assuming the CEO role, the company had been characterized publicly as a "dictatorship," and relations with its employees, unions, and local community had deteriorated to the breaking point. This challenge was not one to which Jamie Houghton was born. Scion of the American aristocracy, he was not naturally given to the Rushmorean traits needed to turn the company around. But he committed himself not only to changing the company but also to starting that process of change with himself. People at Corning now talk of him respectfully as the "CTO" (chief transformation officer), and that transformation began the day he asked a soon-to-retire executive, Forrest Behm, to direct the quality program. Behm gave Houghton just one piece of advice: "*You have to lead the program, not me.*" And lead it he did (with Behm as his coach).

Houghton began by committing a third of his time to the quality effort. He started with a series of meetings with Behm and "the Six-Pack," the group of officers who reported directly to him. Their first task was to agree on what their values were and what those values meant for the change process. The values they identified—quality, integrity, performance, industry leadership, and technology—were not unusual in and of themselves, but they were built on the foundation of another value: the individual. They decided that this meant that "each employee must have the opportunity to participate fully, to grow professionally, and to develop his or her highest potential." (Again, we find Rushmorean leaders coming back to Jefferson's promise of the pursuit of happiness.)

To realize this value, it was obviously necessary that Jamie Houghton would have to eliminate the "management by fear" that had caused Corning to be branded a dictatorship. He did this in part by pledging to introduce self-management among the company's largely unionized workforce, and to make Herculean efforts to attract, retain, and promote women, minorities, and others who had been leaving the company in droves in pursuit of more open and accepting work environments.

But it isn't what you say that counts, it's what you do. Jamie Houghton soon learned that if he were to transform the company, he must lead by example—and that would take more than the third of his time that he had planned to devote to the process. According to Behm, one critical event signaled a fundamental change in Jamie Houghton. Early in the quality program, it became clear that someone had made a very costly mistake. On hearing this bad news, Jamie blurted out, "Who did it?" Then he caught himself. His face reddened with embarrassment, and he rephrased his line of questioning: "Why did it happen?" "How can we fix it?" "What is our responsibility as leaders to make sure that it doesn't happen again?" From that defining moment of leadership, the successful transformation of Corning was assured.

Houghton and the Six-Pack then worked outward in ever-broadening circles, bringing more and more people into the process of leading change. Jamie himself visited fifty worksites a year, explaining his vision and the values of the company and calling on employees to spend 5 percent of their time annually in training to prepare them to lead the quality effort and to become the industry pacesetters in technology. No "benchmarking" for Corning; let others follow Corning's lead! Year in and year out, through patience and repetition, Houghton went back to the same groups with the same message, demonstrating that this commitment to their enablement was not merely a fad of the month. Gradually, they learned to trust him and began to accept responsibility for making change come about.

Significantly, Houghton says that he leads as he does not because it is expedient but because treating employees with respect is the right thing to do. Thus Houghton has cited the need for "redefining leadership":

- We have traditionally viewed leaders as heroes who come forward at a time of crisis to resolve a problem. But this view stresses the short term and assumes the powerlessness of those being led. . . .
- The true spirit of leadership is the spirit that is not sure it is always right. Leaders who are not too sure they are right are leaders who listen. Leadership is about performance over time, not charisma—about responsibility, not privilege. It is about personal integrity and a strong belief in team play. . . .
- Which points to one more element of leadership: developing strong subordinates and potential successors and staying out of their way. Companies can no longer afford leadership by the few. If organizations are to move ahead and not just play catch-up, every employee must become a responsible leader.
- Employees must have responsibility and the power that goes with it; anything less leads to cynicism and skepticism— and nothing is more demoralizing for employees than to find their skepticism justified.

Does Houghton's new definition of leadership work? Is it effective? It does and it is, as the following example illustrates. At the company's Erwin Ceramics Plant, workers responded to Houghton's quality initiative by taking on the process of change as their own responsibility. They prepared a "vision statement," "a set of beliefs and rights that we value and are fundamental to our future," among which were the rights to "be treated with dignity and respect" and to "participate in decisions that affect our worklife." The vision was, in effect, a description of the kind of place where they wanted to work. To implement the vision, they created a joint management-labor team to plan the changes needed in the existing system. This plan called for the elimination of eighty jobs through attrition and changes in work rules and processes that in the first year led to a 38 percent reduction in defects. Here's the Corning lesson: where there is Rushmorean leadership, rights and responsibilities become complementary rather than antithetical, just as labor and management become, in the words of Horace Mann, "fraternal rather than antagonistic."

Robert Galvin

The third corporate leader I would immortalize in granite is Motorola's Robert Galvin. Thanks to Galvin's understated leadership, Motorola has probably done the best job of any large U.S. corporation at institutionalizing change. When Galvin assumed the CEO role in the late 1950s (on the death of his father, Paul, Motorola's founder), he worked with the top management team to lay out a ten-year plan for transforming the company. Galvin quickly saw that the plan could not be realized without the support of all Motorola employees. In fact, he saw that he would have to involve them immediately in creating the plan. To do this, operations were radically decentralized, and employees were formed into teams, each responsible for such things as quality, productivity, cost and inventory control, and customer service.

Because these teams were truly self-managing—and because all employees were rewarded with healthy bonuses when they met the goals they had set for themselves in consultation with management—Motorola created a system in which workers had a greater say and stake than competing Japanese workers had in their firms. Motorola workers also had a high degree of autonomy: in the 1970s, one Motorola worker proudly explained to me that "like Japanese, we play softball on excellent company facilities; unlike Japanese, we play when we want to, not on cue!"

Motorola became the first large company in America to enable its workers to be leaders themselves. Through a system of constant communication and feedback, Motorola employees came to understand what their individual and group piece of the business was, and how that contributed to the grand corporate scheme, and were thus able to make rational decisions without the need for constant managerial coercion. The system grew out of a no-holds-barred analysis of the company's basic assumptions about workers and work, an analysis that led to the conclusion that employees are intelligent, curious, and responsible and hence it was incumbent on management to create a system in which they could exercise their ability to reason.

Motorola ended up with an industrial system under which people are treated with dignity without losing discipline, and power is widely shared without degenerating into anarchy. The means are simple and sensible: all employees participate in the decisions that affect their own work, and all participate in the financial rewards that come about as the result of their efforts. This dual approach works because participation in decision making without participation in financial gains would be viewed as illegitimate by workers who saw the fruits of their efforts reaped by others. And participation in financial gains without participation in decision making would be seen as illegitimate by workers who were powerless to influence the things that determine the size of their paychecks. The results of Motorola's system are well known: perhaps the highest-quality products in American industry; regular introduction of innovations in semiconductors, pagers, and handheld communications; and, of course, high profits.

What did Bob Galvin do to accomplish this? Very little himself. I have heard of few instances where he ever gave a direct order to anyone (with the exception, perhaps, of his son, Christopher, a top Motorola executive—again, nobody's perfect). Basically, Galvin removed the obstacles that might have prevented his employees from being fully effective. He encouraged them to take initiative and to be as fully productive as possible without violating Galvin's strong moral values, the foremost of which is trust. Galvin trusted everyone at Motorola—the people who reported to him and the people who reported to them—to create a system of unusually high productivity: "One's creativity depends on interaction with others—others one trusts, others who feel trusted. For one to be unfettered in risking creative interaction with another, that other must know the trust of openness, objectivity, and a complementary creative spirit. . . . Trust is power. The power to trust and be trusted is an essential and inherent prerequisite quality to the optimum development and employment of a creative culture."

Galvin was a leader of leaders, a leader of such admired executives as William Weisz, George Fisher, Gary Tooker, Christopher Galvin, and others, who in fact ran the company. Moreover, the spoils at Motorola went to employees who successfully challenged inappropriate premises advanced by those at the top. As one manager explained to me, "The expectation is that you will challenge any idea. The top guys disagree with each other in front of their managers. The upshot is a healthy disrespect for the idea that those at the top are necessarily the wisest."

Bob Galvin explains where this comes from:

> Our challenge is to continually evidence a willingness to reach and risk, a willingness to *renew*. I saw at a young age that my father had to change to survive. . . . My father was a "natural" at changing his mind. He would pound on the table telling you he was right. Then you would tell him the consequences of his decision, and he'd change his mind right there. There is no master plan that can anticipate change. That is why my father counseled, "Be in motion." He didn't believe in milking things to the end, until they became failures. We saw what happened to our former competitors Philco, Zenith, and Admiral and swore that we wouldn't let it happend to us. We

looked at the companies that didn't survive, and we learned from them. As a management team we read John Gardner's *Renewal*, and we've lived by its precepts ever since.

The attitude of constant renewal pervades the entire Motorola corporation, not just the executive suite. There is a healthy sense of dissatisfaction with the status quo, which manifested itself when Motorola was on top of the world, having just won the first Malcolm Baldrige Award for quality. Instead of resting on its laurels, the company committed itself to the creation of American industry's most ambitious training effort. At Motorola University, every employee now partakes in at least five days of classwork annually. In fact, at Motorola, everyone has a "right" to training—a Jeffersonian right to make all that they can of themselves in order to participate in the continuing renewal of the company.

Jan Carlzon

The choice of a fourth Corporate Rushmorean was the hardest. With one strong reservation, my candidate would be Jan Carlzon, CEO of Scandinavian Airlines (SAS) and author of one of the few books on leadership by a corporate executive that is worth reading (along with Max De Pree's). His *Moments of Truth* offers a quintessential overview of how to lead change. There is no need to repeat here what he does so well in that book. Instead, we focus on one of the clearest examples of the peculiar kind of resistance to change that is the unique focus of our inquiry. In late 1985, just before his book was published, Carlzon visited Los Angeles, where, at the invitation of Warren Bennis, he addressed some two dozen of the most powerful executives in California, most of them unfamiliar with the story of SAS's transformation, which has since become legendary. On that memorable occasion, I was a fly on the wall.

Carlzon began his talk with an explanation of the conditions he inherited at SAS, a description of the process of change he employed, and a review of the consequent results. He also described his philosophy of leadership, with specific reference to his now-famous notion of "turning the organizational pyramid upside down" so that leaders may serve followers. He explained why and how every SAS employee had been empowered—without the requirement of prior approval from supervisors—to do whatever was necessary to satisfy customers: "You can get people to develop their specific goals not by steering them with fixed rules but by giving them total responsibility to achieve a specific result." To get that result—namely, customer satisfaction—the key resource that employees needed was information: "An individual without information cannot take responsibility; an individual who is given information cannot help but take responsibility."

Carlzon then recounted examples of the exercise of such responsibility from the fifty million "moments of truth" that occurred annually when SAS employees had direct, one-on-one contact with customers. He argued that the sum total of these moments added up to the general level of satisfaction that had made the airline number one in Europe among business travelers.

At this point in the discussion, the American executives started to grow fidgety. After much nervous coughing and paper shuffling, one CEO could take no more. Clearly enraged, he slammed his palm down hard on the table in front of him and with the other hand pointed an accusatory finger at the Swedish guest speaker: "OK, Carlzon, now own up. How many of those fifty million moments went sour? How many times did your employees abuse the responsibility you gave them? How many times did somebody do something dumb that ended up costing your shareholders money?"

Carlzon, soft-spoken and low-key, took no offense at the interruption. Instead, he weighed his words carefully in reply: "Do you want the data from the first year or for the entire six years since we introduced the change?"

"The whole works. Come on, 'fess up!"

"I believe we have had about a half dozen serious instances of the type you mention. Those were times when employees went far beyond what was a reasonable effort on behalf of customers and, in so doing, caused costly errors."

Satisfied that he had made his point, the American turned to his peers and said, "There, I thought so. That's what you get when you let the lunatics run the asylum—anarchy!"

Politely, Carlzon mentioned that at SAS they thought that six errors in three hundred million positive experiences was a pretty good ratio (and I wanted to add that professors fall victim to the same fallacy of the exception when they argue against adopting the honor system on the grounds that "someone might cheat"—but I had sworn a vow of silence during the session).

Tasting blood, and ignoring Carlzon's explanation, the American interlocutor went back for more. "Now that you are shooting straight, tell us what you did about the employees who were ripping off your shareholders."

Either Carlzon didn't understand the CEO's vernacular, or he understood but couldn't believe his ears. "I'm sorry, what do you mean?"

"In plain English, how did you punish them?"

Carlzon got the drift. "Punish them? Why should we have punished them when it was *our* fault? We believe the task of leaders in a large company is to articulate the values of the organization, to create a system in which people can be productive, and to explain the goals that the system was established to achieve. We also believe that people don't act maliciously. If we in top management had done those jobs properly—if we had explained adequately the purpose behind employee empowerment—those few errors would not have occurred. That is why we went back to evaluate our own communication skills."

Carlzon's view, in brief, was that the challenge of change requires more than a leader; it requires leadership. American executives at that time could not see the difference between those two related concepts. I suspect that by now most of them have come to understand the difference, but too few of them are acting on it. The thoughts that the angry CEO expressed a few short years ago may have become "managerially incorrect," but there is little evidence that managers who now know better are as yet willing to entrust others in the manner Carlzon demonstrated.

Earlier I mentioned that I cite Jan Carlzon with reservation. The postscript to this story is inconsistent both with my argument and with what Carlzon practiced and preached at SAS. Shortly after having achieved Rushmorean status, Carlzon threw away much of his credibility in one fell swoop. Competition in the airline industry suddenly heated up, and small airlines like SAS found their existence threatened. In what can only be called a panic move, SAS formed an alliance of convenience with Continental, then headed by Frank Lorenzo, a CEO whose leadership philosophy was the antithesis of everything Carlzon stood for. Thus I end up feeling about Carlzon being on my Mount Rushmore the way I do about Thomas Jefferson being on the real thing: though no leader is perfect, it is the failings of the good ones, not the sins of bad ones, that break your heart.

Other Worthies

If Jan Carlzon doesn't quite fill the bill, there are other candidates for a spot on the mountain. Here are brief profiles of a few other corporate Rushmoreans.

Bill Gore

Recently deceased, Bill Gore was the founder of W. L. Gore & Associates, makers of Goretex and other marvels of chemistry. Gore & Associates practiced "unmanagement," a nonhierarchical, nonbureaucratic form of self-leadership in which there were no titles, no job descriptions, no bosses, and only one rule: all employees had the authority to do anything, as long as they didn't risk sinking the entire ship. Bill Gore wasn't into making decisions or setting rules; he was too busy practicing values-based leadership. He was constantly on the road, talking to all his employees about the vision, the purpose, the objectives, and the philosophy of the company. He was convinced that if his associates understood and shared his values, there would be no need for him to control them. The payoff was a steady stream of innovation from an energized group of employees committed to constant change.

Ricardo Simler

Ricardo Simler is CEO of Brazil's Semco, a manufacturer of industrial equipment, including pumps, mixers, and valves. At Semco, all employees are included in every decision made. Despite this developing country's sorry history of political authoritarianism, all Semco workers set their own hours, rules, and production and sales targets; pick their own leaders; and even decide their own salaries. This freedom is rarely abused because the pool of rewards is tied to the performance of the firm. "It's all very simple," Simler explains. "All we are doing is treating people like adults." So much for arguments that Rushmorean leadership is "culturally determined," that Latins "can't cope with democratic values," and that paternalism is "necessary" in the developing world.

Gordon Forward

The president of Chapparal Steel of Texas is another leader who believes in "management by adultery"—Gordon Forward's cheeky way of describing a system in which all employees are viewed as grown-ups capable of accepting real responsibilities. At this company, responsibilities for quality, safety, personnel, training, and even research and development have been pushed down to the level of the company's self-managing production teams. The company's prime value is continuous innovation, and that is achieved through rewarding all thousand employees for using their heads as well as their hands. The employees—all of whom participate in profits, sabbaticals, research, and decision making—think of themselves as leaders with access to the company's boardroom. What does that leave for President Forward to do? He can be found in the locker room talking technology with workers, or with them in that very boardroom discussing corporate values and philosophy. Everyone in the company is happy to share credit for having made Chapparal the world's lowest-cost steel producer.

Lawrence Phillips and Bruce Klatsky

Lawrence Phillips and Bruce Klatsky lead the billion-dollar Phillips–Van Heusen Corporation, whose products include Van Heusen shirts, Bass shoes, and Geoffrey Beene clothing. Phillips, great-grandson of the company's founder, reinvigorated the firm some one hundred years after it began as a pushcart in the streets of New York (in 1881). He began by rekindling the founder's long-dormant entrepreneurial spark, building several phenomenally successful new lines of retail outlets and then setting the ten-year goal of becoming a "model company." In the garment industry, no company has ever come close to achieving overall excellence (and only one other, Levi Strauss, has made the public commitment to try). But Chairman Phillips and his team, headed by recently named CEO Klatsky, have begun the process by including all employees, foreign and domestic, in company ownership and self-management. Avoiding the Levi's problem of going public in the press with lofty principles that exceed practices, the Phillips team quietly and modestly enunciated its values and ethical standards to vendors, customers, and employees. The company's values are rooted in a clear statement of the "basic rights of our associates." One of the first things they did to put substance behind those rights was eliminate the need for prior approvals for operating units to do whatever was required to serve customers and increase quality. To that end, teamwork among the company's 13,500 employees is now not just celebrated but rewarded. Klatsky is uncomfortable speaking publicly about this because it will take ten years to get where they want to be and should be. But he doesn't hesitate to say they are committed for the long haul. This, remember, in an industry not typically characterized by progressive practices. So much for the contingency rationale that leaders are forced to reduce their behavior to the level of their competitors.

Mac Booth

Polaroid's Mac Booth began his company's still halting transformation with a remarkable transformation of his own leadership. When Booth took over at Polaroid, he had a reputation as a brilliant technician, but as a leader, he expected others to follow him as unquestioningly as he had once followed company founder Edwin Land. In response to the threat of a hostile takeover, however, Booth began a long process of learning as much about leadership as he knew about science. Not only did he open up the company's ownership and decision making to employees, but he opened himself up, too, by listening to others. He has gradually evolved as a leader to become a Rushmorean teacher. Is this transformation merely a response to a changed situation? No, Booth will admit that the process has been one of growth, and there is no contingency in which he could, or would, go back to the rigid old days. Mac Booth's transformation stands as a model countless corporate executives might profitably emulate.

Pete Hart

Pete Hart recently retired as CEO of MasterCard after taking that moribund business and expanding it into sixty-two new countries in the space of four and a half years. Success came, he explains, by breaking with the monolithic and inflexible standards of the industry, freeing the company's representatives around the world to do whatever was necessary to meet the divergent needs of their thirty-three thousand customer banks. If this meant broadening the use of MasterCard so that customers could charge a speeding ticket with the trooper who pulled them over, so be it! Hart admits that he didn't succeed at first in gaining the initiative needed in the field because people kept coming to him for approval before acting. He soon discovered that he could energize them by giving them a general vision of the needed change, then trusting them to carry it out. "If you are successful at that, your people will run past you. At the beginning I thought I had the change process down cold. Now I can't keep up; it is happening too fast." That's the way to use values-based leadership to overcome resistance.

The Visionaries of Ford

Ford Motor Company's leaders in the 1980s succeeded in creating a climate conducive to continuous change in a company that had a history of rigidity and one-man rule. Ask Ford managers who was responsible for the lasting transformation of the company, and fingers will be pointed in all directions. The leaders of the change included Philip Caldwell, Donald Petersen, Peter Pestillo, Ernie Savoie, and even Henry Ford II (alias Henry the Lesser), who had once been a big part of the problem. The process of change, which began in 1979 under Henry's watch with an overture to the United Auto Workers union, grew into the Team Taurus project in 1988 under Petersen, and now extends across the large corporation, involving all its stakeholders: suppliers, customers, dealers, and employees worldwide.

There were several key steps along the way, including the early introduction of Deming's principles and the only instance on record of Donald Petersen's giving an actual order. At a crucial moment when the company had lost $3.2 billion in one year, top management balked at investing money in training as part of the Taurus effort—why spend money on an investment for which there were no hard figures on forecasted return? Petersen replied that no investments would ever be made in training and education if human capital were treated like investments in machines. He argued that it was an act of faith—and common sense—that one couldn't empower an entire workforce without giving it the needed skills to act. A few years later, Petersen's sometime nemesis, Philip Caldwell, told a reporter that the success of Team Taurus had been "due fifteen percent to technology and eighty-five percent to human factors." In the end, Ford's many leaders had overcome resistance to change by involving everyone and reducing the threat of change by avoiding the layoffs and purges endemic to the auto industry.

David Collins and Edward Smith

Schering-Plough Consumer Products president David Collins and his marketing maven, Edward Smith, overcame resistance to changing an entire industry. In seeking to shift the sale of prescription drugs to over-the-counter status, they met predictable resistance from doctors, pharmacists, trade associations, the Food and Drug Administration, from their own internal management, and also, ironically, from customers who stood to benefit from the lower cost. Collins, who had been greatly responsible for the deft handling of the Tylenol tampering crisis as president of the McNeil division of Johnson & Johnson, is a profit-oriented Humanist who saw that he could not command the desired change. He managed to get the resisting parties on board by starting from where *they* were—by addressing their various self-interested concerns—and then letting them buy into the higher-order value of lower health care costs.

Internal change was just as complex. Marketer Ed Smith could not reach all of Schering-Plough's constituencies by acting alone, but most of the managers he needed for the outreach effort had been enculturated in a different environment. To create an entire team devoted to the change, Smith introduced values-based leadership to the firm. Spending none of his time on controls, threats, incentives, or pleas for cooperation, he instead discussed with the team the values that would be enhanced by the change effort. In the end, he created a cadre of "virtual Eds," each as effective at communicating those values as he was himself, and each with full authority to speak on behalf of the company. The lesson here is that to be an effective leader of leaders, one need not be CEO or president or even have much power in the conventional sense. Instead, Ed Smith had a powerful concept of what the proper relationship should be between leaders and followers.

Lodwrick Cook

Atlantic Richfield's Lodwrick Cook led an unusual transformation at the company where he had spent his entire career, working his way up from the Louisiana oil fields to the executive suite. During his tenure as CEO, Cook returned ARCO to the inspiring values promulgated in the 1970s by its deceased president, Thornton Bradshaw—values that had won ARCO wide recognition as the leader of its industry. Unfortunately, much of the force of those values had been lost in the 1980s when Bradshaw left the company. Bradshaw's leadership was based on stakeholder symmetry, the belief that share-owners are best served in the long run when corporations attempt to satisfy the legitimate claims of all parties who have a stake in them—including customers, employees, suppliers, governments, host communities, and the investors themselves. Bradshaw viewed the task of leadership as resolving conflict between the competing claims of these constituencies, providing balance among their legitimate in-terests. To Cook's credit, even in bad economic times, he returned ARCO to the philosophical path pioneered by Bradshaw. Cook was able to do so, in large part, because he was trusted. Lod asked ques-tions, admitted when he was wrong, and practiced the traditional values of the company. That's integrity.

Anita Roddick

Anita Roddick's inclusion here is problematic. She is the founder of England's Body Shop International, a chain of four hundred stores in thirty-four countries that makes and markets products that "cleanse, polish, and protect the skin and hair." Elizabeth Arden once wrote that "the cosmetics business is the nastiest business in the world," but Roddick's intention has been to create a firm that will be recognized for its compassion, caring, and candor. Roddick writes in her firm's one-sentence mission statement, "We will be known as the most honest cosmetics company around."

Cynics call it the trendiest company around: the Body Shop does no animal testing, all its products are biodegradable, all come from ingredients "as close to the natural source as possible," no aerosol containers are ever used, and everything from labels and annual re-ports to the bottles used to contain cosmetics are recycled. Moreover, the Body Shop advertises only to provide information, not to create demand; each shop is required to undertake a community service project (on company time); and it contracts for products in the Third World in imaginative job-creation projects among particularly destitute populations ("Trade, Not Aid" is the motto—critics jeer-ingly accuse the company of "leftist exploitation of labor"). Roddick is many times a millionaire and has been awarded the highest civilian honor, the Order of the British Empire, as much for her Thatcher-approved entrepreneurship as for her self-proclaimed do-goodism. In light of her impressive accumulation of sterling, her critics say that she has merely capitalized on the values of her times in the way that Elizabeth Arden responded to the quite different market demands of her era. So, they ask, what's all the fuss about Roddick's "virtue"? A professor at the Harvard Business School put the cynics' case against Roddick to me in this fashion: "Be a Realist—Roddick has just come up with an *au courant* marketing strategy."

I have no idea what Roddick's motives are, but she is a Rushmorean in the clear distinction she draws between ends and means. To her, the purpose of the Body Shop is to provide society with goods and services that it needs. The measure of its success in doing so—and the reward for its efforts—is profit. The profit is then viewed as the means to improve the standard of living and quality of life of the people whose lives the corporation touches. Let there be no doubt, profits are the irreducible minimum. Anita Roddick is the first person to salute the old notion of "the more profits, the better." "I think profits are jolly good!" she proclaims, but is quick to add that profits are means, not ends. She uses the company's profits for higher ends, and this inspires her employees, customers, and investors. For example, the Body Shop invested £8 million to build a soap factory in Glasgow in what is one of Europe's worst slum areas (unemployment reaches the 70 percent level). The Body Shop plows 25 percent of the profits from the plant back into the community, "and *they* can tell us what to do with it," Roddick says. "Now, *that's* what you do with profits."

Equally able to make money by investing in a nice, safe suburban industrial park or by investing in risky Glasgow, she chooses the latter. Able to make money either through the hard-sell advertising of sex and glamour or by providing consumer information on health and physiology, she chooses the latter. After a thoughtful moral analysis, she has concluded that it is better in the long run for her investors and her company that the people of Glasgow be employed consumers rather than disaffected social burdens, and better that her customers be healthy rather than comparing themselves invidiously with the actor Catherine Deneuve. As a result, in the short term she and her investors may have to be content with being very rich instead of fabulously wealthy, but their hope is that their children may inherit a better world as the result of this small deferment of gratification. In effect, Anita Roddick has made a moral choice, and whether one agrees with her values or not, such a choice is an essential aspect of Rushmorean leadership.

It can be argued that all this may be well and good for Roddick, but isn't she "imposing her values" on investors who prefer a pound note today to two in the future and on those customers who are indifferent to natural products and are shopping only for the lowest-priced items? The answer is that traditionally managed firms also have agendas based on unexamined values—or at least values that they don't make explicit—and they are also governed by assumptions about profit, products, and managerial processes. What differentiates Roddick from her competitors is that she makes *everything* explicit, from her ingredients to her values. Thus her investors, customers, and other stakeholders are able to make more informed choices about whether or not they wish to do business with her.

Still, I would be reluctant to advance Roddick to full Rushmorean status for one major reason: the values of the Body Shop are her values, not necessarily the values of those who work with her. Because employees don't have quite the freedom that investors have to choose where to put their allegiance, there is, ironically, an element of forced conformity at the Body Shop that one gets at traditionally managed firms at which diversity of thought is not celebrated. Anita Roddick has no qualms about imposing her values on her organization, and she is often her own worst enemy in her self-centered public pronouncements that often have little to do with the actual practice of the Body Shop. Thus while I admire Roddick, she falls short of manifesting a Rushmorean level of respect for her employees.

Jacques Raimond and Jacques Benz

Jacques Raimond and Jacques Benz are leaders of leaders at France's GSI Corporation. This computer services company has succeeded without forcing traditional Gallic values on its operations dotted around the globe. Inspired by Robert Townsend's 1969 classic exposition of Rushmorean leadership, *Up the Organization*, Raimond and Benz were among the first European business leaders to predicate their managerial philosophy on the universal principle of "Respect for People." Annually, they survey all their employees to ensure that the company practices that principle—and doesn't promote managers who fail to do so.

A Raft of Women Entrepreneurs

Six and a half million women entrepreneurs head over a third of all businesses in America (up from only 5 percent in 1972). Have you heard about Ruth Owades (founder of Gardeners Eden), Gun Denhart (head of Hannah Andersson), Ella Williams (owner of Aegir Systems), or Sophia Collier (who recently sold her company Soho Cola to Seagrams)? You won't read about them in the traditional business press, but as described in Joline Godfrey's *Our Wildest Dreams*, these and countless other women entrepreneurs are quintessential Rushmoreans. Godfrey's book illustrates that values-based leadership is practiced in a lot more places than one would believe if one's only source of information were the *Wall Street Journal*.

Larry "the Legend" Lewis

My final example, Larry Lewis, is included not because he is rich, powerful, famous, or even a corporate sort but because he belies the notion that leaders must be prisoners of the situations in which they find themselves. In one of the nastiest and most brutish of all environments—the world of Little League baseball!—Lewis practices Rushmorean leadership. As manager of the 1994 world champion Long Beach, California, baseball team, he demonstrated that one needn't be a stereotypical, abusive Little League parent. Not only does Lewis insist that the children on his team not be criticized for their mistakes, but he extends that principle to the kids on the opposing team as well. If a member of the press suggests that the pitcher on the other team has been wild, Lewis characteristically "looks at the floor and waits for the conversation to move in other directions." In his manifest respect for people, Larry the Legend shows that coaches can be winners without being abusive monsters.

Commonalities

Certain themes run through these examples of Rushmorean leadership. Each of the individuals cited is an inclusive leader of leaders. That inclusion is a big tent, extending over all affected parties, constituencies, and stakeholders. Inclusive leaders enable others to lead by sharing information, by fostering a sense of community, and by creating a consistent system of rewards, structure, process, and communication. They are committed to the principle of opportunity, giving all followers the chance to make a contribution to the organization. The values-based leadership they all practice is based on an inspiring vision. And each is dedicated to institutionalizing continuous change, renewal, innovation, and learning. And the bottom line in what they do is adherence to the moral principle of respect for people.

Importantly, that respect is not contingent on anything. On all of the factors just mentioned, the Corporate Rushmoreans are consistent and persistent—which is different from being rigid and inflexible, in that the former attitude accommodates and even encourages disagreement and divergent viewpoints, whereas the latter is deaf to dissent. If this distinction seems somewhat paradoxical, in fact, Rushmorean leadership is often about the management of paradox. Simultaneously, these leaders are concerned with both continuity and change, with the short and the long term, with accountability and freedom, with planning and flexibility, with, in

fact, the intrinsic contradiction between leadership and participation. In a practical, business sense, values-based leadership provides
for internal, strategic unity while at the same time encouraging
independent entrepreneurial initiative.

Let us now analyze the relevant examples of leading change
among the organizations described above—specifically, the Girl
Scouts, Herman Miller, Corning, Motorola, SAS, Phillips–Van
Heusen, Polaroid, Schering-Plough, MasterCard, Ford, and ARCO—
to see what commonalities they might share. Though the leaders of
these organizations shared the philosophical commonalities just
cited, they each changed their organizations—indeed, remade those
cultures, and themselves, radically—by using *different methods*. To
repeat a central theme: Rushmorean leadership is *not* a function of
technique; rather, it is a function of attitudes and ideas. There was
no one formula that enabled these leaders to alter the outmoded
ways of their organizations. Instead, they each institutionalized a
variety of change processes—processes that in some cases took as
long as ten years to show clear results. Though the mechanisms by
which change was achieved vary in detail, all entailed one form or
another of decentralization of decision making, monitoring of stakeholder needs, challenging of assumptions, and providing appropriate rewards and incentives for all of these activities.

In each case, the process began with a sine qua non of change:
a clear, long-term, top-management commitment to the hard work
of altering corporate culture, beginning with themselves as leaders.
Let me clarify what such change really means, as it is not like
changing furniture or changing channels on TV. As the Ford
example illustrates, it is just as absurd to talk of changing the culture of a firm into something radically different as it is to talk about
manipulating your personality to become someone you aren't. In
the 1980s, the usefulness of the concept of corporate culture was
nearly lost when management gurus defined culture in terms of symbols, slogans, heroes, rites, and rituals. These may be *manifestations*
of culture—although any graduate student in anthropology could

come up with more sophisticated examples—but they are *not* culture. A culture is a system of beliefs and actions that characterize a particular group. Culture is the unique whole—the shared ideas, customs, assumptions, expectations, philosophy, traditions, mores, and values—that determines how a group of people will behave. When we talk of a corporation's culture, we mean the complex, interrelated whole of standardized, institutionalized, habitual behavior that characterizes that firm and that firm only. Thus to talk about a culture as "it" is absurd: culture is "us." To talk about top management's role in changing corporate culture is to talk about people changing *themselves*, not changing some "it" or "them" outside the door to the executive suite.

To think in terms of "it" is to fall into the trap that ensnared the deceased shah, Mohammed Reza Pahlavi. He tried to change Iranian culture by bringing the country up-to-date a bit: giving women a few rights, taking away some of the power of the clergy, introducing Western education and material goods. In fact, the erstwhile shah was a champ at manipulating symbols, slogans, heroes, rites, and rituals (just think of the big party he threw in the desert to commemorate the founding of Persepolis—a ritual that set him back a few million smackers, what with the elephants and the helicopter shuttle service and all).

Significantly, it is *exactly* the shah's approach to change that was advocated by the 1980s culture vultures. A favorite story used by consultants at the time to illustrate "how to do a successful culture change" concerned a Silicon Valley company in which the CEO decided to "shake up his troops." He called an off-site meeting at a nearby motel and started into the usual, boring routine with overheads and flip charts when, suddenly, out on the lawn landed several helicopters manned by "guards" who took the executives "captive" and whisked them off to a remote beach. There the executives found the elements of the new "culture" that the CEO had cooked up for them. There were belly dancers with the new company logo on their tummies and elephants sporting banners with the new company slogan, omnipresent during two days of rituals designed to demonstrate a complete break with the past. It was a great story. I have only one trouble with the whole idea: I don't believe it worked—or if it did, it didn't last. For all the shah's fun and games, bread and circuses, rites and rituals, he failed *completely* to alter Iran's underlying fundamentalist Islamic values. Why should we believe that the Silicon Valley CEO would have had any more success than the shah? (That the shah was also corrupt and authoritarian didn't help, either; but even if he had been an honest and decent guy, he was still going about change in the wrong way.)

Effective change builds on the existing culture. A group will reject a foreign system of values the way a healthy body rejects a virus. Anthropologists know that culture change occurs in one of two basic ways. The first is revolutionary. This is always the course of disaster. Whether it is a planned, Maoist-like cultural revolution or the unplanned collapse of a primitive culture that results from contact with the powerful technology, organization, and religions of the West, revolutionary culture change is always shocking, painful, disruptive, and undesirable. The second form is evolutionary. For example, over time, American culture has evolved from a rural European, Protestant, and traditionalist past to an urban, heterogeneous, secular, and modernist present. The agents of change—politicians, business leaders, inventors, union organizers, artists, writers, scholars—moved the country forward by reference to the "things that have made this country great." Can you name a Democratic candidate for president who didn't remind the citizenry that his was the party of Jefferson and Jackson or a Republican candidate who didn't evoke Lincoln, much as Lincoln himself evoked the Founders? Every one of these agents of change has known that success depends on the active support of the people, and for the people to become involved in change, they must see some familiar elements of continuity. Franklin Roosevelt could succeed in changing America because he put the radical reforms he sought in the context of traditions, systems, and beliefs with which the people were familiar;

in contrast, American Communist leaders of the same era failed to make converts because they tried to *impose* a system that was foreign to the traditions and values of the citizenry.

If you are starting to get the idea that altering the culture of a corporation is slow, hard work, you're getting the picture. But when the leaders of a company understand that change must be based on the current culture of the company (Lee Iacocca's "new Chrysler" was still Chrysler at heart—he couldn't have turned it into a cultural clone of IBM no matter what), and when they have the patience to involve the entire organization in the process of change, it is possible to turn a company around—given the better part of a decade to do it.

In general, the successful processes of change initiated at the companies cited in this chapter had the following things in common:

- *Change had top-management support.* Because the process of changing the entire culture of a large organization is a slow one, the leaders of the corporation must make a commitment to the long, hard work involved—including the commitment to change their own behavior.

- *Change built on the unique strengths and values of the corporation.* Organizations don't start with a coherent philosophy or set of values. These evolve over time, pragmatically, and grow out of experience. New values can't be created by fiat.

- *The specifics of change were not imposed from the top.* Instead, all levels of the corporation participated broadly and openly in all stages of the process. Those at the top seldom "do" anything. Rather, leaders create the conditions in which followers may take productive action.

- *Change was holistic.* Because the parts of a culture are all complexly interrelated, changing one part requires changing them all to achieve consistency among objectives, strategies, rewards, structure, training, management style, and control systems.

- *Change was planned.* The long-term process was mapped out in advance, and there was a period of education in which every employee was informed about the what and the why of the effort. The process was broken down into small, doable tasks.

- *Changes were made in the guts of the organization.* Power relationships, information access, and reward systems all must be altered in meaningful ways.

- *Change was approached from a stakeholder viewpoint.* Because the goal of change must be to meet the needs of all corporate stakeholders as efficiently as possible, the primary source of impetus and direction for change usually comes from the external environment, often from customers.

- *Change became ongoing.* Because the environment doesn't stand still and the needs of stakeholders aren't static, the idea is to institutionalize a process of continuing change.

All of this—especially the final point—requires Rushmorean leadership. Indeed, most Rushmorean leaders encourage the challenging of sacred cows as the source of continuing renewal. Max De Pree once explained what that process entails: "The part of our strategy that is renewing is our continuing to question what it is that has changed—the asking of ourselves, figuratively, what day it is. And then asking, if this is the new condition and the new day, what is the need and what is appropriate?"

Max may have inherited the change "gene" from his father, D. J., but how can a company institutionalize what the De Prees did naturally? Verne Morland, an executive at NCR, suggests that the same effect can be had by hiring a corporate "fool." Like King Lear's

Fool, the corporate equivalent would be licensed "to challenge by jest and conundrum all that is sacred and all that the savants have proved to be true and immutable." Though not necessarily dressed in motley, spangles, and bells, the fool would be obligated to "stir up controversy, respect no authority, and resist pressures to engage in detailed analyses." In keeping with William James's observation that "genius . . . means little more than the facility of perceiving in an unhabitual way," management consultant Nancy Reeves suggests that women may be natural to this role because "they have been outside the status quo ante, and are free to marshal historic exclusion for positive ends. . . . Women have not learned, [and] therefore do not have to unlearn, principles no longer pertinent. . . . Women might be the utterers of today's imperative blasphemies." If she is correct, that much misused word *diversity* has a practical application.

No matter how they do it, Rushmorean leaders create a climate in which assumptions can be continually tested and, if proved wanting, revised. And the opportunity to do this is not reserved to one leader (or even a privileged few). Because they recognize that wisdom seldom, if ever, resides exclusively in one powerful source, the corporate Rushmoreans create organizations open to taking long, honest looks at themselves, to identifying their strengths and weaknesses, their warts as well as their beauty marks. Ironically, the least Rushmorean of presidents, Calvin Coolidge, understood the risk of failing to do this and the reward inherent in success: "Progress depends very largely on the encouragement of variety. Whatever tends to standardize the community, to establish fixed and rigid modes of thought, tends to fossilize society. . . . It is the ferment of ideas, the clash of disagreeing judgments, the privilege of the individual to develop his own thoughts and shape his own character, that makes progress possible."

Caveat: All this heady talk about change and flexibility might easily be misinterpreted as supporting contingency, or situational, leadership. In fact, it is exactly the opposite. While the Corporate Rushmoreans are masters at quickly and appropriately changing their strategies, structures, policies, and programs to meet the exigencies of the competitive environment, they almost never change their fundamental values. An even stronger distinction is this: the Rushmoreans change their pragmatics, not their moral principles. Indeed, it is by always remaining true to moral principles, such as respect for people, that Rushmoreans create a climate of trust in which their followers are willing to risk strategic and tactical change.

We conclude this review of the Corporate Rushmoreans with an unsolved mystery: if the benefits of values-based leadership are so great, why don't more executives practice it? We find, in Chapters Three through Six, that the answer to that question is simple, but overcoming the resistance to the practice of values-based leadership is complex and complicated. It turns out that the source of resistance to the Rushmorean approach is so deeply rooted in our collective psyches, experiences, and assumptions that we must dig to painful depths to reveal it. We all resist committing ourselves to the practice of such leadership, and most of us deny that we hold back our commitment. We now turn to the arduous and, for some people, threatening task of revealing why, at heart, so few of us are Rushmoreans.

3

The Realists and the Fallacy
of Tough Leadership

The careers of the Rushmoreans and the painting *Christ's Entry into Brussels in 1889* illustrate the general proposition that there is no alternative to the practice of values-based leadership. The argument has now been advanced that resistance to change in complex democratic societies can be overcome in no other fashion that is both moral and effective. Yet having advanced that proposition, it has not been proved. Moreover, I readily admit not only that it is difficult to do so, but also that the vast majority of scholars and executives with whom I have discussed the matter reject my conclusion. Over the past dozen years, I have had the opportunity to discuss the issue in many diverse settings. After presenting examples of individuals who practice values-based leadership, I typically ask these audiences, "Why isn't this style of leadership practiced more often?" The responses can be grouped into five major categories:

- "It's no different from what [executive so-and-so] is doing." Values-based leadership is rejected as being undifferentiated from traditional models.

- "It's not theoretically sound." Values-based leadership is rejected as being at odds with either contingency theory or the results of social science research.

- "It doesn't work." Values-based leadership is dismissed as ineffective.

- "It's incompatible with human nature." Values-based leadership is considered antithetical to what is known about the nature of such immutable factors as hierarchical dominance, the role of testosterone, and the male ego.

- "It's countercultural." Values-based leadership is said to run counter to the historical fact that there have always been strongly directive leaders in Western (and Asian) societies.

Each of these objections is legitimate, and there are no easy or self-evident refutations to any of them. They each deserve thorough discussion because, until they are demonstrated to be false, the presumption remains in favor of the rejection of values-based leadership. In the chapters that immediately follow, we examine the arguments and evidence against these five tenets of conventional wisdom. We examine them not in any particular order because, as we shall discover, they are all of a piece: they all originate in basic and traditional cultural assumptions about the necessity of "tough," albeit benign, "one-man rule."

In my discussions with business audiences, I usually begin by asking, "Who comes to mind when you hear the word *leader?*" The Rushmoreans are seldom mentioned. Almost invariably, generals (Patton, MacArthur, Schwarzkopf), football coaches (Lombardi, Landry, Shula), and political leaders (Churchill, Thatcher, Lee Kwan Yew) will be cited. Indeed, I would say that Lee and Patton are mentioned more often than any other individuals (in nonbusiness groups, Gandhi, Martin Luther King Jr., Mother Teresa, Lincoln, and JFK are most frequently cited, along with Churchill, who is equally popular with both types of audiences.)

Singapore's Lee: The Ultimate Realist

That Singapore's Lee is a favorite of business managers is now increasingly recognized. Some three thousand foreign firms have established a presence in his tiny city-state. *Time* magazine's Jay Branegan reports the following from a Western financial analyst based in Singapore: "*Fortune* 500 executives love it here because the government runs the country the way AT&T would." More important, Lee and Singapore have been advanced as exemplars of an alternative to Jeffersonian democracy that is increasingly popular in many corporate, government, and academic circles. Francis Fukuyama, author of the influential *End of History*, argues that in the wake of Marxism's demise Singapore "is the one potential competitor to Western liberal democracy, and its strength and legitimacy [are] growing daily."

One can see why. Singapore is an island populated by three million obsessively hardworking people, 78 percent of whom are ethnic Chinese. The nation's per capita GNP recently exceeded that of the United States, and it boasts the second-highest standard of living in Asia, after Japan. In this squeaky-clean mini-utopia, there is no unemployment, crime, pornography, litter, or graffiti—nor are there any dope peddlers, unwed mothers, or illiterate sixteen-year-olds.

Most remarkably, Lee and his government are honest: Singapore is free of the graft and corruption commonplace throughout the developing world. Lee serves not to enrich himself but to increase the standard of living of his people (although he recently retired from public office, I refer to his rule in the present tense because he continues to be the most powerful individual in his nation). When he assumed power in 1965, Singapore was on the verge of civil war, beset by racial unrest between Chinese and Malayans, and the economy was in a typical postcolonial shambles. Lee quickly changed all that, single-handedly resolving the short-term political crises and putting into place the necessary structure for the long-term transformation of Singapore's economy into the world-beater it since has become. Having turned Singapore into a capitalist utopia that runs like clockwork, it is no wonder that Lee is so often cited as a "model leader." To many businesspeople, Lee represents the classic corporate turnaround chief executive, the take-charge guy who knows what needs to be done and has the intestinal fortitude to see that his vision is carried out.

Indeed, Lee brooks little opposition to his will. Singapore's impressive efficiency comes at the price of civil liberty: the nation has no bill of rights, no dissent, no real democracy. The country's Internal Security Act allows the government to lock up dissenters without trial. Even its admirable cleanliness is achieved by the draconian enforcement of laws against littering (there's a $625 penalty) and other forms of antisocial behavior (a $94 fine is imposed on persons who fail to flush public toilets, and feeding birds is a no-no punishable by law). The freedoms of its residents are limited in large things and small (chewing gum is banned, and there is a $312 fine for eating on the subway). Lee argues that the economic efficiency of Singapore has resulted from his enlightened leadership, which has steered a course between the anarchic democracy of the West and the self-serving despotism of the Third World: "What a country needs to develop is discipline rather than democracy. . . . The exuberance of democracy leads to undisciplined and disorderly conditions which are inimical to development."

In early 1994, theretofore hidden public support for Lee's philosophy surfaced in this country when an American teenager living in Singapore was sentenced to be flogged for having vandalized numerous cars. A few American public officials rushed to the guilty youth's defense on the grounds that caning constituted a violation of both a 1982 declaration of the United Nation's Committee on Human Rights and the spirit of the U.S. Bill of Rights, which forbids "cruel and unusual punishments." But these politicians were surprised to find themselves without much of a constituency: opinion polls showed that close to 40 percent of Americans supported the Singapore ruling, and—more surprisingly—a great many thought that corporal punishment should be introduced here. Looking at the issue from a different ideological perspective, other Americans supported the Singaporeans' right to do whatever they please on the grounds of cultural relativism. We return later to that perspective because it constitutes a philosophical justification for contingency theory.

Lee's greatest appeal is to people who value order. He says, "The expansion of the right of the individual to behave or misbehave as he pleases has come at the expense of orderly society." Those who share that perspective are more than willing to overlook Lee's despotic ways. In his defense, they say, "Be realistic—the alternatives to Lee's strong leadership are either chaos or communism."

Consider for a moment that voice of Realism: "In a crisis, whom would you want as your leader, someone who says, 'Let's take a vote' or a take-charge guy who immediately sizes up the situation, assumes control, gives citizens their marching orders, and makes sure that they do what they are told? Be realistic, now—isn't the latter going to be the one who saves lives in an emergency?"

Is "Tough" Effective? Some Data

When it comes to our basic philosophy of leadership, most of us are Realists (as opposed to Rushmoreans). When push comes to shove, we tend to believe that a single, strong individual—like Lee Kwan Yew—must assume full authoritative command. The Rushmorean alternative—"soft," "touchy-feely," "feminine," "democratic"—is thought to lead to ineffectiveness, insubordination, and anarchy. The Realist typically illustrates this proposition with reference to the "heat of battle": troops in combat, firefighters battling a blaze, airplane pilots facing a life-or-death situation. When lives are on the line, says the Realist, that's not the time for "effeminate handholding." By extension, countries and corporations also need tough, no-nonsense leadership when they face crises—Lee fighting communism and Third World anarchy, or the CEO of General Electric fighting for the corporation's survival. In brief, Rushmorean leadership by listening and by inclusion is seen by the Realist as a luxury at best, and in hard times, the leader *must* tighten the reins. Here's how Doug Allen, a management professor at the University

of Denver, explained the Realist (he called it "situational") position to a *Los Angeles Times* reporter: "Yelling and cursing at people
may not be inappropriate in some situations. You may not want a
commander on a bombing run to engage in high levels of participative decision-making while approaching the target."

The National Aeronautics and Space Administration (NASA)
tested that proposition in the 1970s in a series of experiments
reported by Robert R. Blake and Jane S. Mouton. The results do not
constitute scientific truth, but they are directly relevant to the central controversy about leadership: Who is likely to be more effective leading change, the Rushmorean or the Realist?

NASA's research was based on the conventional Realist wisdom
that airline accidents were more likely to occur when "there had
been a general erosion of the captain's authority in the cockpit, and
this could be corrected by strengthening the captain's skill in the
exercise of direction and discipline." In the language of the Realist,
NASA was going to see if it could toughen up namby-pamby pilots
so that they would "act like men" in emergencies. Before undertaking such training, NASA thought it wise to check the Realists'
assumptions. It did so by putting three-person crews into flight sim-
ulators and measuring their effectiveness in dealing with computer-
generated "crises" caused by air traffic, equipment failure, bad
weather, and the like.

They discovered that pilots would react to a crisis in one of two
ways: most responded "with the traditional pattern of authority-
obedience," barking an immediate command, but some consulted
their copilots and engineers before making a decision, asking their
crews, in effect, "Holy cow—whaddya think we oughta do?"

The researchers generally found that the pilots who "took
charge" were less likely to arrive at a safe and valid response to the
crisis than those who sought more information and advice before
deciding what action to take. Hence Blake and Mouton concluded
from the experiment that although "there can be no doubt that the
captain is in charge, and it is his responsibility to reach an ultimate

decision, one key to increased safety is to keep the crisis situation open to interaction, not to shut it down. The captain needs to keep information flowing back and forth rather than to give decisive commands to 'do this, do that.'"

When the command-issuing types were asked why they had acted so decisively to assume complete authority, they would often explain that "a crisis is no time for handholding." Why these pilots assumed that gathering information from others was "handholding" is apparently a question that NASA didn't ask. Yet it seems relevant; after all, the other pilots who had consulted their crews hadn't held hands. In fact, these pilots had remained as firmly in charge of their cockpits as the others and had also made the final decisions about to what to do. Still, the majority of pilots found it threatening—to their egos? their authority? their masculinity?—simply to ask of their subordinates, "What do you know?" or "What do you think?"

Though we can only guess at the psychological factors that influenced the "tough" pilots' behavior, we know for certain that their stated reason for not soliciting information—"no time"—is bogus. NASA had reviewed Federal Aviation Administration (FAA) data and established that, in almost all airborne crisis situations, crews have at least thirty seconds in which to act, and the entire exercise of asking the two questions and listening to the replies takes five to fifteen seconds. In the pilots' defense, one could argue that they might not have known that they had so much time. So let's give them the benefit of the doubt.

But should we be so generous to the equally tough take-charge leaders in corporate management and in government who cite a lack of time or opportunity to consult with others before making important decisions? Here that familiar rationale looks even more like a flimsy excuse, for how often in corporate affairs or the affairs of state is there insufficient time for leaders to consult key staff and affected constituents before making a decision? How often is the leader the only one with relevant information and understanding of a problem? And how often is it that no one else but the leader has a useful perspective to bring to a question? As improbable as these hypothetical conditions may be, they are unstated premises on which Realists predicate their proof that command-and-control leadership is the most effective way to deal with a crisis.

Nearly all arguments in favor of a single, strong commander ultimately boil down to a single question: Whom do you want as your leader in time of war? The entire argument is weak. A far better case could be made for single-person leadership in ad hoc situations. For example, when mudslides threatened homes in my neighborhood, a woman took charge and organized a team of strangers who had volunteered to place sandbags and bales of straw. No one questioned her authority, even though she did not organize the work in the most efficient way. Nonetheless, we were grateful for her willingness to lead, and we followed out of gratitude, in part because none of us wanted the responsibility. It was simply more efficient in the long run to do things her way than it was to call a meeting in the middle of the flood-threatened highway to try to devise a better system. The point is that we all bought into this one-time effort. Yet if we found that we had to go through the drill again the next day, or if it turned into a regular job, we wouldn't be compliant and unquestioningly willing to follow our volunteer commander. In fact, under those real world conditions, it would have been more efficient for us to pool our ideas and find the best way to get the work done. Had our ad hoc leader then listened to us and incorporated the good suggestions made, she would have become a legitimate Rushmorean leader.

Realist Assumptions and Philosophical Roots

The Realist argument breaks down completely when their rationale is extended to noncrisis situations because they claim it is always desirable to have at the helm of any enterprise a leader who is "battle-ready," if not battle-tested. Specifically, Realists say that change is most likely to be effective when it is directed by a leader who, like Lee, is "not afraid to make tough decisions." The desirability of command-and-control leadership in noncrisis situations is supported by a host of Realist assumptions:

- People are by nature evil and self-interested; therefore, they must be controlled.

- Human groups are given to anarchy.

- Progress comes from discipline, order, and obeying tradition.

- Order arises from leadership.

- There can be only one leader in a group.

- The leader is the dominant member of the group.

- Dominance is based on levels of testosterone (high levels of which translate into a willingness to make tough decisions).

- Leadership is the exercise of power.

- Any sign of weakness will undercut the leader's authority.

- Might makes right (the leader is, by definition, worthy of loyalty).

- Loyalty, effort, and change can be commanded successfully.

Such premises are derived from the philosophies of Plato, Aristotle, Confucius, Hobbes, Machiavelli, and Carlyle. They are all based on partial truths that, when applied as a unified philosophy of leadership, constitute the strongest line of defense for the legitimacy of the rule of such political autocrats as Singapore's Lee Kwan Yew. Realism dominates thought about leadership in both Eastern and Western cultures. In fact, Lee Kwan Yew is the quintessential

Platonic leader, and Singapore is the closest thing extant to Plato's Republic. Moreover, Lee articulately defends his rule in Platonic and, especially, Confucian terms. To understand the long-standing hold of the Realist position on the collective mind of the civilized world, we must return to those philosophical origins.

The idea that leadership is a solo act—that it is a privilege, in Plato's words, reserved for "one, two, or at any rate, a few"—has been part of both Western and Eastern philosophy for two and a half millennia. The central practical question that concerned Confucius and Plato was the legitimacy of leadership: who is *entitled* to lead. They concluded that civilization begins when leadership becomes earned rather than inherited. If, as it often turned out, the son of the chief was a dummy, retaining him as leader was both unjust and inefficient (and it could lead to tyranny if the dummy had to resort to force to maintain power). Monarchy would simply never do.

Democracy wasn't the answer either; in the words of Plato (which Lee echoes), it creates a city "full of freedom and frankness, in which man may do and say what he likes. . . . Where such freedom exists, the individual is clearly able to order for himself his own life as he pleases." Such a state may sound agreeable to the modern libertarian, but to Plato it was tantamount to anarchy. Worse, political liberty leads to political equality, a situation that is unjust because people are not, by nature, equal: "Liberty is full of variety and disorder, and [dispenses] a sort of equality to equals and unequals alike." That might sound desirable to modern egalitarians, but Plato found it to be the second-least-acceptable form of government, only one rung above tyranny.

Plato proposed the alternative in *The Republic*, a "well-ordered state" characterized by "the rule of the few." This ruling elite, or oligarchy, is *not* composed of hereditary aristocrats who owe their positions to birth, wealth, force, or the inclination to power. The "guardians" of Plato's Republic—like the Mandarin sages described in Confucius' *Analects*—rule by force of their manifest "virtue."

The characteristics of this leadership elite are their knowledge, wisdom, competence, talent, and ability. In short, Plato proposes a nondemocratic state that is nonetheless just and legitimate because it is a meritocracy in which the leaders practice the "science of government"—which, he tells us, is "among the greatest of all sciences and most difficult to acquire." Again, because the mastery of this science is so rarely achieved, "any true form of government can only be supposed to be the government of one, two, or, at any rate, . . . a few . . . really found to possess the science." One, for instance, such as Lee Kwan Yew.

Plato's elite rule not for themselves but, like Lee, for the good of society as a whole. Though the Cambridge-educated Lee is capable of defending himself on Platonic grounds, when he is on his home turf he calls himself a Confucian. Writing around the time of Socrates, Confucius drew many of the same conclusions as the ancient Greeks, including the superiority of meritocratic oligarchy. And like them, Confucius' motivation in advocating such a form of leadership was his fear of disorder. Indeed, throughout history and across cultures, the dominant view has been that the only realistic alternative to anarchy, on the one hand, and tyranny, on the other, is benevolent despotism. Relatively few philosophers at any time or in any culture have placed much faith in the efficacy of the other possibility, democracy.

Given Singapore's miraculous economic growth, it is easy to understand why Lee is so popular with business managers, even though they tend to be the very same individuals who in the next breath vigorously oppose any governmental encroachment on their own freedoms. One might have expected believers in freedom instead to tout the capabilities of the democratic leaders of Spain and Portugal who, in the 1980s, produced phenomenal economic growth in their countries without the loss of individual freedom. But apparently two and a half millennia of cultural conditioning causes Realists to long for a "strong leader," even though they will rebel against anyone who dares tell them what to do.

When push comes to shove, the two-thousand-year-old attitude about the superiority of strongmen emerges from the collective unconscious. In June 1994, syndicated columnist Cal Thomas voiced the Realist position in defense of Colonel Oliver North (who had lied to Congress when testifying about the Iran-Contra affair in the 1980s and yet was now the Republican candidate for the U.S. Senate from Virginia), and in condemnation of the Rushmorean position taken by moderate Republicans: "Weak men fear strong men. They always have, because it exposes their own weakness. Too many Republicans prefer the way of conciliation and friendship-building with liberal Democrats to all-out warfare over ideology."

Corporate Realists

Of course, most citizens of Western democracies would balk at the prospect of Oliver North or Lee Kwan Yew at the head of their nation. But these same individuals have fewer qualms about the legitimacy of Realist leaders in private corporations. Platonic and Confucian assumptions are frequently used to legitimate the leadership style of such successful contemporary corporate strongmen as Goodyear's Stanley Gault, Allied Signal's Lawrence Bossidy, USF&G's Norman Blake, Compaq's Eckhard Pfeiffer, and Tenneco's Michael Walsh, all of whom were featured in a 1991 *Business Week* cover story titled "Corporate America Calls In a New Cold-Eyed Breed of CEO."

Each of these "cold-eyed" leaders assumed power during a crisis when "a firm hand was needed on the helm to avert disaster," and each took tough, decisive actions that were credited with "turning around" disastrous situations. Conceding those two points, the assumptions of the Realists are nonetheless specious on three grounds.

1. *The tough-guy actions of most leaders are often signs of their own past failures, of the failures of their predecessors, or of their current leadership shortcomings.* Let's examine the conditions in which the "turn-

around" artists cited by *Business Week* became darlings of Wall Street. A corporation was losing hundreds of millions of dollars, and its survival hung in the balance. A CEO was appointed who immediately closed the least efficient operations; sold off unrelated businesses; eliminated waste; postponed dividends; canceled executive perks; cut back research and development, training, and capital investment; and removed layers of fat (people). As a consequence of the savings derived from such actions, the leader balanced the budget and saved the company. Now, given the crisis the leader faced, were these actions (a) necessary steps, (b) commonsense responses to rectify past mismanagement, (c) desperate and unimaginative measures, or (d) evidence of great leadership? Wall Street Realists answer (d); Rushmoreans say any *but* (d). Yet it might be argued that I've loaded the dice and that these four options overlook the overriding fact that these leaders had the guts to take unpopular but unavoidable steps. Perhaps—but if these tough decisions were in fact unavoidable, almost any leader would have taken them; so how can doing the obvious and the necessary be taken as a sign of greatness? Instead, to qualify as a Rushmorean, a leader must have (a) avoided a crisis in the first place, (b) kept an unavoidable crisis to manageable proportions, (c) dealt with it in a constructive way that laid the groundwork for healthy growth in the future, and, in particular, (d) involved the affected parties at all stages, getting *them* to find ways to accomplish (a), (b), and (c).

Though it is probable that the aforementioned CEOs came on the scene too late to implement options (a) and (b), the pages of *Business Week* are replete with stories about leaders who are praised for undertaking massive downsizing of bureaucracies that they themselves created! More to the point, as the longtime Speaker of the House Sam Rayburn once put it, "Any jackass can kick a barn down, but it takes a good carpenter to build one." Should not the highest praise be reserved for those rare corporate leaders who institutionalize the ability constantly to meet competitive exigencies? On this score, the jury is still out on *Business Week*'s "cold-eyed breed."

2. *Tough guys don't lighten up when the crisis has passed.* Will Realist CEOs become Rushmoreans once the crises have passed at their firms? Many leadership theorists would predict that these CEOs will alter their style as conditions warrant. Because "it all depends," scholars argue, sometimes a leader must be tough and sometimes not so tough. We might well wonder if leaders' styles are as changeable as the coloration of chameleons.

The evidence is overwhelmingly negative. In 1965, Lee Kwan Yew assumed autocratic powers in Singapore to deal with racial unrest between Chinese and Malayans and to turn the economy around. By 1980, not only was the unrest a thing of the past, but the per capita income of Singaporeans was second only to the Japanese in all of Asia. By the end of that decade, there was no crisis in Singapore, political or economic. Did Lee then change his spots and begin preparing his country for full democracy? Quite the opposite: he actually increased censorship and further centralized his powers, warning of the moral laxity inherent in freedom. Ditto most strongman corporate leaders. Through fair weather and foul, American Airlines's Robert Crandall engages in a Cronus-like devouring of his own employees. Why? *Because there is always a crisis.* Being tough is not the exceptional behavior of wise leaders faced with five seconds in which to make a lifesaving decision; rather, it is their normal modus operandi.

3. *In the long run, strongmen are ineffective.* Evidence tends to support this assertion. For one thing, political strongmen turn out to be bad for their countries in the long run. Mussolini was the quintessential Realist; yet in the end, not only did Italian trains not run on time, but his country suffered the humiliation of military defeat. Also, the Realist pilots in the NASA experiment were the ones most likely to make bad decisions. Furthermore, corporate history shows that the performance of tough-guy CEOs, once they've done the easy cutting, almost always fades to mediocrity. There are exceptions, of course. The fabled Harold Geneen of International

Telephone and Telegraph (IT&T) was the toughest command-and-control CEO imaginable, yet he retired a clear winner. That is because the operative phrase is "in the long run." Practically the day after Geneen retired, the IT&T empire started to unravel. Geneen managed to beat the bell because he had a rare genius for detail, and he was a seven-day-a-week, eighteen-hour-a-day workaholic; for mere mortal strongmen who need to take an hour off once a year to go to the dentist, the fall comes more quickly.

Today the most faithful practitioners of Realism are such Asian disciples of Confucius as the communist colleagues of Deng Xiaoping in Beijing, Lee's conservative doppelgängers in Seoul and Taipei, and such capitalist business leaders as the American An Wang. Wang, an immigrant from China, founded Wang Laboratories in 1957 at the precocious age of thirty-one. By 1984, his computer firm had ten thousand employees and had increased its profits at the rate of 30 percent per annum for an entire decade. In 1992, then over $1 billion in debt, the firm filed for Chapter 11 bankruptcy protection, and its creditors contemplated liquidation of its few remaining assets. The Economist explains the sudden fall in this fashion: An Wang had "refused employees' pleas to launch general-purpose personal computers." A Confucian to the end, Wang equated employee involvement with anarchy. When a competitive crunch hit the computer industry, he responded by further centralizing power, even appointing his son CEO (much as Lee Kwan Yew turned the titular rule of Singapore over to the one person he was certain he could control, his own son).

The rule of Paul P. Kazarian—erstwhile chairman, CEO, and president of the Sunbeam-Oster company—did not degenerate into nepotism, but the New York Times says that his "intolerant" and "intimidating" leadership led to mutiny on the corporate bridge. Kazarian, like Business Week's tough CEOs, was a turnaround specialist noted for running a tight ship. Like them, he was a success as the Realists use that term. He had quickly turned a nearly bankrupt company into a highly profitable one with a 17 percent profit margin by taking "unavoidable" short-term actions to cut expenses. In the process, he created "more than $1 billion in wealth" for the company's original investors. Despite this success, his fellow executives went to the company's board and demanded Kazarian's ouster.

According to the *Times*, Kazarian couldn't understand what the problem was. Sure, he was "demanding," but what was wrong with that? Kazarian, like most tough leaders, apparently could not see the difference between being legitimately demanding, which is always desirable, and being immorally abusive, which is never acceptable:

- With a wave of his hand, he dismissed notions of trust and empowerment, saying that he trusted only his friends and family. . . .
- He acknowledged that he did grow impatient at times, but for reasons such as having to repeat and re-emphasize points to managers that he felt should have been fully digested the first time. "I come from the school of thought that if you teach someone once, you expect them to take the lesson."

That school of thought is, of course, the Realist school in which leaders expect to be immediately understood and obeyed. In contrast, Rushmoreans view leadership as teaching and dedicate their lives to finding ways to communicate their visions to their followers, recognizing that no one understands the need for change the first time it is presented.

Among the few teachers that businesspeople cite as successful leaders is Bobby Knight of Indiana University, one of the winningest coaches in the history of the National Collegiate Athletic Association (NCAA) and also one of the most abusive. Knight prides himself on his Vesuvian chair-throwing, fist-swinging temper tantrums, which he argues are necessary to motivate his players to do their best on the court. Others—including Lou Campanelli, erstwhile coach at the University of California, Berkeley—have emulated Knight's "winning" style. When Campanelli was fired in mid-season in 1993, the basketball coaches of America rallied to defend him on the grounds that he was simply demanding the best from his players. The coaches apparently believed, in proper Realist logic, that the behavior of a martinet is required to motivate players to perform, and that coaches who show respect for their players will be taken advantage of and hence end up losers. The athletic director at U.C., Berkeley had a different reading of reality: he argued that abusive leadership was anachronistic and that players wouldn't take it anymore. He believed that young people today are motivated not by push but by pull. As if to prove his point, the Cal team, which had had a losing record under Campanelli, won ten of its eleven remaining games under its Rushmorean replacement coach.

Perhaps the greatest myth blocking acceptance of Rushmorean leadership is that only Realists have high standards. In truth, not only can Rushmoreans have standards every bit as demanding as Realists, but they have a far greater chance of bringing out the best in their people. Yet the belief persists that Realist leadership is required for excellence, is necessary for change, and is the only alternative to chaos. In the next chapter, we examine these and several other lines in the defense of Realism.

· ·

Why Amoral Leadership Doesn't Work

Few leaders have been as successful at the art of change as South Africa's Nelson Mandela. On the eve of his ultimate electoral victory, May 1, 1994, the *New York Times*'s Bill Keller recapped Mandela's lengthy career, attempting to elucidate the essence of the Nobel Prize winner's leadership. The reporter concluded that, all things considered, Mandela was a pragmatist, a realist, a man willing to do whatever the situation required in order to succeed:

- Try as admirers will to sentimentalize Mr. Mandela, the president-in-waiting of a reborn South Africa is at heart the most practical of men.
- He is not unfeeling, but passion—even anger at what he has endured—does not drive him or distract him. He enjoys debate, but he is not a great philosopher or intellectual. He has principles, but he will bend them if they stand in the way of his objective—which, for the last half century, has been ending white domination.

In this view, President Mandela personifies contingency leadership, the Realism advocated by so many political theorists since the time of Machiavelli. Indeed, most students of leadership today subscribe to contingency theory—the most thoughtful of whom include Henry Kissinger and Gary Wills. Moreover, most corporate executives who say that how they lead change "depends on the situation" are also Realists; among the most successful of these are Goodyear's Stanley Gault, American Airlines's Robert Crandall, and, the subject of this chapter, General Electric's Jack Welch. They are wrong.

The moral and logical error inherent in contingency theory is *relativism,* the belief that there are no universal truths or objective knowledge save scientific proofs. In the relativist's belief system, there are no rights and wrongs—or if there are, these are purely personal concerns and as such are irrelevant to the practical arenas of statecraft and corporate leadership. We see evidence that relativism is erroneous when we read the career of Nelson Mandela not in Realist but rather in Rushmorean terms. Like Lincoln and Jefferson, Mandela was pragmatically willing to compromise wherever necessary on tactics, policies, strategies, alliances, and the like. But ipso facto, this ability to play the game of politics does not, as Keller implies, make one a Realist with no guiding principles. Keller himself notes that Mandela never compromised on "his objective": the goal of freedom and political equality for his people. Had Keller built his story around this point, he might have concluded that Mandela created followers precisely because they knew he would not compromise that goal, which was *their* goal. They trusted Mandela to act, at all times, in their interest.

The central fact about Mandela's leadership is that the people of South Africa trusted him. Mandela offered a clue why this was so in his response to a question posed by another American reporter on that same historic day. When asked what he had learned from his years of struggle, Mandela said the lesson was that "people respond to how you treat them. If you treat them with respect, and ignore the negatives, you get a positive reaction." You will recognize this as a restatement of the fundamental Rushmorean principle that trust derives from the respect a leader displays for followers. Respect for followers is made manifest by listening to them, faithfully representing them, pursuing their noblest aspirations, keeping promises made to them, and never doing harm to them or to their cause. Significantly, throughout his long career, Mandela was known as the quintessential listener. Though far from an eloquent phrasemaker, when he spoke at his party's victory rally, he addressed the party faithful not as his followers but as fellow leaders from whom he had learned by listening: "I am your servant. I don't come to you as a leader, as one above others. We are a great team. Leaders come and go, but the organization and the collective leadership that has looked after the fortunes and reversals of this organization will always be there. And the ideas I express are not ideas invented in my own mind."

Trustworthiness, respect, promise-keeping, service, faithfulness—these are moral principles. The subtle difference between Realist and Rushmorean leadership is that whereas the former is relativistic, the latter is founded on a few clear, inviolable moral principles. Hence the point of this chapter: lacking a moral compass, leaders in the Realist-relativist-contingency school are prone, when pressed by the inevitable exigencies of public life, to behave in ways that destroy the trust of followers. Because people will not follow the lead of those they mistrust, contingency leaders will often encounter insurmountable obstacles on the road to leading change.

This distinction is simple and basic, but it is not obvious. For example, the confusion between Realism and Rushmorean leadership surfaces when General Electric's Jack Welch is advanced as the model leader of change that young executives should emulate. Because the failure to distinguish between a pragmatic philosophy like Welch's, on the one hand, and a values-based philosophy like Mandela's, on the other, is at the heart of why leaders fail to bring about change, it is essential that we clarify this subtle difference. To do so, we must first take an important philosophical detour to understand the moral error at the root of Welch's contingency leadership.

Contingency in Theory

Contingency theory was developed for historical analysis, where it proved more useful than either determinism or the "great man" leadership theory in explaining why certain events occurred. Here is contingency theory in the words of Tolstoy: "Why did it happen in this and not in some other way? Because it happened so! Chance created the situation; genius utilized it." But as useful as it is in historical analysis, contingency theory is descriptive, not prescriptive; thus it is not a guide to action and not a moral philosophy.

Yet, unwittingly, contingency theory is used prescriptively in the academic study of leadership. For example, the proposition that "leaders of today's complex organizations should always listen to employees, customers, suppliers, and dealers" will be rejected by a large portion of the professorate on the grounds that it is "too extreme" and "not scientific." Why? Because nothing can be called true if one can think of an exception—in this case, an instance when a leader shouldn't listen. That amounts to saying that a leader who listens to an idea and then rejects it might actually generate more opposition to change. Because of that possibility of an exception to the rule, and also because we don't know enough about the role of listening in effective leadership, many professors are unwilling to teach anything about listening to their M.B.A. students—except that "it all depends." They would instead counsel their students thusly: "Sometimes you should listen, and sometimes you shouldn't, but we can't say for certain when you should and when you shouldn't."

Contingency theory is an invalid conclusion drawn from a valid observation. The theory derives logically from the great diversity found among people and from the incontestable fact that most human behavior is not reducible to scientific explanation. From this observation the professorate concludes that nothing prescriptive can be said about leadership other than "it all depends." If listening to one's followers is effective in only ninety-nine out of a hundred instances, the counsel to listen must be completely rejected as untrue and unscientific. That leadership is not a science is considered irrelevant. That social knowledge that is useful in ninety-nine out of a hundred instances (or even fewer) is good enough for practical people is beside the point to the professorate, which demands scientific truth or nothing. We shall see in a moment how, paradoxically, this high standard undermines the validity of contingency theory.

Because so little of human behavior can be proved scientifically, most social scientists end up as relativists when it comes to prescription. Indeed, relativism is modernism's dominant philosophical current, undergirding not only Realism and contingency theory but almost every other facet of serious thought as well. We find relativism in the Marxist notion that all knowledge is socially determined, in the nineteenth-century pragmatist belief that what is true is what works, in the twentieth-century anthropological idea of cultural relativism, and in the newer ethical philosophy known as moral relativism. In its most extreme form today, it is represented in the deconstructionist claim that "all knowledge is subjective" (a statement that, incidentally, is a tautology). Relativism makes for strange bedfellows: Henry Kissinger and his realpolitik, the advocate of "black math," and the news analyst who claims that Americans have no right to condemn Singaporeans for flogging criminals are, despite their apparent differences, all relativists. Oddly, then, many irrationalists and hardheaded Realists find themselves in the same intellectual camp.

Relativism grew to be such a large, accommodating tent both because its opposite, determinism, was so misguided and because it is in and of itself more right than wrong: Few aspects of social knowledge can be proved scientifically; most of what people believe to be true is subjective; and most of our factual knowledge is in fact influenced by our social conditions and environment. Where relativists err is to claim that there is no objective social knowledge at all and, worse, that it is always wrong to make moral judgments.

Putting relativism into practice, the executive director of one of Southern California's largest government agencies explained to me that he refrained from imposing democratic American values on employees from other cultures. As an example, he cited a Hispanic supervisor who, in the tradition of the *patrón*, refused to consult with the people who reported to him and, in the macho tradition, refused to treat his female peers at work as equals. The executive explained why he dared not attempt to change the supervisor's behavior: "Who is to say he is wrong? What right do I have to practice cultural imperialism?" One might argue that the Hispanic supervisor was working in the United States, and that is why. But to the relativist, national boundaries are arbitrary and hence irrelevant. Make the case clearer by moving it farther overseas, and relativists will say, "Who are Americans to say that Iraq should be a democracy?"

Such extreme cultural relativism is, in fact, what philosopher Mary Midgley terms "moral isolationism." She writes, "People usually take it up because they think it is a respectful attitude to other cultures. In fact, however, it is not respectful." For example, how is it respectful to Iraqis to say that we in the West will accept nothing less than democracy, but they are "different"? And who says that Iraqis—at least some of them—don't want democracy? Midgley illustrates this latter point with reference to the classical Japanese verb *tsujigiri*, which was used in the ancient samurai tradition to mean "trying out one's new sword on a chance wayfarer":

> A samurai sword had to be tried out because, if it was to work properly, it had to slice through someone at a single blow, from the shoulder to the opposite flank. Otherwise, the warrior bungled his stroke. This could injure his honor, offend his ancestors, and even let down the emperor. So tests were needed, and wayfarers had to be expended. Any wayfarer would do—provided, of course, that he was not another Samurai. . . . Now, when we hear of a custom like this, we may well reflect that we simply do not understand it; and therefore are not qualified to criticize it at all, because we are not members of that culture.

But hold on a minute—do we really think that no one in Japan ever asked, "Whoa, is this a healthy tradition?" Do we really think that the poor peasant who got sliced in half thought it was morally acceptable to use him as a human razor strop? Midgley asks, "Did he consent?"

Because relativism—and the Realist's contingency leadership it undergirds—is absolutist by its own terms, its logic can be destroyed if we show a single exception to the rule. The philosophy that claims "it all depends" can be shown to be false if we can agree on any principle that is not contingent or situational. The existence of one moral absolute would do the trick. I offer three such principles.

1. *Slavery is never justifiable.* In 1762, Jean-Jacques Rousseau explained why not in *The Social Contract*. Relativists, however, argue that the contemporary rejection of slavery is time-conditional: slavery is wrong now, but it wasn't wrong then. Or as white Southerners were wont to argue, "Slavery is part of our culture; what right do Northern abolitionists have to tell us to alter our traditional way of life?" Ask Mary Midgley: Did the slaves consent?

2. *Torture is never justifiable.* Any activity that inflicts intense pain on others is, like slavery, a violation of human rights. Moreover, it is wrong to apply this principle selectively. As A. M. Rosenthal recently noted on the op-ed page of the *New York Times*, it is morally bankrupt to use the relativistic argument—"Flog Asians only"—in defense of the American sentenced to be caned in Singapore. One should say, instead, "Flog no one."

Female circumcision (genital mutilation) is another case in point. The practice, widespread in northeastern Africa, is designed to make women submissive to male dominance by denying them sexual satisfaction. It is defended by relativists on the grounds that it is a traditional cultural practice and that, consequently, Westerners have no right to pass judgment on it. In a letter published in the *New York Times* on November 14, 1993, a history instructor at Lehigh County Community College in Pennsylvania wrote that even though female circumcision is unhealthy and painful and ushers in a lifetime of torture, it does so only "from the Western liberal tradition, and certainly from a feminist perspective. However, from the African viewpoint, the practice can serve as an affirmation of the value of women in traditional society." The writer goes on to grant that many women become infected when their clitoris and labia are removed in painful surgery—"there were even reports of elder women using their teeth to perform the ritual. Yet, whatever the degree of tissue removed, there is little doubt that for the girls it was a joyous occasion." Why? Because they become marriageable after the operation; without it, they would be social outcasts. Thus, the writer goes on, to condemn "a tradition central to many Africans and Arabs is the height of ethnocentrism."

This relativistic argument is as false as it is hoary. After all, prior to the Civil War, the claim was made that the practice of slavery was a tradition central to Southern culture (as *tsujigiri* was no doubt to samurai traditions). Yet today no Southerners or Japanese would defend either practice or claim that it is central to the culture. Although many Southerners in the past didn't realize that slavery was wrong, and many samurai didn't acknowledge that slicing people in half was immoral, that didn't make those practices right— not now, and not even then. In the future, it is safe to predict that the thinking of the descendants of the practitioners of female circumcision will similarly evolve to the point where they understand that the ritual is, and was, barbaric.

3. *Any violation of natural (human) rights is always wrong.* This moral principle subsumes the first two and adds to them. Slavery and torture are invasions of the liberty, dignity, and personal autonomy to which all humans have an equal right by virtue of their common humanity. That is why rape is always wrong. Further, because disrespect of the rights of others violates this principle, it is always wrong to abuse people. Put positively, there is a moral imperative to respect the dignity, liberty, and autonomy of others that includes, as in the First Amendment, their irrevocable rights to their own opinions, beliefs, and values. By extension, there is an

ethical imperative to include individuals in the making of decisions that affect them seriously and directly. That is why democracy is moral and tyranny is not.

Thus the list of moral absolutes is small. It includes only a few moral principles based on natural law, which would include such time-tested principles as the Golden Rule, *primum non nocere* ("above all, do no harm"), the imperative to protect children, and injunctions against stealing. Though most of the major issues in social life are subjective and relative, not all are. There are, in short, some moral absolutes that are not contingent on circumstances.

Contingency in Practice

We may seem to have strayed far from the contingency philosophy of leadership, but in fact we are now better able to see its inherent flaws. The moral error inherent in "it all depends" is that there is no limit to it. The practical error, in the words of contemporary philosopher Mario Bunge, is that "when anything goes, nothing goes well." We can now see that what is wrong with contingency theory is that it stands on the quicksand of relativism: It says to the leader, in effect, sometimes it is OK to be tough, even abusive—*it all depends*. As long as "it all depends," Realists will believe that they must be abusive to be effective. That is because *in the eyes of the Realist, there is always a crisis*. The essence of the crisis is the evil and anarchic nature of humans, which must be controlled by a firm commander. In this way, contingency theory, like moral relativism, lends itself to abuse. Once one admits that tyranny is at any time permissible, existing conditions henceforth will be defined as the permissible exception. The Rushmoreans therefore draw a firm line and insist that it is never permissible to behave like Singapore's Lee Kwan Yew or Sunbeam-Oster's Kazarian. People must always be treated with respect; no crisis justifies abusive behavior. Simply put, it does *not* all depend.

Hence contingency theory should be rejected on the grounds that it is always immoral to treat people paternalistically or disrespectfully. Continginency theory also fails basic tests of moral philosophy. For example, by turning its tenets into prescriptions or guidelines for action, we can test its validity. Thus we might ask: When is it appropriate to abuse and disrespect people? When should we not include people in decisions that directly affect them? When is it right for leaders to break faith with followers and betray their trust? When should a leader behave immorally toward followers? In answering such questions, situationalists can only justify their line of reasoning with reference to a world totally devoid of civilized behavior—the world of Machiavelli—in which leadership is no more than an exercise in power.

Still, it might be objected that this is not the intent of continginency thinking. It is *not* a moral philosophy but instead an empirical observation about pragmatic behavior. As such, one goes too far afield to cite the morality of slavery and the like in what is simply a discussion of practical business matters. After all, business leadership is solely about effectiveness. The proof is that stockholders judge CEOs on how effectively they meet the challenges of change, not on if they obey the Golden Rule or respect natural rights. Thus have we not introduced extraneous questions and confused a straightforward issue of effectiveness?

Over the past several years, a small library has sprouted up on the topic of leadership, and with only a few notable exceptions, the distinction we are drawing here is blurred or contradicted therein. At the core of these texts one is almost certain to find statements along the following lines:

1. A prime task of leadership is to bring about constructive change.
2. How the leader acts to effect change will depend on the situation.
3. Few leaders succeed at achieving constructive change.

Because the first and third of these assertions are based on verifiable observation, we can accept them as true enough for practical purposes. The second assertion, a restatement of contingency theory, is of a different order. To verify a theory requires one or more intervening steps between observation and assertion, steps associated with logical reasoning. This higher barrier to validation notwithstanding, almost all social scientists—and the vast majority of civilians—accept it as true. Whether they are familiar with the jargon of contingency or not, nearly everyone finds it self-evident that there are no universal truths about leadership.

To most observers, it is as clear as the Saharan sky that no basic, immutable principles constitute a single "best way" to lead. Even Gary Wills, whose adherence to contingency theory is weak, nonetheless cites sixteen different types of leadership, the differences among them being situational. One need only consider famous personages as Wills does in *Certain Trumpets* to conclude that each leader must do different things to bring about change. Reviewing the familiar careers of leaders from Pericles to Ross Perot, we might also conclude that leaders must each act with different styles, behave in different ways, and pursue different methods of power and persuasion in light of the exigencies of their particular times, places, challenges, and constituencies.

Hence we may quickly confirm by casual observation that leadership is situational, that "it all depends," and that leaders must do whatever it takes to overcome the resistance to change. Moreover, this commonplace observation is strategically buttressed by prevailing conventions in the social sciences and, as noted, by the ascendant academic values of cultural and moral relativism. Thus a powerful troika of casual observation, science, and ideology all conspire to reinforce the theory of contingency. So powerful and persuasive is this triumvirate of scholarly virtues that contingency advocates ignore countervailing sources of knowledge—in particular, those derived from logic, history, and moral reasoning. For example, advocates of contingency fail to note possible links among the three assertions listed earlier. They do not consider the possibility that so few leaders succeed at leading change (assertion 3) *because* so many are adherents, consciously or unconsciously, of situational leadership (assertion 2).

Moreover, if assertion 2 were valid, there would be no rigorous way to think about leadership. A logical consequence of "it all depends" is that there is no body of knowledge about leadership and hence no "thing" to be learned. If there are no generalizable truths about leadership, it follows that what does not exist cannot be taught. Like the theory of contingency itself, there is more than partial truth here. Obviously, some things about leadership cannot be taught; for example, no cookie-cutter approach to organizational transformation can be applied across the board at IBM, GM, and wherever else leaders seek to bring about change (if there were such a magic formula, all companies would succeed and none would fail).

In fact, only a very few things about leadership can be said to be universally true. Fortunately, these are the most important things; unfortunately, these things are lost on leaders who believe in contingency because they do not know where to look, what to look for, or how to look—because they do not believe that such things are even there to be discovered. Indeed, leadership can be learned only if we change our lenses of perception from the dominant trio of casual observation, social science, and ideology to the more useful triad of logic, history, and morality. Having changed focus, one begins to see that leaders fail to bring about constructive change because they fail to apply the lessons of moral experience. Leading change may be the most difficult of social endeavors, but certain leaders have done it nevertheless. Analysis undistorted by the warped lenses of contingency will reveal that successful leaders share certain core values that allow them to overcome ever-present resistance.

Jack Welch: Contingency Leader Par Excellence

That is not to say that all leaders who bring about effective change are Rushmoreans. To clarify what values-based leadership is, we must understand what it is not. Let me illustrate by reference to General Electric's CEO, Jack Welch, who is today's most admired, most studied, and most quoted corporate leader. In late 1993, *Fortune* said of Welch that he "is widely acknowledged as the leading master of corporate change in our time." The general approbation that accompanies the mention of Welch's name stems from two sources. First, during his tenure, GE's financial performance has been second to none among the largest U.S. corporations. Between 1981 and 1993, the company eliminated more than two hundred thousand jobs while increasing its market value by some $68 billion and tripling its net annual income. Second, he stands out among corporate executives in his ability to articulate the era's dominant leadership philosophy. American executives and scholars are therefore comfortable with Welch not only because he makes a great deal of money for his shareholders, but also because he says the right things about leadership (and says them with remarkable consistency). One thing he invariably says is, "It all depends."

A 1984 *Fortune* story had also featured Welch. His picture on the cover was the captioned "America's Toughest Boss." What *Fortune* meant by "tough" most people would call "abusive." The distinction is essential. Neither Welch's many defenders nor his few detractors argue that he did not have tough choices to make in the 1980s—the toughest of which involved closing factories, selling businesses, and laying off workers. Facing the demise or survival of a firm, a CEO may have little choice but to make such tough calls. Therefore the toughness controversy was not about workforce reductions; it was about Welch's day-to-day treatment of the people who reported to him.

In the early 1980s, journalists started to use the now-famous sobriquet "Neutron Jack" in describing Welch's relationship with subordinates (at the time, the media were obsessed with the neutron bomb, a test weapon storied for its ability to wipe out entire populations while leaving buildings unscathed). In terms meant to be flattering to Welch, *Fortune* said that employees who brought Welch news of unsatisfactory performance were berated, insulted, scolded, and ridiculed—often in front of their peers: "According to former employees, Welch conducts meetings so aggressively that people tremble. He attacks almost physically with his intellect— criticizing, demeaning, ridiculing, humiliating."

At GE, Welch was said to set the standards and the rules; if his underlings didn't meet the former or follow the latter, they were punished. (Such behavior is still prevalent—and still admired by the editors of *Fortune*. In a 1993 feature article, the magazine used the following phrases to characterize a group of America's "toughest" CEOs who were held out as masters of the art of change: "doesn't listen," "impatient," "unreasonable," "micromanages," "humiliates employees," "slams doors and kicks over chairs," "advises to 'fire 'em so they'll understand you are serious.'")

Welch brooked no nonsense from his troops, whom he treated as wayward children when they strayed from the path he had set for the firm. He argued that he alone knew best what was needed to change GE, and it was irrelevant if the people who worked for him didn't like it. He was in a competitive war, and he had no choice but to act as any general would under those circumstances. "Empowerment and transformation are California talk," he said— and he left no doubt that they were inappropriate for the conditions GE was facing in the early 1980s. Anyhow, the proof was in the pudding: he was succeeding in turning GE around and making money.

Then, in the mid 1980s, something unexpected happened: like Saul on the road to Damascus, Welch became a sudden convert to a different—some would say opposing—school of leadership from the one he had so recently espoused. He went from being a general to being—if we may borrow the metaphor from a previous chapter—almost a good shepherd. Seemingly overnight, there was a "new" Jack Welch, a CEO who now spoke as passionately in favor of a humanistic style of management as he had recently done in defense of command and control. In books, articles, and videos, he was seen treating Americans to the thoughts of the new Welch, especially the necessity that leadership be built on integrity and trust. He spoke eloquently about the need for employee voice, involvement, participation, inclusion, and, yes, even a dollop of the California-style empowerment he had so recently ridiculed.

The leader's job, he informed the world, was not to command but instead to articulate a set of principles that would energize all members of the firm, gaining their voluntary adoption of the firm's values. The CEO's "vision" would allow all employees to understand their roles in the enterprise and thereby motivate them to perform at the peak of their abilities and contribute ideas that were essential for the company to increase productivity. No more did GE want macho leaders bent on dictating; the company now sought out, in Warren Bennis's words, maestros who would engage in coaching. Welch's most quoted observation was that GE was no longer hiring tyrants like the old Jack Welch!

By the early 1990s, Welch had become the nation's most authoritative spokesman for a style of leadership that he had forcefully opposed for most of his managerial career—the "new management" philosophy that had been advocated for forty years by such theorists and consultants as Douglas McGregor, Peter Drucker, J. Edwards Deming, and Bennis himself, and practiced for as long—longer in some instances—by the corporate executives we have begun to call the Rushmoreans, Robert Owen, James Lincoln, Robert Townsend, Thornton Bradshaw, Robert Galvin, Jan Carlzon, and Max De Pree. There is more than a touch of irony in this. Welch came to be known as dedicated to overcoming unreasonable resistance to change among his followers. But equally interesting is why Welch himself had resisted necessary change for so many decades!

Welch was unlike his predecessors in one important way: *he couched his arguments and actions in terms of contingency*. In his many interviews, he has always been careful to say that Neutron Jack did no wrong in the 1980s. Instead, he goes out of his way to say—even now when he acts in the opposite fashion—that he was right to do what he did *then*. Understand that Welch is no hypocrite; he is completely consistent in word and deed, and there is no evidence that he prevaricates to curry favor with the press, stockholders, or anyone else. We must take him at his word.

What is refreshing about Jack Welch is that he never engages in mea culpas about his former behavior. He shows no sign of regret for having been abusive, for having treated employees with disrespect, for having approached people as means and not as ends. Quite the opposite; in the tradition of General George Patton, he proudly claims to have been right to act that way at that time. Consistent with his philosophy of contingency, he argues that the circumstances of the time necessitated his actions and behavior. He merely did what he had to do to succeed. He had to be tough because GE was starting to lose its competitive edge: the company had gotten fat, dumb, and unproductive; its workforce was unmotivated and complacent; and nearly everyone in the company was resistant to the changes that were necessary to ensure its survival in the long run. In the early 1980s, he saw that GE was about to enter a competitive war, and to win it he would have to whip the troops into battle-ready shape. Here relativists warn that no one has standing to condemn Welch for having abused his employees. He had no choice: *they were resisting change*. And doesn't history now offer support that he was right to have acted as he did? Simply compare GE's record to that of the other denizens of *Fortune*'s top ten in the 1980s—GM, IBM, U.S. Steel, et al. They didn't change, and look what happened to them.

Hence his insistence that he was correct to have acted as he did then. And today? "Our current values are the only ones that will work in this decade," he asserts. The contingency theorists argue that he has again been proved right, as demonstrated by GE's impressive economic performance so far in the 1990s. He was right to be a tough, take-charge authoritarian in the 1980s, and he is right in the 1990s to be a listener concerned with drawing out the ideas of all employees. Contingency theory—the philosophical basis for his leadership—is again validated by observation.

But what about the future? Welch remains consistent: he says it all depends. Maybe he will have to be tough, maybe soft—who can predict? He consequently refuses to rule out the option that some future situation may require the reinvention of Neutron Jack. And why not? Remember, there was nothing wrong with that style; leadership is a matter of expediency, he tells us, not a question of right or wrong. In an instructive video discussion with Warren Bennis, Welch deftly fielded a question about the appropriateness of the leadership styles of such tough-guy college basketball coaches as Indiana's Bobby Knight and the University of California's Lou Campanelli (who, we recall, lost his job over the issue of abusive treatment of his players): "They are dealing with young minds for two or three years, then [the players graduate] and go on. The coaches can brutalize them, kick them, yell at them, motivate them to a high standard for a short time. [That's because] the coaches don't have to deal with them for a lifetime. College coaches grab a kid by the shirt and shake him, but you can't do that for twenty years to the same person."

Welch—always philosophically consistent—thus refused to criticize abusive coaches on moral grounds. To him, the issue is not whether it is ever right to abuse people but rather whether it is expedient to do so in a corporate setting. He concluded only that it is inexpedient in the long run. In contingency terms, he left open the possibility that it might be pragmatic to be abusive "for two or three years," especially when the leader has sufficient turnover that he doesn't have to deal continually with the abused parties. Again note Welch's total absence of hypocrisy: his argument in defense of the coaches is exactly the one he uses to explain his own tough behavior toward GE employees in the 1980s (many of whom he no longer has to deal with because they were among the two hundred thousand whose positions were subsequently eliminated): a leader must do whatever it takes to achieve the objectives. To his credit, Jack Welch practices the contingency leadership he preaches.

Welch and De Pree

Most businesspeople seem to agree with him that leaders must be tough in times of crisis. In discussing Jack Welch with corporate executives, I have seldom heard negative comments about his leadership style or philosophy. Indeed, for as long as GE was making money, Welch was commonly portrayed as unflawed by his many admirers. This is in sharp contrast to similar discussions that I have had concerning the leadership of Max De Pree, the recently retired CEO of Herman Miller, whose values-based philosophy I describe in Chapter Two. I have seldom gotten through a seminar on leadership when De Pree's philosophy was not attacked, dismissed, or rejected, often virulently. On one memorable occasion, a theretofore phlegmatic and unemotional executive confessed to a roomful of seminar participants: "I don't like Max De Pree." This was surprising—particularly in light of the fact that De Pree is a patient, gentle, avuncular man completely devoid of arrogance, while Welch is a feisty, ex–hockey player with little tolerance of others, be they fools or geniuses.

For the longest time I puzzled over why corporate audiences who viewed videos of the two leaders so often warmed to Welch and turned cold to De Pree. The root cause could not be financial success: during De Pree's long tenure at the helm of Herman Miller, the company was among the most profitable of the entire *Fortune* 500. It could not be hypocrisy: throughout his career, De Pree practiced what the new Welch only began to preach in the late 1980s. It could not be differences in their current messages or practices: when asked, few executives were able to identify more than minor differences between the recent statements of Welch and what De Pree had always said. After many sessions of listening carefully to the reactions of businesspeople, I finally came to understand that they were not reacting to what Welch or De Pree said or did; rather, their acceptance or rejection of each was based on philosophical grounds.

The philosophical difference is this: Welch now advocates the necessity for employee voice, participation, and inclusion on the pragmatic grounds that such practices *work*, while De Pree argues in favor of such principles on the grounds that they are *right*. Put another way, Welch's starting point is that leadership is *a pragmatic exercise* in getting the leader's will enacted through the efforts of followers; to De Pree leadership is, at base, *a moral activity*. In my experience, businesspeople are more comfortable with a philosophy of leadership rooted in expediency than with one rooted in morality. That they are so is understandable because if they were to abandon contingency theory, they would surrender a broad range of options relating to their exercise of power.

De Pree's philosophy is, in the eyes of many executives, not only impractical but also moralistic. By this I do not imply that De Pree's open admission of Christianity is offensive to them; in fact, unlike many Christians today who seek to impose their values on others, De Pree's faith is personal, and he is refreshingly tolerant of those sinners (like myself) who are patently not of the Christian persuasion. Yet one can see why executives view the fundamental premise of his leadership philosophy in such a harsh light. To follow his basic moral premise that all men and women are created in the image of the same Maker—which, as we have seen, is at the root of humanistic natural law as well as Christian ethics—would greatly restrict the options of a leader. For example, from this starting point De Pree concludes that all employees have certain inalienable rights; in particular, that all are entitled to be treated with respect and all are entitled to be treated as ends and not means. At the highest level of abstraction, as we have seen, these rights are absolute. For example, there are *no* circumstances in which it is permissible for a leader to treat followers with disrespect; there is *never* a valid reason for leaders to abuse followers. In essence, then, he says, it does *not* "all depend."

In sharp contrast, contingency theory rejects the notion of any "higher law." As Welch so clearly articulates it, in the final reckoning, the call belongs to the leader, who is free to do whatever is necessary to get followers to perform. In effect, the leader reserves the right to act however he or she sees fit. Under contingency theory, it is always right for the leader to do whatever is necessary, given only one limitation: that the action works to advance his or her ends. Pragmatically, "whatever is necessary" includes anything that the leader decides is required by circumstances to achieve the goal being pursued. For example, if the situation requires disrespect of followers—in other words, abuse—so be it. Of course, contingency theorists seldom discuss their beliefs in these terms. In the hard-nosed, practical world of observation, science, and ideology, there is little room for soft questions of morality.

Efficiency is the ultimate defense of contingency leadership, and, as discussed, the example invariably given is the necessity of efficacious action in an emergency, with war offered as the extreme of such situations. As we have seen, contingency theorists are on their strongest ground when they claim that "leaders must do whatever has to be done in a crisis." After all, the opposite is unthinkable— who would advocate indecisive leadership when lives are at stake? "Do you want the troops to take a vote in the middle of a battle?" they ask.

Welch himself makes this case. In the early 1980s, he saw the need to downsize quickly. This requisite for bold, decisive action necessitated running roughshod over certain niceties of participation (niceties that he now calls, in perfect contingency thinking, necessities for the 1990s). Today he argues that his only regret is not having been tough enough in the midst of the 1980s crisis: "My biggest mistake was agonizing too long over difficult decisions. I should have done it faster. But we're all human. We don't like to face up to some of these unpleasant things. . . . And I didn't want to break this company. In hindsight, I was generally erring on the side of being afraid of breaking it. GE would be better off if I had acted faster."

Let us try generalizing this contingency argument beyond the confines of GE. A company finds itself in a crisis and needs a decisive leader to take firm, bold, quick action. Because contingencies demand such speedy, authoritative steps, the participation of managers in the decisions that affect them would be both inefficient and inappropriate. To save the sinking ship, the leader has no choice but to bark firm directions—and to worry about hurt feelings later. If the leader doesn't act quickly and decisively, there will not be a later to worry about. And if one requires a moral justification for this unfettered exercise of power, it is this: without a strong hand at the helm in a time of chaos, the vessel will not survive.

Consider an alternative scenario: the leader must act quickly to save the company. She calls in the people normally involved in the decision-making process, as well as those who will be directly affected. She quickly and candidly explains the nature of the contingency to these individuals. What is likely to happen next in this scenario? I suggest the following as the most probable dénouement: if the leader has built the trust of those around her in the past, it is a good bet that they will say to her in this moment of clear crisis, "It's your call. We trust your judgment. Let us know how we can be of help." Then, even if the leader makes a bad call, there is some basis for rebuilding trust after the crisis has passed. Admittedly, this scenario will be viewed as hopelessly naive and optimistic by the cynical standards of the situationalist. But even in purely expedient terms, doesn't a leader have more power if it is granted than if it is unilaterally usurped?

NASA's series of experiments in the 1970s (reported in Chapter Three) add further evidence that the contingency of a crisis demands more than speed and "taking charge" on the part of a single strong leader. Furthermore, the issue isn't the theoretical one posed by Realists: no one advocates "taking a vote in the middle of a battle." The mundane issue is what happens *after* a crisis when a leader has arbitrarily excluded from the decision-making process the people who were affected and who were accustomed to participating. In almost all instances, the people excluded will sense a betrayal of trust. Whatever credits for trustworthiness the leader may have accumulated in the past will thus be expended in one furious round of decisive command. Such credit is not easily reclaimed; in many organizations, trust once lost is never regained. I stress this issue of trust because it is the factor that Welch himself says is most required for his new style of leadership.

If in fact crisis situations demand the infringement of basic morality, contingency theory is valid on practical grounds. But if a crisis can be handled without suspension of moral principles—for example, if one can fight a war without suspending democracy—the philosophy is invalid in practice. Bear in mind that Welch, ever consistent with contingency thinking, does not claim that the leader's only path to success is along the authoritarian route; he merely says that *sometimes* the leader must be a tyrant. In particular, he says that the contingency of a crisis demands an authoritarian response. In sum, we question his conclusions on moral, logical, and historical grounds:

- Morally, is it ever right for a leader to be a tyrant? We have seen that there is an absolute moral prohibition against the infringement of basic human rights.

- Logically, is it a fact that only tyrants are effective in emergencies? The NASA experiment and the careers of the Rushmoreans offer evidence that the contingency of a crisis may be handled effectively without resorting to tyranny.

- Historically, has it proved necessary to suspend basic rights during crises? During the Civil War, didn't Lincoln keep Congress in session—and didn't he himself stand for reelection in the darkest days of the conflict? During World War II, didn't Churchill maintain parliamentary democracy even during the Battle of Britain?

Here, no doubt, the contingency theorist will object: Welch isn't talking about the high value of democracy; he is concerned only with the low value of productivity. He is wrong. In all cases, we are discussing the process of effective and moral leadership, be it of a nation or of a corporation. In this context, it is irrelevant if the goal is Mandela's freedom or Welch's productivity. What concerns us is how followers are included in the process of defining and achieving goals.

Even if we were to accept Welch's singular and circumscribed measure of leadership effectiveness, questions may still be raised about his performance: Would productivity have been higher over the long term at GE had Welch behaved with moral consistency throughout his tenure? Doubtless he succeeded in the past while being abusive, but would he have been even more successful had he treated people with the same respect during the crisis of the 1980s as he says he does now? And would he be even more successful now if GE employees knew that they could trust him never to revert to being Neutron Jack? No one knows the answers to such questions, but is it more logical to accept the assertion of no than to consider the possibility of yes?

Welch and Patton: Must a Leader Be Tough to Be Demanding?

Finally, Realists will argue that the proof is in the pudding: Jack Welch's tough style brought out the highest performance among his troops. In essence, the argument goes, a leader must be tough to elicit the best from followers. I would argue that GE might have been more productive had Welch understood the moral nuances among the words *demanding, tough,* and *abusive.* All great leaders are demanding in that they inspire the best in their followers—and such leaders are willing to accept nothing less than the highest performance from them. On this score, Max De Pree was a thoroughly demanding leader, unwilling to accept from Herman Miller employees anything but the highest levels of product design and quality, customer satisfaction, and overall financial performance. Yet in the many years I studied Herman Miller, I never heard of De Pree having abused anyone.

Perhaps the most demanding CEO in America is Walt Disney's Michael Eisner, himself a friend and admirer of Welch's. Indeed, like Welch, Eisner pushes all of his people hard and incessantly to improve their performance. Eisner never seems satisfied with the results; he always believes that his people can do better. Because he never lets up, some employees have told him to his face that he can be an irritating perfectionist. Yet I have never heard a Disney employee say that Eisner has ever treated anyone with less than perfect respect. He is obviously flawed as a leader, but his flaws are related to his ego rather than to his morality. Eisner may not have handled his parting of the ways with Jeffery Katzenberg with aplomb, but the severance was downright humane compared with Neutron Jack's old style. Indeed, one Disney manager told me, "I don't think Michael knows how to be abusive."

It is important to recognize that Welch does not argue that abuse is moral; he doubtless sees abuse as an evil necessity. Like General George Patton, he believes that it is sometimes necessary to treat people with less than respect to motivate them to perform. We must ask if this is true—particularly now that Welch is being advanced as a role model for young leaders. If Welch's philosophy is flawed— if, for example, it is possible to be demanding without being abusive—then it is incumbent on us to find a more appropriate philosophy and a better role model. Let me suggest one test of Welch's effectiveness as a leader: the behavior of his followers. To test Welch's leadership, one might ask the following questions of, and about, his managers around the world:

- Is there consistency between what Welch preaches and the actual practices of GE?

- Is the organization in fact encouraging the free expression of ideas at all levels in the firm? Is this translating into change and innovation?

- Do the people who report to Jack Welch, and the people who in turn report to them, behave toward their followers like the new Welch or like the old Neutron Jack?

- Is GE's culture both moral and effective? Do the names of GE's divisions appear in the news in connection with legal, ethical, and regulatory violations?

On such judgments, the jury is still out. But as this book went to press, evidence continued to mount that Welch's leadership of GE is seriously flawed on the dimension of morality, if not on the dimension of effectiveness:

- In 1989, the company paid $3.5 million to GE employees who claimed their division had defrauded the government. One allegation by the GE whistleblowers was that the company had faked test results on defense contracts.

- In 1990, GE paid $30 million in penalties for defense contracting overcharges.

- In 1993, the company's NBC subsidiary apologized and paid court costs to GM when it was revealed that the network had rigged a test crash of a GMC pickup.

- In 1994, it was revealed that a trader at GE's Kidder Peabody subsidiary faked $350 million in sales.

Perhaps more than any other large American corporation, GE is faced with an imposing backlog of lawsuits relating to environmental transgressions and fraud in defense contracting. Moreover, its ham-fisted handling of its Hungarian acquisition, Tungsram, has soured relations between U.S. business and the growing economies of Eastern Europe. All of this, of course, may be clouds that will have passed by the time this book is in print. Welch himself pooh-poohs all of the above, pointing to the profits he has earned for GE's shareholders. Indeed, as he has moved the company away from domestic manufacturing and into the more ethically freewheeling world of financial services, there is no gainsaying that GE's billions of dollars worth of divestitures and acquisitions have proved profitable in the main. Be that as it may, the issue is that Welch clearly is not practicing values-based leadership. To what transcendent, higher-order values has he dedicated himself and his company?

There is no question that Welch has been a success. Much like General Patton—who was recognized by admirers and critics alike as a military genius—Welch achieves his objectives at least as well as his competitors and definitely faster. On this point, my former colleague Morgan McCall calls attention to the perhaps unconscious parallels between the following epigrams:

> *"War is a very simple thing, and the determining characteristics are self-confidence, speed, and audacity."*
>
> —General George Patton, 1947

> *"[Leadership requires] speed, simplicity, and self-confidence."*
>
> —Jack Welch, 1993

Indeed, the question we should ask about Welch is the same question that Generals Eisenhower and Bradley raised about Patton: Is there a better way? Can one have the same level of success without incurring high human costs? Indeed, would Welch have been even more successful had he taken the higher road? What might have happened at GE had the old Jack Welch been like the new one all along? What would have happened to GE's bottom line if there had been no necessity for Welch to change styles? In light of the answers to those questions, one might revisit the basic issue: Is contingency theory merely a rationalization for certain kinds of otherwise indefensible behavior? In short, does "it all depend"?

When introduced, contingency theory was an improvement over the competing theories advanced by such great minds as Plato, Confucius, Machiavelli, Carlyle, Emerson, Tolstoy, and Weber. Their theories—each intriguing and partly valid—were found to be too confining to serve as guides to effective leadership. The challenge remains to identify a moral alternative to contingency theory that does not founder on that failing of oversimplicity.

Justice Oliver Wendell Holmes once said, "I wouldn't give a fig for the simplicity this side of complexity, but would give my life for the simplicity the other side of complexity." What Holmes meant is that we should not be seduced by facile theories—for example, leadership theories based on such concepts as charisma, chance, natural hierarchies, or testosterone levels. Such ideas foster the most dangerous exercise of simplicity: unidimensional thinking in a multi-dimensional world.

An advantage of contingency theory is that it acknowledges leadership's many levels of complexity. That would make it a marvelous step forward were it not for the unfortunate fact that so many leaders get lost in the maze. Leaders who see only the complexity of situations become confused and indecisive and consequently allow their organizations to drift into deadlock, gridlock, paralysis. More often, as we have seen, contingency theory is used as an excuse for expedient behavior, encouraging leaders to cut through complexity with the confidence that "this is one of those times when I have to be tough." The epigrams cited attest to the attraction of such simplicity to Patton and Welch.

Indeed, almost all advocates of contingency theory are tempted to interpret the ever-present complexity of life—the confusion and chaos endemic to modern society—as a crisis demanding toughness. This is perhaps better than getting mired in complexity, but neither option seems ideal.

Leaders must act, and to act requires an element of simplicity. Leaders must ultimately reduce complexity to a manageable size, reformulate it, and clarify it in terms simple enough for followers to understand. But leaders cannot succeed at this task unless they themselves understand that the complexity of the modern world derives from an absence of certainty—that is, from disagreement fueled by the differing values of followers. To cut through this complexity requires the creation of transcendent values, a collective view that followers recognize as morally superior to their own narrower interests even while encompassing them. As Nelson Mandela understood, people will follow only leaders who take them where they want to go. Leaders thus beget followers, and they do so by allowing the followers to take the leader's dream as their own. This can occur only when leaders acknowledge the legitimacy of followers' competing beliefs and diverse values. Hence the overall conclusion of our inquiry: for leadership to be effective, it must be moral, and the sine qua non of morality is respect for people. Significantly, this concept of leadership that we are calling Rushmorean is not new. It has coexisted and competed with Realism for centuries. It was first expressed by the Chinese philosopher Lao-tzu some six hundred years before the birth of Christ:

> A leader is best
> When people barely know that he exists,
> Not so good when people obey and acclaim him,
> Worst when they despise him.
> "Fail to honor people,
> They fail to honor you;"
> But of a good leader, who talks little,
> When his work is done, his aim fulfilled,
> They will all say, "We did this ourselves."

The cynic might argue that what Lao-tzu advocated is no different from the philosophy of Jack Welch because at base it is manipulative. But in fact there is a great difference in that the leadership called for by Lao-tzu is constrained by the moral principle of respect for people. As Jefferson told Du Pont, moral leadership requires the full inclusion of followers. That is why Jefferson trusted the American people to be the best judges of their own interests in the long run. He trusted the citizenry because in the final analysis, he respected them. In contrast, it was said of Richard Nixon that he trusted no one, and the American people returned the sentiment. Moral and effective leadership always comes down to that basic attitude about people. Gandhi observed that ultimately, immoral leaders always fail because their followers feel disrespected. Amoral contingency leaders fail for the same reason.

We do not know what, along his private road to Damascus, changed in Jack Welch. Was it his attitude toward trusting others? If he now truly respects the value of others, he may go down as a great leader. But the jury is still out. As Sophocles cautioned, "Count no man fortunate until you know his end." If Jack Welch ultimately stumbles and falls, it is likely to be because he does not believe in the Taoist principle "Fail to honor people, and they fail to honor you"—a principle shared, as we must again note, by all major religions and humanistic philosophies. It is not too late, of course, for Welch to renounce contingency leadership and go into history in better company than George Patton! But to embrace the Rushmorean approach, he will first have to overcome the Pattonesque belief that such leadership is "soft" and unacceptably "feminine." We turn to that considerable obstacle in the next chapter.

. . . .

Leaders of Leaders

Why Values-Based Leadership Is an Unnatural Act

The Realists' position is firmly based on the hard, immutable facts of life. Their starting point is the data, derived from history, sociobiology, and the social sciences, that all add up to incontestable proof that a single strong leader is necessary in any society or organization. Let us test the evidence from these three sources, beginning with a little recent history.

In the 1960s, the Ford Motor Company tried to sell badly designed luxury cars known as Edsels. The few people who purchased them were often subjected to public ridicule: strangers would point at their silly-looking cars and make derisory remarks. Eventually, when those belittled souls had suffered as much abuse as they could take, they cleverly transformed their folly into a badge of honor by establishing an "exclusive" Edsel owners' club. No such effort of consumerist revisionism has been attempted by the purchasers of early-1980s Texas Instruments personal computers. Apparently the embarrassment attendant to that acquisition is still too profound for folks to admit to owning a TI lemon. The TI computer took the "stand-alone" marketing concept to its illogical extreme: at the dawn of the era of "plug compatibility," its hardware and software were compatible with nothing in Christendom. Thus buyers soon discovered that they had plopped down several thousand smackers each for a machine of extremely limited versatility. When word got around—and it took about six minutes to spread to every nerd and hacker in this fair land—TI was left with several million dollars in wasted investment. The upshot was that TI's CEO and president at the time—Messieurs Bucey and Shepherd, respectively—soon found themselves bereft of gainful employment.

In hindsight, we can say that Mr. B. and Mr. S. seem to have done nearly everything wrong in developing the product. Yet—and this is why the story is instructive—they did what most other red-blooded American managers would have done under similar circumstances. They behaved exactly as leaders have always behaved in history books and in legend, as they were taught in business school, and as many of the greatest Realist thinkers have said they should in theory. They behaved, in short, like perfect corporate clones of Lee Kwan Yew.

Here is the TI leadership tale in brief. Bucey and Shepherd began by calling in their top product development and marketing people and handing them "specs" for a personal computer that they had drawn up themselves (in consultation, apparently, with only the computer muses). Their colleagues balked at the command to create the bosses' brainchild and suggested that TI's customers, dealers, and suppliers had all recently started to hum the mantra of compatibility. They politely suggested that perhaps B&S should rethink their proposal in light of such information. B&S then became abusive, asking their subordinates, in effect, If you're so smart, why aren't *you* in the executive suite? Who's running the company, anyway—the dealers? the customers? *the employees, for Crissake?* Because no self-respecting leader will stand by while the inmates run the asylum, B&S put the order in plain language that all could understand: *Button your lips and do as you are told.* The employees acquiesced. With great fidelity to the bosses' desires, they created TI's turkey of a personal computer, and the story ends in a sea of red ink that nearly engulfed the company (and in which B&S figuratively drowned).

The lesson here is a complicated one. Suppose that B&S had guessed right about the kind of computer the world needed. In that event, they might have gone down as geniuses (and their employees would be viewed as having obstinately resisted change). Indeed, didn't Henry Ford behave in much the same command-and-control fashion, and isn't he now hailed as the greatest leader the business world ever produced? That is a nice question for a student essay; however, it is irrelevant, for two reasons. The first is that narrow effectiveness, by itself, is an insufficient measure of leadership. (Would Saddam Hussein have been a greater leader had he succeeded in conquering Kuwait?) Had B&S produced a winner, they might have been prescient, talented, or lucky, but they would not have been great leaders. Warren Bennis makes the crucial distinction: leaders don't just do things right; they do the right thing. Abusing people is never the right thing to do (a point developed in Chapter Four).

The second reason was stated best in 1965, ironically, by the then president of TI, Pat Haggerty. He was one of the first U.S. managers to observe that "there is probably no greater waste in industry today than that of willing employees prevented by insensitive leadership from applying their energies and ambitions in the interest of the companies for which they work." In essence, Haggerty meant that Henry Ford could do it all himself in an era when technology was simple and markets didn't change overnight; today even geniuses need a little help from their friends. (A further challenge to the myth of the Great Man is the fact that geniuses have always needed help—witness Jefferson's reliance on Madison and Gallatin. And Ford's stubborn need to do it "my way" eventually brought him to the brink of bankruptcy in 1927.)

Platonic rule "by one, two, or at any rate, . . . a few" is so much a part of Western culture that we can understand why it seems not to have occurred to B&S to listen to others who might have had something to contribute. Everything—experience, myth, upbringing, education, social science, the clichés of everyday language—conspired to make them act as they did. Let's look at it from B&S's perspective: they had worked their way to the top of TI, loyally and successfully doing the bidding of their bosses. Hence they, the crème de la crème of TI managers, had earned their positions in a merit-ocratic competition in which high performers rose to the top. Now they were responsible for the firm's fortunes. The top, as everyone knows, is no place for shrinking violets. The buck stops at the executive suite, and it is incumbent on the people whose names are on the door to give direction to the firm. By definition, those who climb to the top of the hierarchy know best what needs to be done, and it is therefore their duty to call the shots. The alternative is a sloppy ship at best, anarchy at worst. As we are taught from the cradle, somebody has to be in charge. Ultimate authority must be invested in a single person: the father, the principal, the coach, the mayor, the CEO, the boss (from the Dutch *baas*, meaning "master"). The tasks of this individual are to plan, to command, to motivate, to evaluate, to reward, and to control. B&S learned all that in church, in scouting, on the gridiron, and, if they were at all typical, especially at Father's knee.

They probably learned it in business school, in boot camp, and on the job, too. The most frequently used visual aid in leadership training in academia, government, and business over the past four decades has been the World War II film *Twelve O'Clock High*. In this movie, the leader (played by Gregory Peck) whips a squadron of whimpering fliers into shape, and they respond gloriously with a successful bombing run over Germany. Unquestionably, Peck's style of leadership by intimidation and fear worked during World War II. The question is, would it work today in business or government? (I am told that the military has stopped using the film.)

Consider how the world has changed since World War II. In the film, Peck operates with absolute authority over his men in a life-and-death struggle against an unambiguously evil adversary. In contrast, a leader in contemporary organizations has relatively little punitive leverage over the firm's employees, most of whom are volunteers in the theoretical sense that they can quit and go to work for another organization at any time. And the "enemies" of a McDonald's or an IBM are not Hitlerian tyrants but the very institutions where workers are most likely to seek alternative employment. Moreover, Peck's men (all of them white, middle-class thirty-somethings with similar values) are unlike the employees of today, who are as demographically diverse as American society. The metaphor of the leader as general crumbles to dust like old celluloid. Significantly, it was not even accurate during World War II. Peck had other options; he just couldn't see them because he was blinded by cultural myths.

The Rushmorean Who Longs to Be a Realist

While we are talking about movies, director Francis Ford Coppola had the following to say about leadership in *Hearts of Darkness: A Filmmaker's Apocalypse*, a documentary about the making of his prize-winning feature film *Apocalypse Now*: "A film director is kind of one of the last truly dictatorial posts left in a world getting more and more democratic."

Coppola claimed that his inordinate dictatorial powers stemmed from the fact that he was writer, director, and producer of *Apocalypse Now*, a film made with his own money. Indeed, what mere weakling CEO of a publicly owned firm could claim such a basis for authority? In comparison to the all-powerful Coppola, the head of General Motors is simply an elevated hired hand whose power is constrained by investors, board members, unionists, environmentalists, and fellow managers.

In acknowledging that the head of GM is in ways the prisoner of forces beyond his control, we ought also to recognize how much actual power the "last dictator" had on the set of *Apocalypse Now*. In the documentary, we see actor Dennis Hopper flatly refusing to play a scene as written. Coppola begs, pleads, reasons, and finally gives in and does it Hopper's way! When production falls a week behind schedule, Coppola is forced to telephone Marlon Brando in Tahiti, asking him to come a week later than planned to the shooting location. Brando tells Coppola he's booked then, so he'll just pocket the million bucks he's been advanced. After Coppola has groveled to his satisfaction, Brando finally arrives on location (when he pleases) and proceeds to show everybody who the *real* dictator is.

In subsequent scenes, "dictator" Coppola finds himself dependent on the technical skill of his cameraman, the artistic judgment of nearly everyone in the company, and the whims of his hosts, the Philippine government. Even with the enormous powers—unparalleled in our democratic age—at Coppola's disposal, the gofers and gaffers in his employ insist on doing things *their* way. In the hour-long documentary, we never see him give an order that is obeyed directly. Imagine, then, being a leader who really is powerless—say, the CEO of General Motors!

As much as any corporate manager, Coppola is a prisoner of the myth of the Strong Man, the solo leader who is entitled to rule because he is wiser and more virtuous than everyone else (and, not incidentally, because he is a he, a point to which we turn later in this chapter). The truth is that nobody—not the CEO of Texas Instruments, not the head of state of Singapore, not the commanding World War II officer played by Gregory Peck, not even dictator Francis Ford Coppola—is capable of doing it all alone.

In the documentary, Coppola ironically fails to recognize the true source of his influence—and considerable genius—as a leader. He is not, in fact, powerless; he is actually shown in the film to be a superbly effective motivator and change agent. In several scenes, we see Coppola acting not as the commander he thinks he is but as the great teacher he is in actuality. One scene in particular shows him limning his vision to the entire assembled crew, explaining his philosophy, describing the obstacles they face, acknowledging their contributions as a team, thoughtfully responding to their questions, listening to their concerns, and articulating in clear language what they are to accomplish. He talks about their common goals and aspirations. It may be his vision, but he leaves no doubt in the crew's mind that it is *their* film. His "troops" end up wanting to make a better movie for him than if he had had the power to force his will on them. Because Coppola was a cultural prisoner of the myth of Realism, he could not acknowledge even to himself that he was, instead, a Rushmorean leader.

Here's the Coppola lesson: Without despotic power—which no one has these days—no leader can command or compel change. Change comes about when followers themselves desire it and seek it. Hence the role of the leader is to enlist the participation of others as leaders of the effort. That is the sum and essence not only of leading change but also of good management in general.

I have made this sound too easy. In reality, such leadership is extremely difficult because it is unnatural. What comes naturally—particularly for men—is the style of leadership personified by Bucey and Shepherd at TI. Why? Because of the natural instinct to use force to overcome resistance. This tendency to feel that we must "take charge" is magnified by the frustrations of working in groups, functioning in organizations that seem inert and bent on self-destruction. Jean-Paul Sartre was partly right when he wrote that "hell is other people." Actually, hell is organizational life. What makes it hell is the tyranny of custom that invariably defeats the spirit of change in all groups. When left to run a natural course, all organizations become more important than the individuals in them. They become hierarchical, bureaucratic, rule-dominated, and change-resistant. That is the course of inertia. And the individuals who lead organizations become uncaring, cautious, overly conservative, and obsessed with retaining their own power. Even if they decide, like B&S, to side with the angels and advocate change, they will do so in a self-defeatingly autocratic way. Indeed, they will feel compelled to use the powers of command because the group behaves with the obstinacy known as institutionalized irresponsibility. It is natural to conclude that when they will not do what we want, we must force them to do so. That was Peck's mistake.

How, then, does one overcome these natural tendencies and practice the management of inclusion? How does one become a leader of leaders if the natural instinct is to be a solo commander?

Although good management is unnatural, it is nonetheless commonsensical. It is counterinstinctive—particularly for men—but it is *not* counterintuitive. Thus the leader must begin by understanding that change is necessary and by admitting that the change must start with himself (for some women the starting place may be different, as we will discuss later). That's what Ben Cohen did.

The Hippie CEO

Cohen is the ex-hippie cofounder of Ben & Jerry's, a company that, in the 1980s, made fabulous ice cream, marvelous contributions to society, and heaps of profits for its long-term owners. During the period when Ben & Jerry's was growing like crazy, a friend of mine visited headquarters in Vermont to ferret out the secret of the company's success. She put the question directly to Ben:

"Why has Ben & Jerry's been so successful?"

Ben, who looks like Santa Claus, characteristically stroked his handsome white beard while giving long and careful consideration to the question before answering: "We've succeeded, in a word, because of *participation*."

"What do you mean precisely by participation?" my friend asked.

"The goal is for everyone in this company to be empowered to address every issue, problem, and opportunity we face."

"You really take participation seriously, then?"

"I believe that it is the *only* way to succeed in the long run." Then Ben's face turned red, as it does when he is getting ready to say something he finds embarrassing. "Please, I want you to understand that participation is merely the goal, the ideal. I believe in it, but personally, *it is damned hard for me*."

Ben went on to explain that it was not natural for him to ask questions of his employees when he felt he knew the answer, not natural to involve them in planning when in his gut he already knew what he wanted to achieve, not natural to listen to them patiently when he knew that what they were saying wasn't right, and not natural to ask them their ideas when he was bursting to tell them what to do. Now, if participation isn't easy for the nation's most successful ex-hippie CEO, imagine how hard it is for the majority of executives who were more likely to have been ex-scouts or ex-Marines!

Today Ben admits that the hardest task for him as a leader has been to work on not doing what comes naturally. He now says, after years of trying to constrain his natural instincts, that he is "ready to let go." He has learned that he must do so to get everybody in the company working on the constant management of change. The institutionalized participation at Ben & Jerry's is paying off in spades—as the story of Gail Mayville illustrates.

Some time back, Ben & Jerry's publicly dedicated itself to a concept called linked prosperity, the belief that the central role business plays in society gives it tremendous leverage—and responsibility—to improve the quality of life in the broader community. To employee Gail Mayville, that pledge opened the door for her to search for ways to link the company's business activities to efforts to improve the environment. While working as an office manager, she had noticed that Ben & Jerry's wasn't "being as proactive as we might be in managing our solid waste and conserving our resources." So Mayville took the initiative, beginning with the company's chronic sewage problem: the sludge left over from the manufacture of ice cream she sold as pig feed and as farmland fertilizer—for a profit. Next she recycled the ten bales of cardboard that the company was dumping each week—saving $17,500 a year. After that, she found a "technically impossible" way to recycle the fifty thousand 4.5-gallon plastic buckets the company uses to hold ice-cream ingredients—at a saving of 78 percent of the cost of dumping. On and on she went, each activity requiring moral and entrepreneurial imagination to turn social costs into company savings and profits. Her program became so successful, in fact, that it is now being copied all over the United States by companies that had never before been concerned with conservation.

What Gail Mayville achieved at Ben & Jerry's required no act of selfless altruism. But that she was able to find ways to do well through doing good in no way detracts from her impressive display of moral imagination, initiative, and—dare we say it?—leadership. Technically and financially, what Mayville did could have been done by any other company; that it was done first at Ben & Jerry's is a direct outcome of the company's commitment to the enlightened capitalistic value of linked prosperity. By stating this value as a corporate premise, Ben & Jerry's created an environment in which a morally imaginative and enterprising employee like Gail Mayville would feel empowered to act. Certainly, such leadership is most likely to flourish in an organizational atmosphere that encourages and rewards it. In some organizations, an employee like Mayville who took initiative independently would have to pay a price for her virtue. Indeed, in organizations where such behavior is punished, only rare and "saintly" individuals are willing to risk defiance of the corporate norms. The reason why Mayville took the initiative and not only did good but did well for Ben & Jerry's bottom line was that Ben Cohen had become a leader of leaders.

Of course, Ben has since undercut the impact of this story by announcing his early retirement. But we shouldn't be surprised to learn that Ben believes that the company doesn't depend on him for success. In fact, right from the start, Ben surrounded himself with other leaders, like the company's first president, Fred "Chico" Lager; Gail Mayville; and, of course, partner Jerry Greenfield. Not only can one not be a leader without followers, but one cannot effect change without energizing a cadre of disciples. Unlike despotic leaders, who may survive by the judicious disposal of rivals, those who would lead a moral cause must surround themselves with individuals who themselves are capable leaders. George Washington, Thomas Jefferson, Abraham Lincoln, Winston Churchill, and Martin Luther King Jr. were such leaders of leaders—Washington of Jefferson and Alexander Hamilton; Jefferson of James Madison, Albert Gallatin, and James Monroe; Lincoln of William Seward, Salmon Chase, and Ulysses Grant; Churchill of Harold Macmillan and Anthony Eden; and King of Jesse Jackson, Ralph Abernathy, and Andrew Young.

In contrast, perhaps the most tragically flawed leader of our own time, Mikhail Gorbachev, was incapable of attracting followers. The last leader of the Soviet Union was a courageous visionary who failed to surround himself with people who would put his ideas into practice. To the bitter end, Gorbachev remained a solo agent—a brilliant, Platonic, nonlistening apparatchik whose fatal flaw was that he could not create disciples. As a leader, he was no Ben Cohen.

Women Rushmoreans

Because Realist leadership is as much Asian as European, it is not, strictly speaking, "politically incorrect." That is ironic because its roots stem from primitive notions of male dominance. The leader of the tribe (or band of protohuman apes) was the male whose system was most infused with testosterone. Today Realist leaders are still characterized as strong, aggressive, decisive, and masculine—even if that leader is a female like Indira Gandhi or Margaret Thatcher (who was often called "the only real man in the British cabinet"). This is in keeping with the observations of sociobiologists and primate ethologists who have experimented with injecting female baboons with testosterone. They have shown that by increasing male hormone levels, a previously submissive female can be turned into the leader of the pack. Findings have been similar in wild hyenas.

This is all very interesting, but people are not baboons or hyenas. Moreover, groups of modern men and women no longer rely on the physical aggressiveness or strength of their leaders for their survival. Instead, they depend on such traits as integrity, sense of moral purpose, and capacity to communicate a vision. They depend not on the leader's ability to force followers to do what must be done for the survival of the group but on the leader's ability to get the members of the group to identify for themselves and then want to do what must be done for their own good. Such a task is of little utility to baboons and hyenas—and a high level of testosterone is of no use to a human engaged in such tasks. In fact, the macho aggressiveness of "Alpha males" is counterproductive because it generates among associates resentment at being commanded and controlled.

In a controversial article in the *Harvard Business Review*, Judy B. Rosener argued that male leaders are more likely than female leaders "to use power that comes from their organizational position and formal authority." In contrast, female leaders get "subordinates to transform their own self-interest into the interest of the group through concern for a broader goal." In sum, Rosener found that most men lead by "command and control," whereas most women "actively work to make their interactions with subordinates positive for everyone involved. More specifically, the women encourage participation, share power and information, enhance other people's self-worth, and get others excited about their work."

If Rosener is right, the "feminine" style of leadership is more appropriate than the "masculine" style in overcoming the tyranny of custom because it does not provoke the resistance to change that arises from being forced to do something against one's will. The key to the success of "feminine" leaders is the inclusion of the followers in the process of leading change. People become energized when they are included because they feel respected. In contrast, when they are ordered to do something, they become angry because they are being treated as inferiors. When one is treated as an inferior (or a child), one's sense of self-worth is eroded, and one becomes defensive and resentful, hurt at not being treated as a competent adult. The effect of paternalistic commands is thus to suck the excitement and energy out of an organization. When that occurs, followers will be submissive, offering only begrudging compliance as they go about their halfhearted efforts. Even this assumes that the leader has sufficient power to exact compliance; in many organizations, the reaction will be to ignore the order or, as in the Sunbeam-Oster case, to fight back.

Hence the "feminine" style is more effective in modern organizations in which everyone's best efforts are needed—that is, in any organization that requires employee initiative, self-motivation, innovation, and willingness to take the extra step to serve customers or to meet competitive challenges. Importantly, "feminine" leadership does not mean weak leadership—nor does it mean that only women can or do practice it. In fact, without calling it such, it is the style long advocated by W. Edwards Deming, Douglas McGregor, Warren Bennis, Rosabeth Moss Kanter, Tom Peters, James MacGregor Burns, and other authorities on leadership. The Rushmoreans practiced it, too—not because they thought of it as "feminine" but because they knew that it was both just and effective (and the same holds true for Ben Cohen).

In a democratic world characterized by intense competition, in which organizations must move quickly to cope with environmental turmoil, in which all members of the organization must be aligned with the vision of the leader, and in which all must be willing to lead the constant changes needed for effectiveness, the "feminine" Rushmorean style is almost without exception more effective and appropriate than the "masculine" Realist style. (The exceptions are the extremely rare life-or-death emergencies noted in Chapter Three when there is no time for the leader to do anything other than bark an instinctive command.) I hasten to add that this conclusion does not constitute a scientific law; rather, it is a "good enough" working theory for practitioners.

In so saying, we bid adieu to the Theory Class because this conclusion is a direct challenge to the prevailing notions in academia of contingency, political correctness, and scientism. Indeed, this is such a controversial position that Rosener herself refuses to embrace it as the logical conclusion to be drawn from her own data and arguments.

Recall that contingency theory denies the existence of universal principles of leadership. Sadly, this "scientific" position gives

Realist leaders an escape clause. Let me illustrate. I once attended a workshop at which Rosener presented convincing data about the desirability of the "feminine" Rushmorean leadership style. During the question-and-answer period that followed, she was asked, "But aren't there contingencies in which the masculine style is called for? Doesn't a leader have to get tough in certain circumstances?" Rosener responded that, certainly, "it all depends." An audible sigh of relief was voiced by many men in the audience who appreciated that they had just been let off the hook: there was no need for them to change their behavior. After the session, I spoke with a man who had the reputation of being one of the toughest, most abusive no-nonsense tyrants in his industry. I asked him what he had taken away from Rosener's session. He replied, "I can sum it up in three words: It all depends."

In contrast, what I had taken from Rosener's talk was that women "actively work to make their interactions with subordinates positive for everyone involved. More specifically, the women encourage participation, share power and information, enhance other people's self-worth, and get others excited about their work." I only wish that Rosener would have asked of her audience when that style was *not* appropriate.

Furthermore, to claim universal support of the "feminine" Rushmorean style is politically incorrect because it posits that women leaders are indeed different from men leaders. Many feminists cannot abide the existence of a peculiarly "feminine" style because it opens the door to unequal treatment (because it is seen in our society as better to be tough than to be soft, women leaders can too easily be dismissed as "weak" and therefore inferior). Though I sympathize with this concern, I believe that feminists would have a better case if tough leadership were in fact better than soft. But as we have seen, the so-called "feminine" style is better than the masculine, regardless of the gender of the practitioner. (The "feminine" style is *not* a sex-linked trait; men can learn it by unlearning the anachronistic macho lessons of childhood and youth.)

So why concede an incorrect sexist argument? Why not instead embrace fully the tremendous untapped contribution to leadership that women can make? Rosener's data show that women are far more likely to be comfortable with the Rushmorean style than men, so why deny them the chance to practice it by denying that it is better? Why would women want to act like men when men's Realist style of leadership has so often proved belligerent, bullying, and ineffective? Instead of joining the ranks of the failed, we should all try to adopt the more successful and desirable style by both recruiting more women leaders and working to teach men to become "feminine" Rushmorean leaders.

The last major theoretical obstacle in the way of implementing the "feminine" Rushmorean style of leadership is the thinly veiled societal fear of the dreaded D-word: *democracy*. We turn to that subject next.

Why Democratic Leadership
Is *Not* an Oxymoron

It is by now clear that the Corporate Rushmoreans, like their political counterparts, were not perfect people or perfect leaders, nor did they always succeed in their efforts to bring about change. Like all humans, they had flaws, failings, and foibles. They made mistakes, and from time to time they may even have slipped into Realist leadership practices. But they were most effective at leading change—and their actions were consistent with their own stated moral aspirations—when they practiced values-based leadership. Given the academic and media pressures on them to conform to the prevailing standards of leadership as exemplified by Robert Crandall and Jack Welch, it is to their credit that they were almost always able to resist the temptation to act like the tough guys featured on business magazine covers and lauded as exemplars of contingency leadership in scholarly texts.

But Corporate Rushmoreans are not simply up against an invalid academic theory; thousands of years of human experience give Realists the upper hand. Everything in Western culture—and in the dominant culture of the Asian Far East, as well—reinforces the Realist position. Even people who know better will call for "strong leadership" in times of crisis or gridlock and in chaotic situations such as governing large and diverse nations or directing movies. If one doesn't listen carefully, even the words of someone as antiauthoritarian as Peter Drucker can be misinterpreted to reinforce the

Realist model. In a 1987 speech I heard him give in London, Drucker offered the conductor of a symphonic orchestra as a metaphor for corporate leadership. It was a brilliant, but risky, performance—as I discovered during the coffee break when it became clear that several executives in the audience had visualized the legendary Herbert von Karajan as the embodiment of the leadership traits Drucker had advocated. That had not been Drucker's intention, but the now-deceased conductor of the Berlin Philharmonic was apparently quite alive in the collective memory as the personification of the maestro.

The von Karajan model of the ideal conductor is a solo star who controls every aspect of the orchestra, commanding the absolute obedience of all its members by virtue of his skill, character, position, power, and prestige (not to mention testosterone). Such a conductor makes marvelous music—not exactly by himself, but by bending the will of a hundred musicians to his own. He is above them, better than them, with no need to consult with them or to ask anything of them other than to do as they are told. Drucker, who is a noted authority on East Asian art and culture, could not have offered a clearer restatement of Confucian leadership than this easily misinterpreted metaphor of the conductor as corporate leader.

Around the time that Drucker was advancing this metaphor, one of his most successful disciples in the business world was finishing work on a book that came to a quite different conclusion. In *Leadership Jazz*, Max De Pree offers the leader of a jazz band as a metaphor for effective corporate leadership. In a jazz band, the leader does not control or command; rather, the leader sets the tone, which the followers use as the basis for making their own special contributions, personal variations on the theme established by the leader. The jazz leader is not aloof from the members of the group but is rather a working member of the ensemble who leads by example.

In the summer of 1992, I discussed both the symphonic and jazz models with students at the renowned Aspen Music School and asked them which they felt was likely to be the more effective style of leadership. The students knew next to nothing about corporate life and, as classical musicians and members of the Aspen symphonic orchestra, were not necessarily experts on jazz (though they certainly knew enough to understand that their orchestra couldn't tolerate a clarinetist doing a riff on a Beethoven theme!). Nonetheless, they posited that the day of the dictatorial conductor had passed and that Karajan had been the last of that breed. A woman violinist summed up the conclusions of her fellow students in this way: "The role of the conductor today is to energize the orchestra, not to command it." (In this context, Francis Ford Coppola is a Duke Ellington who longs desperately to be seen as a Herbert von Karajan.)

One of the most respected of the new breed of conductors-as-energizers is Michael Tilson Thomas, musical director of Miami's New World Symphony. He confessed that he was once enamored of the Karajan maestro model, but he now practices "collaboration" with the members of his orchestra: "As a conductor I am utterly uninterested in going out on the stage and giving beats and having people follow them. That is not my style of music making. What I'm interested in doing is helping to create a kind of musical space, a kind of space in time and spirit in which music can take place. And I enter this space with my ideas, and all of my colleagues with me enter this space with all of their ideas, their past experience, their perspectives. And somehow in this space we find one another."

All that talk about space is a bit too New Age for my tired old blood, but in a May 1994 interview in the *Los Angeles Times*, Tilson Thomas explained his conducting goals and philosophy of orchestra leadership in a manner that sounds remarkably similar to De Pree's leader of a jazz band. Tilson Thomas explained that his goal is to encourage innovation. Whereas he used to think he could command change—assuming both that he had all the "right ideas" and that others would willingly follow and emulate the exact vision he carried inside his mind—he now recognizes that that philosophy was impractical on both counts. He finds, first, that others often have "better" ideas and, second, that others are more willing to embrace his vision when he listens to them and tries to accommodate their visions within his. In the process of embracing this new approach to leadership, Tilson Thomas concluded that he has become more of an "idealist." Paradoxically, his new idealistic Rushmorean approach is more effective than his old Realism. And because the new approach is based on genuine inclusion of the people affected by his leadership, it is also more moral than the totalitarian approach of maestros in the past.

Still, Realists are not convinced of the effectiveness of values-based leadership. Inevitably, they will make their last stand on the following grounds: they will accuse Rushmoreans of wishing to grant every member of the orchestra a vote. In the end, the Realist's trump card is the dreaded D-word, *democracy*. It is odd how ambivalent we all are about this inclusionary process of self-government, particularly given that the foreign policy of this country has for most of the twentieth century stressed the importance of "making the world safe for democracy." We may wish democracy on the world, but we draw the line in our own lives and organizations. Calvin Coolidge hailed political democracy for all the right reasons—it encourages new ideas, innovation, and progress and it protects individual freedom—yet, his present-day libertarian disciples balk as the prospect of introducing those virtues into the workplace. Democracy is fine, they seem to say; just don't try it on my turf. It may seem politically incorrect to knock the distinguishing virtue of our way of life—indeed, the very foundation of our political system—but opponents of democracy know that they can get away with it, and even get nods of agreement from progressives who might be expected to be the first to defend government of, by, and for the people.

In fact, those who doubt the wisdom of democracy are legion. Deep in the collective unconscious, we all harbor fears of chaos. Consequently, Realists often carry the day when they claim that Rushmoreans like Tilson Thomas believe that members of an orchestra should vote on what tempo to use in a symphony, that airline crews should vote in crisis situations, and that the governance of General Motors should be a representative democracy like the United States. The Realists claim that Rushmoreans would, in the name of democracy, destroy discipline in every organization. Hence, they argue, the choice comes down to either anarchy ("mobocracy"), on the one hand, or Platonic-Confucian rule by the few who know best, on the other.

This argument is specious because it assumes that "democratic leadership" is an oxymoron. It is simply not true that Michael Tilson Thomas is less a leader than Karajan. Different? Yes. More effective and more moral? I would also say yes. A passive wimp? No. His contribution to the orchestra is every bit as profound as Karajan's was. Realists also assume that democracy degenerates into anarchy. This "fact" is belied by hundreds of years of experience in the United States, Great Britain, and Switzerland. In fact, over the past century, civility has unraveled primarily in Western nations with strongman rulers. Realists also assume that Rushmoreans wish to introduce something like political democracy in work organizations. They are partly correct in that Corporate Rushmorean leadership is based on democratic values, and they are right to point to democratic trends in the workplace. Yale's Robert Dahl, an authority on political democracy, predicts that the next stage of social development in the West will be the democratization of workplaces: "I have no doubt that many people will immediately reject the idea of extending the democratic process to business firms as foolish and unrealistic. It may therefore be helpful to recall that not long ago most people took it as a matter of self-evident good sense that the idea of applying the democratic process to the government of the nation-state was foolish and unrealistic."

In particular, this "foolish and unrealistic" notion was derided by philosophers like Plato and Confucius who believed that wisdom rests with an elite group of guardians. Dahl says that not only has this belief been belied for society as a whole, but it is also not true inside work organizations. Though he admits that democratic workplaces would be as flawed as democratic societies and would have a

similar "tendency toward minority domination," they would nonetheless be more effective (and viewed as more legitimate) than
those managed by a small class of expert guardians. Indeed, Dahl's
point is supported by the examples of the Corporate Rushmoreans
and by recent research that indicates high levels of effectiveness and
productivity in decentralized, participative companies in which
workers are included in decision making.

But let us be clear about this: the day when people in work organizations will "have the vote" is far off—after all, it took twenty-five
hundred years for everyone in the West to become politically enfran-
chised. As Max De Pree explains about his own highly participative
company: "Everyone has the right and the duty to influence decision making and to understand the results. Participative management guarantees that decisions will not be arbitrary, secret, or closed
to questioning. Participative management is not democratic. Having a say differs from having a vote." Indeed, the entire workforce
at Herman Miller has voted on one occasion only: a plebiscite on
whether or not to continue the company's Scanlon plan.

Voting is unnecessary in most work organizations and almost
always undesirable. Voting makes sense within a sovereign nation,
but it is far less useful in other contexts. As the statesman Harlan
Cleveland writes about the United Nations, "Voting is a good way
to take a snapshot of disagreement; but voting is not very useful in
bonding sovereign peoples to do something together." Cleveland
argues that outside the instance of single, sovereign nation-states,
we should be talking not about voting but about fostering "democratic values," the foremost of which is a commitment to human
rights. In the words of Vaclav Havel, democracy depends on the citizenry's sharing such values as "decency, reason, responsibility, sincerity, civility and tolerance." In short, what is needed is a "civic
culture" with commonly held values. And that is the goal of values-
based leadership in corporations.

To this end, Max De Pree has taken the same first step toward
democracy inside his organization that the Rushmorean presidents

took long before the introduction of full political democracy in this country: he has acknowledged that his employees have *rights*. "Each of us, no matter what our rank in the hierarchy may be, has the same rights: to be needed, to be involved, to have a convenantal relationship, to understand the corporation, to be accountable, to appeal. . . ."

In sum, Rushmorean leadership is not about voting; it is about the democratic value of *inclusion*. There is nothing oxymoronic, chaotic, or ineffective about leadership based on that moral principle.

• • • • • • •

Having concluded our inquiry into how leaders may bring about effective and moral change, we now turn to the half of the leadership equation typically overlooked: followers. In the second part of this book, we seek to discover why we all resist change that would be in our self-interest to embrace. Indeed, in the chapters to come, we seek an explanation of why followers so often resist the very leadership that they claim to crave. We also address an even more puzzling phenomenon: Why do leaders themselves resist adopting ideas that would energize their followers? To keep this analysis practical, we focus on why employees of corporations—and business executives themselves—almost always resist changes that would benefit their organizations greatly. To prevent the natural defensiveness likely to arise in such an analysis, our main subjects will not be business practitioners but instead three familiar would-be agents of organizational change. Based on analysis of the relative failures of these thought leaders, we draw general conclusions about the sources of resistance to change. We learn that Shakespeare had it right: in all cases where change is resisted, "The fault, dear Brutus, is not in our stars / But in ourselves."

Part Two

. . . .

Followers (and Leaders) Resisting Change

. . . .

Change Resisted

Thirty-Three Hypotheses Why

I n October 1992, the board of directors of General Motors forced
Robert C. Stempel to resign as the company's chairman and chief
executive officer, posts he had held for more than three years. The
board gave two reasons for the action: Stempel had failed to halt the
long-term erosion of GM's domestic market share (which had slid
from a high of 52 percent in the early 1970s to below 35 percent at
the end of his tenure), and he had failed to bring about the massive
changes needed to make the company competitive in the future.

Contrary to many media reports, Stempel's problems were not
the result of textbook incompetence. In fact, knowledgeable observers considered Stempel among the most able managers to head
the giant corporation since the retirement of the legendary Alfred
Sloan in 1956. Stempel was a skilled engineer who understood the
necessity to make changes in the company's strategy and structure,
and, even more important, he was free of the hubris that had handi-
capped his predecessors in GM's fabled fourteenth-floor executive
suite. Unlike the arrogant men who had recently been at the helm
of "Monolithic Motors," Stempel was good with people, and he
knew the car business from the bottom up—that is, from the van-
tage point of the people who actually designed and made the company's Chevrolets, Buicks, and Cadillacs.

As early as 1987 he had discussed publicly GM's "seventy-five
years of culture that really had to get turned around" to improve the

company's economic performance. To that end, he had called for "a new quality ethic," for "entrepreneurial-type management," for eliminating "a number of vice presidents and a number of layers of communication," for building a relationship with the United Auto Workers union based on "an understanding between us about our common goals that will let us work away from an adversarial framework to a cooperative one," for increased investments in training and in the latest production technologies, and for dealing with "issues like trust, sharing, and making sure that managers are properly informed." Clearly, Stempel knew what to do; the problem is that he didn't do it. He couldn't turn GM's culture around.

That problem—being unable to do what one knows should and must be done—is a common cause of failure among would-be leaders. If the press had been correct and Stempel's problems were sui generis—"the death throes of the last corporate dinosaur"—we could shake our heads, say, "Well, that's GM for you," and get on with our business. But Stempel's experience was not a singular manifestation of the "GM disease." The heads of nearly all corporations that have fallen on hard times in recent years have suffered from the same misdiagnosed ailment that proved fatal for Robert Stempel: they could not lead change.

Why couldn't they? For three decades it has been assumed that corporate failure results from a lack of know-how. The familiar problems of industrial decline, diminishing productivity, technological obsolescence, the absence of innovation, and the other manifestations of shrinking profits and contracting corporations have been attributed to management's failure to understand or apply the techniques used by "excellent companies." This assumption has led business professors, consultants, and corporate culture spin doctors to proffer up a cornucopia of New Management delights: programs, policies, and practices distilled from the experiences of the world's best-managed firms.

This advice is basically sound; indeed, it is all the same commonsense advice offered in different guises and packages. Beginning in the early 1970s, a legion of New Management storm troopers succeeded in getting their message out to nearly every sentient businessperson, from the proprietors of Mom n' Pop's store right on up to Robert Stempel and his fellow executives in their terrorist-proof fourteenth-floor aerie in Detroit. They could not have missed the message, yet nothing happened. One of the first and best of the intrepid breed of New Management experts, Edward E. Lawler, suggests that fewer than 5 percent of major corporations practice the techniques pioneered at America's most-admired companies. Worse, even those few companies hailed for being in the vanguard don't practice faithfully what they pioneered.

Thus it turns out that the experts' diagnosis of the problem was inaccurate. It isn't a lack of know-how that keeps managers from doing what they should do. The problem runs deeper, and it has taken me nearly two decades of running furiously in place to gain some useful insight on the real causes of mismanagement.

I was attending a conference at one of America's largest high-tech corporations when it first occurred to me that we had all been working on the wrong problem. At the conclusion of that meeting, I was introduced to a well-known author, a consultant recognized for his knowledge of eminently productive corporations. He just had delivered a thoughtful speech to the top managers of the company, and they had responded with apparent enthusiasm to what he had told them. In light of their deafening applause, I had expected to find him flushed with success. Instead, he was downhearted. He explained to me in private: "I've conducted three other seminars for this company over the past few years. At the end of each one, they applauded as wildly as they did today; but they have *never* acted on a single thing I've proposed. I don't get it," he said dejectedly. "They keep telling me I'm 'right on target'—but they never do anything about it. *They never change*."

When I reflected a moment on this company's mediocre performance, I began to appreciate the source of the famous author's frustration. If there were ever a company that could benefit from his exemplary advice, this was it. The company wasn't a basket case, but it could easily soon become one if the obvious changes the author advocated weren't made. Moreover, nothing he had said was so radical or controversial that it should have frightened the managers in the room from taking action. On the contrary, what he had proposed was in keeping with the sound guidance offered in literally hundreds of how-to business books. It then occurred to me that the author probably wasn't alone in his frustration—nor was this company singularly retarded in its inability to learn and to change. In fact, as Ed Lawler points out, precious little of the essential managerial knowledge in general circulation is put into practice in many American corporations.

If Lawler's estimate was anywhere near right, the famous author—and thousands of business executives, management consultants, writers, and professors who, like me, shared his "customer-oriented, employee-centered" philosophy—were focused on the wrong issue. Like everyone else, we had all assumed that corporate mismanagement results from businesspeople not knowing what to do. But if Lawler was correct, that was not the sticking point. Instead, the problem was that managers were not doing what they know full well they should and must do!

In fact, Robert Stempel knew what to do at GM. Like most other chief executives at the time, he said all the right things. Moreover, he acted on some of those: he introduced the latest quality programs, cut red tape, and laid off tens of thousands of unproductive middle managers. But he didn't—or couldn't—overcome the deep-seated resistance to changing GM's culture. For all his manifest managerial skills, he lacked the proper Rushmorean attitude to lead. He was unable to bring about the changes at GM that he knew were necessary because he, personally, was never fully comfortable with them. It was as if he had found someone else's stylish shoes that he admired and wore daily, even though they never quite fit. In other words, he couldn't change the minds of others because he hadn't made the new ideas completely his own. Without doubt, he knew what had to be done intellectually—his head was full of how-to—but his heart wasn't there. He had lived his entire life under the old GM system, and while he understood its shortcomings, he could not forget that he had done well for decades by conforming to its precepts. He couldn't help but remember what was positive about the old culture, and so in his every good-intentioned call for change, there was just a hint of reticence. For example, when management consultant John Simmons asked him in 1987 if it was "a fair observation" to say that "there is still a very conservative culture at the top" of GM, Stempel replied:

> I suppose from the bottom looking up, it might be. From here looking out, I'd hate to be taking much more risk right now. . . . I think what the critics are really concerned with are the things they associate with the fourteenth floor that have not changed—such as the traditional meetings and meeting structures. We've got some of the traditional check and balance meetings in there to make sure things are moving. My objective will be to accelerate even faster, because I share the view that once we're really operating as a business, we could do away with some of the redundant meetings and reports.

The "risks" to which Stempel referred were attendant to eliminating, by his own reckoning, "a number of vice presidents and a number of layers of communication," changes that in fact put at risk only the bureaucracy's "check and balance" powers of command and control. Doubtless he was unaware of his own reluctance to embrace change fully, but others noticed: they did not follow. What he said didn't ring true. Down the line at GM, people knew that when push came to shove, nothing really fundamental—nothing threatening to the old ways and the old boys—would occur. In sum, he couldn't inspire others to change because he wasn't inspired to change himself.

Paradoxically, countless managers in the 1970s and 1980s rejected the very knowledge outlined in the first part of this book that would have allowed them to transform their corporations before the competitive crisis of the 1980s, and before they had to downsize and reengineer in a panic. Like Stempel, they resisted the changes that might have spared the decimation of their industries and, in many cases, might have saved their own careers.

Hence understanding the source of resistance to change among both leaders and followers is key to any attempt to transform management. That understanding is both the subject and the object of the following chapters. The subject is a straightforward analysis of why change is resisted among followers. But my object is also to understand the persistent reluctance to accept long-available knowledge about leadership. In doing so we will address the paradox that caused our famous author's frustration: leaders resist the very knowledge that would allow them to overcome the resistance to change!

Since the 1980s, it has become more widely accepted that change is the prime task of leaders and that the best measure of effective leadership is the behavior of followers. To the extent that followers embrace needed change, leaders can be said to be effective. Thus a sine qua non of effective leadership is the ability to overcome resistance to change among followers. But addressing that resistance has not been the focus of most leaders whose mind-set has instead been on their own tasks, visions, and roles, to the near exclusion of the needs, aspirations, and roles of followers. Moreover, the focus of most writing and research about leadership—and the common wisdom on the subject—has been on the personality and characteristics of the leader. But as Peter Drucker notes, there is really only one characteristic common to all leaders: *followers*. Hence in this part of the book the focus will be on why we all resist change—in effect, on why we refuse to become followers. Without that basic knowledge, there is no chance of overcoming humankind's innate conservatism. What we will find is that people in organizations resist change advocated by their leaders for exactly the same reasons that the leaders of organizations resist change advocated by outsiders.

Why Is Change Resisted?

In 1991, citizens of Albania went to the polls in that country's first contested election since 1923. The Albanians had just emerged from a forty-seven-year nightmare of Stalinist rule that had left them Europe's most impoverished people. The Western press had trumpeted the newly minted Democratic Party as the odds-on favorites to win the election because only that party had pledged to create genuine liberty, to seek Western financial aid, and thus to bring long-isolated Albania "into Europe." But apparently the Albanians were not as interested in change as the foreign observers had assumed: they voted their Communist rulers back into power.

Friedrich Hegel, the eighteenth-century German philosopher, would not have been surprised by the outcome of the Albanian election (or, for that matter, by the failure of GM's Robert Stempel). He had offered one of the most pessimistic conclusions imaginable about society: "What experience and history teach is that peoples and governments never have learned anything from history, or acted on principles deduced from it." Let's be clear about this: Hegel did *not* believe that the conditions of society would not or could not improve. He just didn't believe that such change came about as the result of anything that you, I, the king of Prussia, or the CEO of GM might consciously do; instead, Hegel posited that history unfolded in its own sweet time and way. In effect, Hegel's historical determinism rejected the possibility of leadership. He was particularly scornful of the Enlightenment idealists—such as my own personal hero, Thomas Jefferson—who thought that they could create a just society by winning people over to the ideas of democracy, liberty, and equality. That's why I hate Hegel.

Yet it was Hegel's quote that immediately came to mind when the famous author mentioned in this chapter told me that despite continually lavishing heavy praise and unconscionable honoraria on him, the high-tech firm at which we were guests never changed. To me, this was another instance that supported Hegel's counsel of pessimism. In my gut, I knew that Hegel was wrong; but, confound it, the facts all appeared to be on his side. Like Albanians, GM employees, and nearly everyone else I could think of, we all seemed to fail to learn from history and experience, to reject social knowledge, and to deny the necessity to pursue the obvious course of action that would lead to our own self-preservation. On this score, E. F. Schumacher may have been even more pessimistic than Hegel, concluding that people "tend to try and cure a disease by intensifying its causes." That was at least partly true for the Albanians and for two generations of GM executives.

The twentieth century provides myriad instances of similar phenomena: Britain slept through Churchill's repeated warnings of the danger to Western civilization posed by Nazism—as Britain had slept in the 1905–1910 era when Churchill, then a young Liberal Party politician, had advocated progressive social legislation as an antidote to his nation's crippling class warfare. In America, Theodore Roosevelt's remarkable 1912 echo of Churchill's social program was similarly resisted (only to be enacted in its near entirety two decades later in a moment of crisis—as, ironically, Churchill's long-fermenting social program would be enacted in a most intemperate form by the Labour government that had unseated the wartime leader before the echoes of the last Nazi cannon had subsided). More recently, and in a quite different arena, Rachel Carson's early warnings about potential ecocatastrophes required some thirty years to gain popular acceptance. The consequence common to each of these examples is that society paid an enormous price for its resistance to necessary change. Thus we are concerned here not with costless curiosities, but with events of considerable and—if Hegel was wrong—*avoidable* consequences.

Given these enormous costs—and potential opportunities—it is curious that little serious consideration has been given to the phenomenon of resistance to change. That absence of serious thought may result from the overabundance of popular wisdom available on the subject. Nearly every one of the great minds of civilization has offered a pet theory. After my little epiphany with the famous author, I started collecting these casual observations. I discovered that the great minds were as one on the point that groups resist change with all the vigor of antibodies attacking an intruding virus. However, that consensus completely disintegrates upon asking the follow-up question: *Why?* A foray to the library reveals hundreds of speculations about the root causes of resistance to change. Here's a sample of some of the most popular hypotheses.

1. *Homeostasis.* Continual change is not a natural condition of life; hence resistance to change is a healthy human instinct. According to Montaigne, the stability of society is so important that it is "very iniquitous . . . to subject public and immutable institutions and observances to the instability of a private fancy."

2. *Stare decisis.* In common law, the presumption must always be given to the status quo. The burden of proof must always be on the change agent.

3. *Inertia.* When a large body is in motion, it takes considerable force to alter its course.

4. *Satisfaction.* Most people are perfectly content with the status quo. Prince Bolkonski, in *War and Peace,* "could not compre- hend how anyone could wish to alter his life or introduce anything new into it." In fact, most people can't imagine any alternative to the status quo. Said Voltaire's Pangloss in *Candide:* "This is the best of all possible worlds."

5. *Lack of ripeness.* Change occurs only when certain precondi- tions have been met. Such conditions are rare and cannot be forced.

6. *Fear.* Humans have an innate fear of the unknown. We prefer to take our chances with the devil we know.

7. *Self-interest.* Change may be good for others or even for the system as a whole, but unless it is specifically good for us, we will resist it.

8. *Lack of self-confidence*. Change threatens our self-esteem. New conditions require of us fresh skills, abilities, and attitudes, but we lack the confidence that we are up to the new challenges.

9. *Future shock*. When people are overwhelmed by major changes—as they are in modern society—they hunker down and resist because the species is capable of only so much adaptation.

10. *Futility: plus ça change, plus c'est la meme chose*. Since all change is largely superficial, cosmetic, and hence illusory, why would people take part in the charade when they know that the power structure of society will remain unchanged?

11. *Lack of knowledge*. We don't know how to change (or what to change to). Ignorance and faulty analysis get in the way of effective change.

12. *Human nature*. We are innately competitive, aggressive, greedy, and selfish. Because planned change assumes a degree of altruism, it is doomed to fail.

13. *Cynicism*. In light of assumption 12, we must suspect the motives of the change agent.

14. *Perversity*. Change sounds like a good idea; unfortunately, the unintended consequences will be the exact opposite of the stated objective.

15. *Individual genius versus group mediocrity*. Einstein wrote that "great souls have always met with violent opposition from mediocre minds."

16. *Ego*. Change requires that the powerful admit that they have been wrong.

17. *Short-term thinking*. People can't defer gratification. Said Hume, "People are always much inclined to prefer present interest to the distant and remote."

18. *Myopia*. Because we can't see beyond the tips of our noses, we can't see that change is in our broader self-interest. "Worse,"

writes historian John Lukacs, "when people do not see some-thing, this often means that they do not wish to see it—a con-dition that may be comfortable and profitable to them."

19. *Sleepwalking*. Because most of us lead unexamined lives, we have, according to Karl Mannheim, "somnambulistic certainty" about the rectitude of the status quo.

20. *Snow blindness*. Groupthink, or social conformity, is the problem. As early as the sixteenth century, Francis Bacon con-cluded that consensus-seeking causes us to share common myths and misconceptions.

21. *Collective fantasy*. According to Barbara Tuchman's *March of Folly*, people in groups "often act contrary to the way reason points and enlightened self-interest suggests." This "wooden-headedness" derives from the inability to learn from experience and from viewing situations in light of preconceived notions.

22. *Chauvinistic conditioning*. The way *we* do it is right; *they* are wrong. And if you are one of us and you advocate what they do, you are disloyal.

23. *Fallacy of the exception*. Change might work elsewhere, but we are different. In fact, we can't learn anything from others unless their situation is exactly the same as ours.

24. *Ideology*. Because we each have different worldviews—inher-ently conflicting values—any plan for change will divide the community into hopelessly adversarial camps.

25. *Institutionalism*. Individuals may change, but groups do not. Indeed, the prime task of the organization is self-preservation and self-perpetuation.

26. *Natura non facit saltum*. "Nature does not proceed by leaps" was the gradualist philosophy of Leibniz and Linnaeus. In the words of Darwin, change occurs only in "very short and slow steps." Applying this observation about nature to the affairs of human-kind, Macaulay argued that things are constantly improving at

their own unalterable rate, which constitutes the natural and sensible pace of change.

27. *The rectitude of the powerful*. The best and the brightest have set us on the current course. Who are we to question the wisdom of our leaders?

28. *"Change has no constituency."* Machiavelli suggested that the stake that a minority of individuals have in preserving their certain place in the status quo is far stronger than the stake that the majority have in bringing about an uncertain alternative.

29. *Determinism*. As we have seen, Hegel posited that there was nothing anyone could do to bring about purposeful change. Though change might occur, it is not as the result of conscious human action.

30. *Scientism*. The contemporary academic corollary to Hegel's hypothesis is that society *shouldn't* learn from the lessons of history because they aren't scientific.

31. *Habit*. William James remarked that habits are "the flywheel of society." And habit, according to John Dewey, "covers the formation of attitudes . . . , our basic sensitivities and ways of meeting and responding to all the conditions which we meet in living." This is more than positive; it is "the principle of continuity of experience."

32. *The despotism of custom*. In sharp contrast to Dewey, habit is a negative factor according to John Stuart Mill. He hypothesized that individuality is viewed as an affront to custom. Because the ideas of change agents are seen as a reproach to society, progress is thwarted by "despotic" habit.

33. *Human mindlessness*. "It is hard to free fools from the chains they revere," wrote Voltaire. This is the most pessimistic hypothesis of all.

Whom are we to believe? The difficulty with these hypotheses is that they all seem to be correct. All of these sources of resistance may be seen at play in society and in organizations from time to time. Moreover, several of these factors may act in concert, and, I admit, the lines of distinction between the various hypotheses are blurry (Is James's "habit" the same as Montaigne's "stability"?). So even though it may be difficult to distinguish which one or other of these factors is the specific cause of resistance, it would be easy to draw the conclusion that *everything* in society seems to conspire against the receptivity to change.

Yet there's another way of looking at this list. Each of these hypotheses, analyzed alone, fails the simplest test of logic: we can easily imagine an exception to each "rule." Consider Einstein's pithy observation that "great souls have always met with violent opposition from mediocre minds." This myth of the rejected genius—the unappreciated great artist starving in a garret—is a well-fished stream in Western literature. In the twentieth century, that stream was stocked by biographies of a handful of painters who died in pathetic circumstances before their genius was recognized—including van Gogh, Toulouse-Lautrec, Pissarro, Seurat, and, by his own account, at least, our friend Ensor. Though there is no denying that fin-de-siècle France was particularly slow to appreciate emerging trends in art, it is nonetheless difficult to build the general case that great souls have always suffered at the hands of an indifferent society. In fact, it is probably the case in the arts and the sciences that the vast majority of geniuses have been recognized as such during their lifetimes—witness Einstein, himself—the obvious exceptions notwithstanding.

Contrary to Einstein's formulation, rejection seems to be the rule only in the special case of geniuses who dared to challenge prevailing *social* conventions. The personalities of such visionary individuals who met resistance while seeking to persuade their fellows to pursue a course of social progress has become the subject not only of biography but of what today is known as leadership studies. Alas, there is scarcely a useful clue in that voluminous literature to the puzzle before us. We can read about the remarkable strength of character displayed by Churchill during his twenty-odd years in the desert of rejection, but we can find little or nothing about the motives of those who rejected him. The focus of rigorous historical inquiry has been on the personality of the leader, and not on *us*—the vast majority of whom didn't, wouldn't, or couldn't listen, learn, and act.

Insights from the Social "Sciences"

Nonetheless, the discipline of psychology lends limited assistance to our inquiry. A major thrust of mainstream psychology since Freud has been to explain (and overcome) the individual's resistance to change—to changing oneself, to be precise. These insights are relevant, however, only to the extent that collective behavior can be viewed as the sum of individual behaviors. But as members of fraternities, sororities, corporations, unions, or—to take the most extreme example—university faculties will attest, group behavior is not a simple sum of individual traits, reactions, and quirks. Groups behave differently from individuals. To demonstrate the point, social psychologists have devised experiments to show that an individual will act one way when alone and in a quite different manner when a part of a group. Individual psychology, then, may help us understand the attitude of leadership but not the attitudes of collective resistance. Hence individual psychology is a useful, but not sufficient, guide to our inquiry.

More fruitful are speculation and research directed toward the *collective* resistance to change. As we have seen by way of our intimidating list, this focus has drawn the attention of the likes of Bacon, Machiavelli, Hegel, Mill, and Mannheim. But these eminent humanists, philosophers, and social scientists dealt with the issue only peripherally—their main interest was typically the related idea of progress.

The most notable exception is the overcited—and hence often misunderstood—study of the process of change in modern science by Thomas Kuhn. He found collective denial at work among people who are arguably the most rational members of society. He showed that outmoded scientific explanations live on long after facts that belie them have been brought to light, and he posited that this unscientific behavior of scientists is rooted in the collective investment that members of an established discipline have in a discredited paradigm.

Kuhn's explanation is useful to our inquiry but not wholly relevant: even granted the time lags that he documents (during which outdated thinking prevails over more modern explanations), scientific knowledge is nonetheless cumulative. In effect, with regard to science, one can delineate a direction called progress. In contrast, the progression of social knowledge is not linear (or even an advancing spiral or ratchet). For example, democracy was invented by the Greeks—who then turned around and rejected the system for the next two and a half millennia. Still, we find parallels between the "collective conservatism" that Kuhn described among the scientific community and the denial at work in the corporate resistance to the New Management paradigm. In particular, Kuhn's focus on ideas rather than on individuals is helpful. In his view, it was heliocentrism—and not the individual personalities of Copernicus, Kepler, and Galileo—that was rejected in the late Middle Ages and early Renaissance. Similarly, it was clearly the New Management ideas, and not the originators of those ideas—Drucker, Deming, and others—that were rejected in the United States for decades.

Perhaps that *clearly* is not as incontestable as I have asserted it to be. The common wisdom is that resistance is explained by fatal character flaws in the individual who proposes change. Here is the obverse of Einstein's thesis: Churchill's ideas are said to be rejected because of a personal failing of the would-be leader. Therefore, it is argued that, had Churchill not been so egoistical, he would have been able to generate more, and earlier, parliamentary opposition to Nazism. The persistence of this interpretation requires that we explore its merits in the next few chapters.

Another potentially fruitful vein was mined by a small number of authors who, earlier in this century, addressed the process of collective resistance to change in primitive societies. The anthropologist E. E. Evans-Pritchard and the philosopher Michael Polanyi both observed that groups suppress information that runs counter to their basic social premises. Evans-Pritchard and Polanyi—writing separately on the same theme—sought to understand why witchcraft was prevalent in so many different societies. In particular, they analyzed the social process by which the Azande of the Sudan maintain the belief that all natural disasters—floods, droughts, pestilence, human disease, and accidents—are caused by evil spells cast by sorcerers. If an Azande farmer's crop is destroyed by a pest, he looks neither to God nor to the local purveyor of pesticides; instead, he immediately consults an oracle to find out who cast a spell on him. Evans-Pritchard lived among the Azande, and he found it infuriatingly impossible to prove to them that the causes of most misfortune were natural. In fact, he was surprised to find that, "logically," the Azande were right! They could explain the causal links between calamitous events, on the one hand, and the "spells" cast by their enemies, on the other.

Of course, the Azande had learned to avoid putting their entire belief system to a real test. When Evans-Pritchard challenged them on some specific instance of witchcraft—and succeeded in demonstrating that witchcraft could not have been the cause of the misfortune under investigation—the Azande were always able to show that there had been some fault in the procedures used in that particular case. This is, of course, the good Western argument "Well, this case is different" (our hypothesis 23) that we use when confronted with a particular refutation to a fervently held generalization. Evans-Pritchard found, moreover, that the Zande belief system is circular, and each particular objection he raised served only to strengthen their fundamental convictions: "Let the reader consider any argument that would utterly demolish all Zande claims for the power of oracles. If it were translated into Zande modes of thought it would serve to support their entire structure of belief."

What Evans-Pritchard found is that *if* one accepted the basic assumption of the Azande, everything else followed logically. Accept witchcraft, and there were no holes in their explanations of death, disease, pestilence, flood, or drought.

Evans-Pritchard thereby discovered that to understand the behavior of any group of people, it is necessary to get down to the basic premises of their belief system, to root out, in effect, their most fundamental social and ideological assumptions. These assumptions—he called them collective representations—are the glue that holds a group of people together and binds them in such a way that they can act purposefully. The ideas that people in a group hold in common, and hold absolutely, allow for effective social action—as opposed to less efficient individual action. For any social organization to function, then, it is necessary for all its members to share a common worldview. In the words of Polanyi, "By holding the same set of presuppositions they mutually confirm each other's interpretation of experience." This is, of course, an anthropological restatement of the observations made in our list by Montaigne, James, Dewey, and several other philosophers.

Stated positively, this shared worldview that allows for concerted action is much like the transcendent values that leaders call on to unite their organizations and give common direction to the group. Stated negatively—as the process of "collective suppression of countervailing evidence" that Evans-Pritchard and Polanyi found among the Azande—it is, paradoxically, also a source of resistance to change. This form of denial of reality appears to operate in all societies—advanced, rational, scientific ones as well as primitive preliterate communities. Such denial perhaps reached its nadir in modern society during World War I when evidence of the senseless deaths of hundreds of thousands of soldiers in the muddy fields of Flanders was collectively suppressed. Herbert Asquith wrote that the British War Office "kept three sets of figures, one to mislead the public, another to mislead the Cabinet, and the third to mislead itself." And this, of course, is a restatement of the cited observations of Bacon, Tuchman, and Lukacs, among others.

Does this pattern of collective representations explain the resistance to change found at General Motors and in most modern organizations? In the chapters that follow, we test this and several of the other more promising hypotheses on our list against actual experience. Because the roots of collective behavior may be too deep for us to uncover, our goal cannot be to find an explanation that clears the high hurdle of "scientific proof." Instead, we search for an explanation of the resistance to change that meets a lower, more practical standard: Is it useful to practitioners of change? For our purposes, that will be good enough.

8

Drucker Unheeded

Two Potent Sources of Resistance to Change

It is not enough to be right. According to Peter Drucker, leaders—whether of nations, organizations, or social movements—also need to be able to create followers. Why is it then that many would-be leaders fail to attract followers? Drucker himself is an instructive case in point. Though he is not usually thought of as a leader in the organizational sense, he is the founder of an influential school of thought. Widely recognized as the father of modern management studies, for nearly five decades he has espoused a consistent philosophy that today represents the prevailing wisdom. Practitioners such as Max De Pree and gurus such as Warren Bennis credit Drucker with having been first and having been right. For example, had General Motors executives listened to Drucker, the company might have avoided many painful years of retrenchment.

Events may have proved Drucker right, but I was shocked not long ago to hear him upbraid himself when Warren Bennis praised him publicly for his foresight. Drucker's reply to Bennis's admiring words was surprising: "It was meant as a compliment, but I winced because, bluntly, I was at least ten years premature with every one of my forecasts. And *that's* not a compliment. That's saying that one has no impact." Drucker said he had cringed when Bennis spoke because he was reminded of that most common failing of leadership, advancing an idea that is not yet ripe: "What is the environment ready for? One has to do it at the right time."

What surprised me was not Drucker's humility—it was not feigned—but his implication that the art of leadership often hinges on little more than good timing. My immediate reaction was to reject the notion as unworthy of the great leaders whose names came immediately to mind. Certainly Lincoln, Gandhi, and Churchill possessed skills more admirable than an actor's sense of timing, did they not? But as I thought about the experience of those leaders, historical evidence seemed to support Drucker's contention: in leadership, as in making love, position may be important, but you can't beat timing.

But does it all come down to that? Is poor timing a sufficient explanation of why two generations of GM executives failed to follow Drucker's good advice? Or was the explanation to be found in the GM executives' high level of resistance to change? Or in Drucker's shortcomings as a change agent? Or was it a combination of two or three explanations (or more)?

As we have seen, Robert Stempel recognized what needed to be done at General Motors. It would have been remarkable had he *not* known because that knowledge had been in general circulation for forty years before he succeeded Roger Smith to the pinnacle of power at GM. Even in that sloth-paced hierarchy, forty years is sufficient time for word to reach the top. The word was first leaked in Drucker's classic 1946 study, *Concept of the Corporation*. Drucker had spent a year in Detroit near the end of World War II preparing recommendations for GM's return to civilian auto production. He was a great admirer of Alfred Sloan and of the influential managerial system that Sloan had created at GM in the early 1920s. Sloan was the smithy on whose anvil the modern managerial corporation was forged, and Drucker respected the man and his considerable accomplishments.

Drucker was then, as he is today, thoroughly imbued with Old World charm. Throughout his long professional career, he has studiously avoided giving offense and is unfailingly positive in his attitude, even when giving criticism. His report to GM's top management was vintage Drucker: respectful, laudatory wherever possible, and accentuating the positive. But when GM's executives took a gander at it, all they could see was red. They viewed the study as a condemnation of what they stood for and a repudiation of what they had accomplished. They angrily showed Drucker the door and, to this day, have kept him from darkening it again. (As late as 1985, a young GM manager, ignorant of this history, innocently nominated Drucker to receive GM's highest honor, the Alfred Sloan Award. On hearing this blasphemy, then-CEO Roger Smith flew into one of his patented rages—although witnesses recall that neither he nor anyone else in the room could recall why it was de rigueur for GM loyalists to detest Peter Drucker!)

Here is why: in 1946 Drucker had dared to imply that GM must change. Without doubt, Drucker had praised the thoroughly logical theoretical concept of the corporation developed in Sloan's renowned 1919–20 "Organization Study" and had acknowledged that the study had contributed to GM's quarter century of unparalleled success. But Drucker had also dared to ask if Sloan's system would be appropriate for a world soon to be characterized by global competition, changing social values, automation, a knowledge-based economy, and consumer demands for quality. Drucker worried that the bureaucratic hierarchy of commands and controls that Sloan had painstakingly created would be insufficiently responsive to such massive changes: "G.M. is an organization of managers and management," he concluded. "It is a managerial and *not* an innovative company." Drucker was careful to say that this was an observation, not a criticism—many big companies are simply not as innovative as entrepreneurial firms. But that distinction was of small comfort to GM.

In the epilogue to a 1972 reissue of *Concept of the Corporation*, Drucker recapitulated his criticisms, explaining that GM was too impersonal, too addicted to technique, and too concerned with scientific measurement and controllable facts when "what is needed is not facts but an ability to see facts as others see them." Though

Drucker avoided any direct criticism of GM's chief, the implication was that Sloan had vision but lacked perspective. With craftsman's care, Sloan had constructed a company that paid too much attention to policies, systems, and structures and not enough to people, principles, and values. Sloan, the quintessential engineer, had worked out all the intricacies and contingencies of a foolproof system. This was a tour de force, Drucker admitted, but "management is not a science, but an art."

Sloan's system anticipated every problem, establishing rules, procedures, checks and balances, and especially committees empowered to handle anything unforeseeable that might fall between the cracks. Drucker was impressed, but he felt obligated to point out that this system left out customers, employees, and society. Hence his major proposal (which doomed his 1946 report) that GM should abandon adversarial labor relations and seek instead to create a sense of community in its numerous manufacturing facilities. He called on GM to draw a lesson from the company's recent wartime experience during which productivity had been higher than before the war, even though the workforce was less experienced and there were many more workers per supervisor. Wasn't it remarkable, he asked, that a ragtag industrial army composed of housewives, minorities, the aged, the halt, and the lame could work so successfully as partners with management? Drucker asked GM's top brass to consider why this industrial cooperation had led to higher productivity—and then to ask how they might create a similar culture when their regular workforce was demobilized and returned to Detroit. GM's management rejected Drucker's idea of labor-management cooperation as "hostile to business."

Sloan himself was silent on the report. Although there is no record of his ever mentioning it by name in speech or in writing, he immediately set to work on his own version of the GM story. He answered Drucker in a book that he would not publish until 1963 (he patiently withheld the finished manuscript from publication until after the last of his original team at GM was securely in the grave). My *Years with General Motors* is, in Drucker's words, "perhaps the most interesting, most revealing, but also the most frustrating book on business ever written by a businessman." The frustration comes from the inexplicable fact that "there are no people in Sloan's book, no mention of Sloan's own great strength, the leadership of people." Sloan had discounted to zero the value of his own leadership and had instead focused entirely on what he wrongly assumed had been the cause of GM's perennial ranking at the top of the *Fortune* 500, a brilliantly conceived and executed system of controls. Much like Francis Ford Coppola (see Chapter Five), he ignored the human side of the enterprise in favor of a tougher, more economically correct message. Significantly, the next two generations of managers—not only at GM, but in large companies around the world—would listen attentively to what Sloan wrote and miss entirely what he had in fact done.

My *Years with General Motors* stands not only as the clearest expression of the managerial philosophy that dominated American corporations for more than four decades, but also as a thumbnail sketch of what is still the curriculum of most of the nation's business schools. Not that either of these had been Sloan's purpose in writing the book. He had merely set out to correct Drucker, telling his version of how General Motors, under his system, grew from a nearly bankrupt enterprise to the greatest industrial corporation the world had known. The book begins in 1908, when GM was formed by the maverick entrepreneur Billy Durant, and covers the downs (in the early years) and ups (from about 1928 onward) of the company during the forty-five years of Sloan's active service.

First Source of Resistance: Organizational Culture

The book is remarkable for many things, but perhaps the most important (and certainly the most overlooked) is its unwitting expression of a *value system*. Only in the writings of F. W. Taylor is there such a relentless commitment to the engineering worldview that Sloan elucidates on every one of the 522 pages of his book. Whereas Taylor occasionally backs off to justify his ardor for efficiency in human terms, not once does Sloan make reference to any other values. Freedom, equality, humanism, stability, community, tradition, religion, patriotism, family, love, virtue, nature—all are ignored. In the one personal element in the book, he makes passing reference to his wife: he abandons her on the first day of a European vacation to return to business in Detroit.

His language is as calculating as that of the engineer-of-old working with calipers and slide rule, as cold as the steel he caused to be bent to form cars: *economizing, utility, facts, objectivity, systems, rationality, maximizing*—that is the stuff of his vocabulary. He writes, "And since, therefore, no one knew, or could prove, where the efficiencies and inefficiencies lay, there was no objective basis for the allocation of new investment. . . . [So we developed] statistics correctly reflecting the relation between the net return and the invested capital of each operating division—the true measure of efficiency." To Sloan, the highest goal for the corporation was efficiency. Profit and growth were also bright stars in his firmament of values, but efficiency was his North Star, his measure, his navigational guide. On some pages the word *efficiency* appears three times.

Sloan's bugbear is the "human element" that threatens constantly to gum up the efficient operation of his intricately organized and smoothly functioning machine. He writes that GM's great strength "is that it was designed to be an objective organization, as distinguished from the type that gets lost in the subjectivity of personalities." Two such personalities are called out for special scorn: GM's founder Billy Durant, whose sin it was to manage by hunches and impulses, and Henry Ford, who stubbornly and "illogically" had felt a quaint attachment toward the cars he made. Both men get their comeuppance: Billy's career ends in bankruptcy, and Henry loses forever his leadership of the auto industry. Sloan uses these as cautionary tales. The entrepreneurial way, he concludes, is the way of the past. The engineering way, the way of scientific management—what Daniel Bell calls "the economizing mode"—is the way of the future. Sloan writes, "Mr. Durant was a great man with a great weakness—he could create but not administer." No such weakness had Mr. Sloan.

That creativity gets one in trouble is a leitmotif of the book. The one truly creative man to survive at GM during Sloan's reign—the inventor Charles F. Kettering—is treated with gentle disdain. Kettering dared to attempt to develop an air-cooled engine (nearly twenty years before one was successfully introduced by Volkswagen), and Sloan details at painful length how Kettering's attempt at innovation was simply bad business. Sloan concludes that "it was not necessary to lead in design or run the risk of untried experiments." And true to Sloan's word, after the air-cooled-engine fiasco, GM was never again to be a technological leader. The company was to become the domain of the engineer, not the innovator, the arena of the bureaucrat, not the creative scientist, the world of the administrator, not the entrepreneur.

So successful were Sloan and his "associates" (he does not tell us if they were also his friends) that their administrative techniques were taught to two generations of managers at the nation's leading business schools. (As far as I know, no significant new idea has ever been *created* at a business school. Instead, professors steal the best ideas from managers, repackage them, and sell them back to corporations at an unconscionable markup. The only value added is jargon.)

American business schools swiped the accounting and financial controls pioneered by Sloan's alter ego, Jakob Raskob (who had brought modern managerial accounting to Du Pont and later introduced it into GM when the two companies were both briefly under the leadership of Pierre S. Du Pont). And the business schools lifted Sloan's product policy, his system of market research, and his use of committees to coordinate policy. Unconsciously, they even absorbed and transmitted Sloan's social philosophy—his antagonism toward unions, government, and anyone who preached corporate responsibility to any constituencies other than stockholders or managers themselves. They also soaked up his low regard for the business of exporting and for international trade in general.

In particular, business schools came to advocate the Sloanian model of organizational structure. There is no doubt that Sloan solved the problem of how to structure a giant corporation. His secret was to decentralize manufacturing while centralizing corporate policy and financial controls. With this single stroke of genius, Sloan laid the groundwork for a managerial model and philosophy that would dominate American industry for the next fifty years.

Organizational ideas, however, are seldom developed in this fashion from theory or by design; they evolve from practice and experience. In fact, pressures from competition, human foibles and follies, demands from shareholders, and the human tendency toward bureaucracy led GM to stray from Sloan's decentralized model as early as the 1930s. When Marx was on his deathbed, he surveyed the state of world communism and is reported to have said, "I'm no Marxist." Had Sloan taken such an honest look at what had become of his marvelous idea, he might have issued a similar disclaimer. For by 1945, Sloan's system had become a caricature of what he had originally proposed. And in his book he had perpetrated a caricature of himself as a hard-hearted engineer instead of the warm leader of people he actually was, according to Drucker.

But none of that mattered. The book became the corporation's bible, and GM socialized its managers chapter and verse in the gospel according to their forebears. Roger Smith, Robert Stempel, and their predecessors on the fourteenth floor had all been raised on the precepts of Sloan's good book. The GM way, as articulated by Sloan, coalesced and hardened into a narrow value system—an ideology. GM's managers could be forgiven for concluding that they had, once and forever, "solved the problem of management." After all, the company was the greatest corporate success story in history—so great that the guiding principles behind it were crystallized into operating assumptions for all subsequent generations of managers. Here, gleaned from the pages of *My Years with General Motors*, are some of Sloan's major operating assumptions (significantly, many of these remained current even as the company entered the 1980s):

1. GM is in the business of making money, not cars.

2. Success comes not from technological leadership but from having the resources to adopt quickly innovations successfully introduced by others.

3. Cars are primarily status symbols. Styling is therefore more important than quality to buyers, who are, after all, going to trade up every year.

4. The American car market is isolated from the rest of the world. Foreign competitors will never gain more than 15 percent of the domestic market.

5. Energy will always be cheap and abundant.

6. Workers do not have an important impact on productivity or product quality.

7. Consumer, environmental, and other social concerns are unimportant to the American public.

8. The government is the enemy. It must be fought every inch of the way.

9. Strict, centralized financial controls are the secret to good administration.

10. Managers should always be developed from inside the company.

There were many more assumptions, some conscious, others inexplicit; but ten will suffice. It is important to acknowledge that these guiding assumptions were based on the pioneering policies that had made GM one of the most successful industrial organizations in the history of the world. By repeating what had made it successful in the past, the company became ever more successful. This in turn reinforced the legitimacy of the operating assumptions. These assumptions then became unchallengeable—and remained unchallenged. Why challenge an idea with eternal validity? Only a fool would knock success!

Alas, nothing fails like success. Though there was nothing intrinsically invalid about the company's operating assumptions, something happened in the 1970s that made them anachronistic: as Drucker had predicted a quarter of a century earlier, the environment changed radically. Gasoline became expensive; the auto market became internationalized; the rising budget for retooling, in cost and time, made it necessary to be a leader rather than a follower in the introduction of new products and new technology; consumer values shifted from style to quality; the size of families shrank; people could no longer afford to trade their cars in every few years; worker values and attitudes changed; successful government relations required cooperation rather than adversarial spirit; the few "kooks" in California who bought Volkswagens and read *Consumer Reports* became an important segment of the auto-buying public; the world economy began to globalize; and much more. By 1980, the environment had changed so thoroughly that the brilliant assumptions that Sloan had made to meet the exigencies of the 1920s had become inappropriate.

Thus GM's very success was at the root of its inability, beginning in the 1970s, to innovate to meet the changing environment. As the Japanese captured more and more of the market in California, and the Germans did almost as well on the East Coast, John Z. De Lorean described GM's top brass complacently looking down from the fourteenth floor of their headquarters onto the parking lot and adjacent streets below and saying, in effect, "Wow! Look at all those big cars. Who says Americans want small ones?" I hesitate to cite De Lorean as an authority on this matter, but quote him I must. De Lorean contributed the third important insider's account of GM, *On a Clear Day You Can See General Motors*. De Lorean's book documents the organizational reasons for GM's managers' inability to perceive, let alone challenge, the outmoded assumptions that held them prisoner. Here we see the deep roots of resistance to change.

In one of the most hilarious and telling vignettes in the book, De Lorean describes what he calls a "typical" meeting of the GM executive committee in which the top two or three managers would pontificate while the remaining dozen or so executives present "would remain silent, speaking only when spoken to. When they did offer a comment, in many cases it was just to paraphrase what had already been said by one of the top guys." De Lorean writes that Richard Terrell, then–vice chairman of the board, was "the master of the paraphrase," able to parrot the views of the chairman and big boss, Richard Gerstenberg. According to De Lorean, the following was typical dialogue:

Gerstenberg: Goddamnit. We cannot afford any new models next year because of the cost of this federally mandated equipment. There is no goddamn money left for styling changes. That's the biggest problem we face.

Terrell (after waiting about 10 minutes): Dick, goddamnit. We've just got to face up to the fact that our number one problem is the cost of this federally mandated equipment. This stuff costs so much that we just don't have money left for styling our new cars. That's our biggest problem.

Gerstenberg: You're goddamn right, Dick. That's a good point.

I cite this neither to damn GM nor to praise De Lorean. Whether this hypothetical dialogue is accurate or not, it illustrates the essence of a behavioral problem found in most organizations. People in groups form fixed ideas (Evans-Pritchard's "collective representations"), and all of the forces within the group conspire to protect those notions, no matter how outmoded or inaccurate they may be. GM's managers were, in effect, corporate Azande, all clinging to the same worldview, all sharing the same limited values, the same strong corporate culture. And it was that mentality—fifty years in the making—that all of Roger Smith's huffing and puffing, all his commands and orders, failed to change. It was that mentality that

Robert Stempel was unable to change even though he was a "bubba," a trusted insider, a loyal member of the team. And it was that mentality that Peter Drucker was unable to change by way of analysis and logical persuasion.

Shared assumptions—common cultural values—are thus the powerful force that, like subatomic gluons, bind together the many facets of a culture. Without this gravitational force, tribes, societies, and organizations would disintegrate at the slightest challenge. Though such forces are necessary for efficient and effective cooperation, paradoxically, they are also a prime source of resistance to change. Thus when Drucker's logic called for a new spirit of community within GM, for new practices built around innovation, customer service, and worker empowerment, he inadvertently pressed the cultural hot button, causing the executives to scramble to protect what they felt was the essence of the cultural bond between them.

Second Source of Resistance: Values of Western Society

That might explain a good part of GM's resistance to change, but why would the Sloanian model have such a hold on managers in other corporations as well? One reason is that the GM organizational form had deep roots in long-held values of Western—and Eastern—culture. Although there is no evidence that Sloan (or the other developers of the modern corporation) borrowed consciously from philosophy or history, many time-honored philosophical premises are consistent with his modern concept of the corporation. For example, Sloan's corporation is a modern embodiment of the organizational form first described in Plato's *Republic*.

As we recall from Chapter Three, the Platonic ideal was the "well-ordered state," a government characterized by "the rule of the few." Importantly, this ruling elite, or oligarchy, was not composed of hereditary aristocrats who owed their positions to birth, wealth, force, or the inclination to power. No, that was the stuff of tyranny, and Plato would have none of it. Instead, the "guardians" of his ideal republic ruled by force of their manifest "virtue." The characteristics of this leadership elite were knowledge, wisdom, competence, talent, and ability. In short, Plato proposed a nondemocratic state that was, nonetheless, just and legitimate because it was a meritocracy in which the leaders practiced "the science of government"—which, he wrote, is "among the greatest of all sciences and most difficult to acquire." Because the mastery of this science is so rarely achieved, "any true form of government can only be supposed to be the government of one, two, or, at any rate, . . . a few . . . really found to possess the science."

Plato's elite ruled not for themselves but for the good of society as a whole. The purpose of the republic "is not the disproportionate happiness of any one class, but the greatest happiness of the whole." In the realm of the economy, the rulers seem to be charged with providing a high standard of living—a "state at fever heat"—not for themselves, of course, but for the benefit of the ruled.

Indeed, the guardians of the republic might be seen as analogous to the managers of Sloan's concept of the modern publicly held corporation. These executives hold their positions not by dint of ownership, heredity, force, or election. Instead, in theory at least, they are a meritocratic elite who sit atop their hierarchies thanks to their manifest virtue—their skill, talent, intelligence, experience, and wisdom (as warranted by the possession of the M.B.A. degree!). Sloan tells us that corporate managers should be the ones found to be the most qualified to guide the organization in pursuit of the common good of its constituencies. Moreover, like Plato's guardians, they must sacrifice their personal self-interest to maximize the wealth of the people they serve: the shareholders. (Galbraith calls this paradoxical self-sacrifice by professional profit maximizers the "approved contradiction.")

Inherent in Plato's—and Sloan's—scheme is the notion of hierarchy. Efficiency requires a division of labor; an orderly division requires a hierarchy based on ability; and a hierarchical system will be, by definition, stratified by class. Plato was unapologetic about the antiegalitarian, antidemocratic nature of his republic. He agreed with Aristotle that inequality based on merit was how things *should* be run. Moreover, Plato agreed with Aristotle that the organization takes precedence over the individual ("personalities," or "the human element," in Sloan's words). And from classical Athens to the present day, all hierarchies have been justified in terms of their efficiency and the necessity of putting the organization ahead of the individual to achieve collective progress.

Hence the ultimate measure of a system is not the freedom or equality of individuals but rather an efficient, "well-ordered" state or organization. The most extreme expression of this "corporatist" view was advanced in the seventeenth century by Thomas Hobbes, who argued that humankind is willing to abandon its natural liberty and equality for the security of the state. He believed that individuals form a combination—literally, a corporation—in the guise of the Leviathan, which is superior to the individual, in effect "an artificial man, though of greater stature and strength than the natural, for whose protection and defense it was intended." (We recognize this today in the legal notion that a corporation is an "artificial person.") The function of the Leviathan is to foster the safety necessary for economic progress. Enlightened despotism is preferable to democratic freedom on the grounds of efficiency. For, without hierarchical order, "there is no place for industry, because the fruit thereof is uncertain: and consequently no culture of the earth; no navigation; nor use of the commodities that may be imposted by the sea; no commodious buildings; no instruments of moving and removing such as require more force; no knowledge of the face of the earth; no account of time; no arts; no letters; no society."

Though Sloan would part company with Hobbes on the granting of total power to a Leviathan for the collective good, he accepted the view that a well-ordered organization is the fount of progress, a necessity for the advance of civilization. And such organizations are, by definition, hierarchical and governed at the top by a small number of individuals possessed of a level of wisdom and virtue far superior to that found down the ranks.

Most of the foregoing ideas are consistent with Eastern philosophy as well. As we have noted, rule by a few wise and virtuous men has been the preferred mode since 400 B.C., the era of two influential near contemporaries, Plato in the West and Confucius in the East. Both believed that chaos is the enemy of efficiency and that it can be averted only by the strong leadership of an enlightened elite. Moreover, convention holds that adaptive change is most likely to occur in the type of state first described by Plato and Confucius—an organization with a directive leader at the helm who has both a clear vision of the requisite elements of change, and a willingness to use the power of position to overcome natural resistance to organizational transformation.

In part because it was based on—or at least is consistent with— such traditional cultural assumptions, Sloan's concept came to be adopted by most large U.S. and many foreign corporations, and to constitute the unexamined premises of U.S. business schools in the post–World War II era (and that is perhaps why Singapore's Lee Kwan Yew—both a quintessential Confucian and an admirer of Plato—is so respected by corporate leaders around the world). In essence, then, the Sloanian model is a corporate manifestation of deeply ingrained cultural assumptions about leadership and organization.

Because the internal assumptions of GM were thus reinforced by powerful, traditional social values, we can begin to see why that company proved so hard to change. The tribal forces of cohesion, when coupled with the "wisdom of the ages," make for two potent, complementary sources of resistance. Hence we have the beginnings of an explanation for why GM managers in particular—and the leaders of American industry in general—were able to resist the ideas of Drucker and others like him whose philosophies were based on countercultural assumptions.

A Third Source of Resistance?

In subsequent chapters we shall discover that this dual-cause explanation has more than casual validity. But we know already that it is incomplete. Drucker makes the case that he was himself partly responsible for failing to get his "premature" ideas accepted in American industry. Over the years, I have asked several older, retired GM executives who were working for the company in the 1950s and 1960s why they suppose Drucker's report was ignored by the company. Most can barely remember because "it was never discussed." But to the extent that they had thought about the matter in hindsight, their explanation—or excuse?—was this: Drucker wrote his report and disappeared. Over their careers they had met other analysts and consultants who apparently assumed that their work would be embraced and implemented because of its obvious brilliance. In effect, then, no attempt was made by GM executives to implement the report's recommendations because they saw it as Drucker's report, not theirs. If their interpretation is accurate, Drucker unintentionally created resistance by issuing an outside challenge to the cohesion of the group. He was seen as forcing his ideas on a group that was doing quite well without his interference.

Drucker recalls the events differently. He gave GM's top management the report, and they treated it like a hot potato, no one knowing quite what to do with it or willing to take any responsibility for it. Not only did they not offer comments on its content, but they adopted a "don't call us, we'll call you" stance toward its author. As an outsider—a guest in the corporation—he had no leverage to get them to respond or to act. Apparently hoping that the matter would just go away, they didn't even bother to stop him from publishing the report.

Considering that these two versions are not completely at odds, let us rewrite the history ourselves. What might have happened had Drucker attempted to create some disciples by allowing the GM executives most open to change to embrace the report as their own?

For example, he might have involved them in the writing and presentation of the document. And he could have couched the document in terms of their needs, their aspirations, and their values. Of course, we do not know how much of this Drucker attempted, or if this approach would have been successful. What we do know is that Drucker's report not only had no impact but also made him persona non grata at GM for nearly half a century.

Doubtless the failure to bring about change was the result of shortcomings on the parts of both leaders and followers, shortcomings attributable to Sloan, GM's other executives, and, to some degree at least, Drucker himself. By the standard of leadership that Drucker applies to others, he "failed to create followers." I believe that it is not coincidental that Drucker honed his skills as a change agent over the course of his career and that now, in his eighties, not only is he among the wisest scholars of the subject, but he is also one of its most adept practitioners.

In assessing his own career, Drucker's explanation of his early leadership failure was poor timing. If this explanation is indeed correct, Hegel's deterministic model of change (discussed in Chapter Seven) gains merit. But as we have seen from Drucker's experience at GM, the problem with the timing explanation is that it can become an excuse—would-be leaders can too easily rationalize that the time isn't ripe for change. To test how we feel about this assertion of moral responsibility for change, we might each ask ourselves the following: Do leaders have a responsibility to act even when the world isn't ready for change? And we may then ask a practical question: If they do act, are they merely engaging in a quixotic quest?

Shortly after this book appeared, Peter Drucker generously offered a response to this chapter. He feels that my criticism of Alfred Sloan is unfair in that I score him for dealing only with the objective aspects of management. Drucker points out that in all disciplines—medicine, for example—basic texts stress the objective factors that make for professional behavior. At the time Sloan was writing, managerial practices were characterized by self-indulgence and sloppiness. Sloan was thus right to stress the dangers of subjectivity.

Moreover, "GM probably would have done extremely well" had Sloan lived because one of his great strengths was his willingness to change. In Drucker's view, Sloan "always faced up to harsh reality." Further, Sloan was not just a leader, he was an excellent manager. To Drucker, "good leaders without managerial ability rapidly become misleaders," or autocrats. In contrast to most CEOs of his time, Sloan did not operate a one-person show. He recognized the need to have a team of effective managers at the top of the organization.

Drucker takes exception to my conclusion that he failed to create followers at GM. In fact, he had influence with GM's CEO-designate, Charlie Wilson, who wanted Drucker to join the company as V.P. of Employee Relations. Drucker recalls that he had Sloan's "half-hearted" support, and "substantial support" among younger executives who wanted "radical change in the approach to workers and union." To GM's old-line managers, this made Drucker "a dangerous man who had to be rejected." To Sloan's credit, he protected the young Druckerites from reprisals by the old guard.

Drucker writes that there were other sources of opposition to his ideas: the union, and the leadership of the National Labor Relations Board, who had a common interest in maintaining labor-management hostility and thus were threatened by a community of interest between the worker and the company.

That resistance to the changes Drucker advocated came from all sides provides a link to Robert Owen, whose experiences we next examine. In a 1938 book, Drucker had written off Owen as a failure whose ideas were rejected in his lifetime by both labor and management. Now Drucker sees Owen as a "prophet" whose work has inspired every leader since who has sought to create a sense of community at work. Drucker reminds us that people of action seldom create ideas, and that leadership is nothing without the ideas of prophets.

9

Deming Ignored
Premature Articulation or Flawed Leadership?

A curious and troubling aspect of human behavior is that reasonable men and women often resist acting on *social* knowledge that would advance their collective self-interest. The stress is on the social because the acceptance of scientific or technical knowledge is clearly a different matter. Such twentieth-century inventions as television and xerography, and medical discoveries like penicillin and polio vaccine, were immediately embraced by all but an insignificant number of religious fundamentalists, curmudgeons, and flat-earthers. Even such esoteric scientific concepts as relativity in physics, the double helix in biogenetics, and black holes in astronomy were readily accepted—if not understood—by all but a small minority of educated men and women. Unquestionably, there is always some opposition to new technology and to advances in science, but the level of resistance to social knowledge in the modern world is more widespread, deeper, and, experience suggests, different.

A peculiarly virulent form of resistance can be illustrated with reference to the familiar story of American industry's decades-long rejection of J. Edwards Deming. In the words of MIT's Myron Tribus, "The ultimate curse is to be a passenger on a large ship, to know that the ship is going to sink, to know precisely what to do to prevent it, and to realize that no one will listen! This is the curse that has been visited for a quarter of a century on W. Edwards Deming."

Significantly, the Deming story starts at the same time and emerges from the same impetus as the Drucker story: the experience of American industry during World War II, a conflict that was won as much in America's factories as on the battlefield. Historians, politicians, and military analysts on both the Allied and Axis sides credit the quantity of high quality American matériel produced for the war effort as a decisive factor in the Allied victory.

As Drucker had noted at GM, this feat was the more remarkable because it was rapidly achieved with a labor force inexperienced in factory work. When the young and middle-aged men who had manned the nation's factories prior to the war were drafted for military service, their places were taken by women who had theretofore not been involved in heavy industry, and in many instances these white women were joined by black men and women from the rural South, many of whom were leaving a sharecropping economy for the first time (until near the end of the war, black men were barred from combat roles by the Pentagon's Jim Crow practices). Perhaps most remarkable about this neophyte industrial force is that the workers had been trained very quickly for their complex tasks, had functioned with a relatively small number of supervisors (compared to the staffing levels that had existed in the same factories prior to the war), and had helped develop ideas that contributed greatly to the quality of their production. All of this amounted to a managerial system significantly different from the peacetime system it had replaced.

Yet across American industry, when the regular managers and workers returned to their old jobs, they brought back with them the hierarchical command-and-control system of management, the layers of supervision, and the lack of concern for quality that had prevailed before the war. This phenomenon was not the special province of General Motors. When Rosie the Riveter was sent back to home and hearth, and black workers were unceremoniously evicted to the streets, the new managerial system that had served American industry during the war years was tossed out as well.

Among the major contributors to the design of that discarded system had been a young statistician by the name of W. Edwards Deming. As a consultant to the Department of Defense between 1942 and 1944, Deming had conducted some twenty-three seminars, each eight days in duration, in which he taught techniques of statistical quality control to engineers engaged in war production. Although his techniques were not then nearly as developed as they would become in subsequent decades, they were already unusual for a statistician in that they had a marked managerial component: Deming stressed the human factor of production as much as the technological elements that preoccupied most statisticians and engineers. When asked years later about this wartime experience, Deming would recall that "the courses were well received by engineers, but management paid no attention to them at all."

In fact, American managers would pay no attention whatsoever to Deming for most of the next four decades. In the years following the war, not just American management but labor and academia as well remained deaf to his ideas. But in 1950, Deming found his audience (at which point a writer of fiction would be hard pressed to put a more ironic turn on events than the actual twist provided by history). Working in Japan for the second time in three years as an adviser to the occupying administration of the de facto mikado, General Douglas MacArthur, Deming was invited to conduct a series of seminars under the auspices of the Union of Japanese Scientists and Engineers. At those lectures, some 340 Japanese industrialists were exposed to the pioneering ideas of a man who had had an influential role in producing the planes, trucks, ships, and tanks that had won World War II—a man whose ideas had helped outproduce *them*. Not only did the Japanese manufacturers listen politely to Deming—one would expect that much from the Japanese—but they then acted uncharacteristically quickly to put Deming's system to the test. According to one authoritative account, "Within six weeks, some of the industrialists reported productivity gains as much as 30 percent *without purchasing any new equipment.*

When the industrialists compared notes, they realized that Deming's Way really worked."

Deming not only taught the Japanese statistical quality control techniques that have since become synonymous with his name, but also convinced them of the need for an entirely new philosophy of management, a system that would actively involve workers in finding ways to improve the quality of the goods they produced. Although this system was an outgrowth of the successful industrial relations that had prevailed in America during the war, it would be refined greatly by Deming and his Japanese disciples over the next quarter century (and would eventually give rise to such familiar practices as quality circles and just-in-time inventory). Among the most radical aspects of this system was Deming's belief (shared by Drucker) that the entire process should revolve around serving the needs of customers. In his 1950 lectures in Japan, Deming contrasted two opposed industrial systems: the "old way," in which the customer is an object or an afterthought, and the "new way," in which product quality is defined by the customers themselves as determined through consumer research. Deming sketched a now-famous diagram for the benefit of the Japanese:

OLD WAY

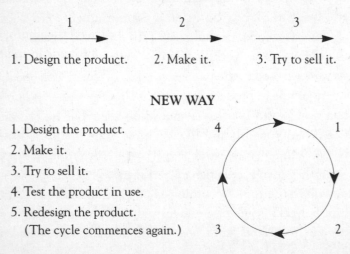

1. Design the product.   2. Make it.   3. Try to sell it.

NEW WAY

1. Design the product.
2. Make it.
3. Try to sell it.
4. Test the product in use.
5. Redesign the product.
    (The cycle commences again.)

As every student of business history—or purchaser of Japanese consumer goods—now understands, Deming and the Japanese would perfect this idea and apply it to the task of overtaking what was then the leading manufacturing power in the world. In the process, Deming came to be so revered in Japan that the nation's highest industrial award was named in his honor. To complete this bizarre circle of events, the recently inaugurated Malcolm Baldrige Award given by the U.S. government for eminence in manufacturing quality is modeled after Japan's Deming Prize.

I call this recent emulation of the Deming Prize bizarre because Deming's way was anathema in this country during the years when American manufacturers were self-indulgently slipping behind the Japanese. Perhaps *anathema* is too strong a word; in most cases, the resistance to Deming's way was passive. I have been unable to unearth a single book, article, speech, or letter by an American manager, scholar, or engineer during the relevant 1945–1985 era in which Deming's methods, theories, or practices were challenged, let alone refuted. *He was simply ignored.* The act of ignoring him, however, was no mean feat. It amounted to collective denial on a massive scale, to an entire continent of intelligent, powerful, and successful people burying their heads in sand. Deming, Drucker, and a host of others tried every trick in the book to make the ostriches look up and around: Deming republished the famous speech he gave in Japan in 1950 in American engineering and marketing journals; the quality guru, J. M. Juran, hammered away at American industry with a message similar to Deming's; in a series of books, articles, and speeches in the 1960s and 1970s, Drucker described for American audiences the successful managerial techniques that the Japanese were using to turn their economy into a world leader; and such management theorists and consultants as Douglas McGregor and Joseph Scanlon pressed managers to place emphasis on the "human side of enterprise"—all to no avail.

This is not to say that Deming (or any of the others mentioned) had discovered the "truth." All that I claim for Deming's way is that it was more effective than the traditional managerial practices it sought to replace. It was more effective not by any objective standard—such a standard, at any rate, does not exist—but by the standards of the people who resisted it. Ultimately, any claim for the superiority of Deming's way must rest on the fact of its ultimate acceptance—in rough outline, at least—by most American managers. That is the only standard that is not itself a matter of irreconcilable controversy.

Nor is any claim made here that Deming's way is the truth, the only truth, or true in its entirety. For example, even some of Deming's admirers question his controversial belief that financial incentives are inappropriate as rewards for worker efforts to improve quality. His belief was based on experience in Japan where workers' pay has traditionally been based on seniority rather than performance. This practice may or may not be effective today in Japan, but it flies in the face of social knowledge about the motivational power of cold cash in the West. Hence the claim is not that Deming's way is wholly right, but that managers were extremely shortsighted in rejecting it.

We must keep in mind that our subject is not the ideas of Deming and Drucker but rather the resistance to the changes they advocated. In this context, it was simply not in the self-interest of American managers to reject 100 percent of Deming's system because it may have been 10 or 15 or even 25 percent wrong. Had managers borrowed from Deming, had they experimented with key aspects of his system, had they attempted to tailor what he taught to the needs of their own organizations, had they pragmatically taken what worked for them and rejected the chaff—in short, had they acted the way they themselves would have defined as rationally pursuing their own self-interest—we could rightly conclude that Deming's ideas had had a fair test, and we would have no phenomenon of resistance to explore. But the fact is that nearly all American managers rejected Deming's way in its entirety. Moreover, many now admit that a terrible price was paid for their many years of negligence.

About a decade ago, when Deming was still a young man in his eighties, he was asked why American managers had rejected his ideas. He recalled that managers would tell him that "things weren't bad enough to justify change." The memory of that rationalization drove Deming to the point of anger: "The supposition that everything has to be wrong must be banished!" He might also have added that the supposition that everything must be right with a proposed solution is equally self-defeating.

In a nutshell, here is the tale of Deming's way: managerial methods initially developed to help the American war effort were subsequently refined and employed by the Japanese to win world markets (who says Japan is closed to American imports?). The final irony is that, in the early 1980s, the besieged leaders of American industry finally turned to Deming in desperation to learn the secrets of "Japanese management." Thus two generations after his statistical techniques and human-centered managerial philosophy had been proved to work, the octogenarian Deming was "discovered" by American managers. (To be recognized as a prophet in your own time, it pays to have sturdy genes that permit you to live until your time comes.)

Over the years, I have made it a habit to ask older managers why their companies didn't adopt Deming's way in the 1970s when it had become clear that American competitiveness was on the wane. Most answer that they don't know or can't remember. When pushed, they say that they hadn't heard of Deming until quite recently, and hadn't known about his alternative philosophy of management when they needed it most. Perhaps, but they had certainly been aware of the ideas of Drucker, Juran, Scanlon, McGregor, and the scores of scholars, consultants, and others who advocated methods similar to Deming's. Were these answers merely rationalizations? I do not know because it is difficult to distinguish rationalization from reality. The motives of individuals are seldom understood by anyone, including themselves. Individuals cannot say if the source of their resistance is rationalization or not (if you knew that you were consciously rationalizing, you would not be rationalizing—you would be lying).

Today, of course, the excuse of ignorance is not available. Managers might just as well admit to living under a rock as claim unfamiliarity with Deming's way. Thus prematurity, or lack of "ripeness," is no longer a valid explanation—if it ever was—for failure to change. When Deming was old—and his reputation finally secured—I would often ask younger managers why the ideas of Deming (like those of Drucker, Scanlon, McGregor, and Warren Bennis) were still so seldom put into practice. Few said that Deming's ideas were wrong. Instead, they often attributed the continuing rejection of Deming's way to the undeniable fact that Deming could be "prickly" at times. When I asked why their companies still did not practice Deming's way, a common explanation was that "Deming is hard to work with." He was described variously as "gruff," "inflexible," and "too demanding." But could this have been the real reason why Deming's way failed to establish a toehold in America for nearly half a century?

I do not pretend to know the motives of the managers I interviewed, but I must now admit that I suspect that the real causes of the historical and continuing rejection of Deming's way had little to do with his personal failings. I base this supposition on three facts. First, only a tiny percentage of American managers had ever met Deming or heard him speak, so how could millions of managers over the years have rejected Deming's ideas based on his personal shortcomings? Second, Deming's way did not depend on Deming, and this would be the case even if Deming himself had thought otherwise. One need not like Jonas Salk personally to benefit from his polio vaccine. Furthermore, managers were free to borrow selectively from Deming's ideas without Deming's permission and to hire a different consultant if so desired. Third, there exists the 1960 testimony of the director of the Japanese Union of Scientists and Engineers, which I quote at length not only because it sheds light on the reasons why Deming's ideas were accepted in Japan and rejected in America, but also for the charming way it captures a moment in Japanese-American relations that seems so distant today:

Special mention must be made of the fact that the Deming Prize was instituted with gratitude to Dr. Deming's friendship as well as in commemoration of his contributions to Japanese industry. When Dr. Deming gave his 8-day course in 1950, Japan was in the fifth year of Allied occupation. Administrative and all other affairs were under rigid control of the Allied forces. Most of the Japanese were in a servile spirit as the vanquished, and among Allied personnel there were not a few with an air of importance. In striking contrast, Dr. Deming showed his warm cordiality to every Japanese whom he met and exchanged frank opinions with everybody. His high personality deeply impressed all those who learned from him and became acquainted with him. He loved Japan and the Japanese from his own heart. The sincerity and enthusiasm with which he did his best for his courses still lives and will live forever in the memory of all the concerned. . . . Featuring all these educational activities was his deep love and high humaneness. Herein lies why we loved and respected, and still love and respect, him.

Unfortunately, I have not gone much further with my exploration of the resistance to Deming's way. I have found an insurmountable defensiveness among managers who had long resisted his ideas that prevents me from obtaining more useful information. If nothing else, this lends credibility to the hypothesis that resistance to change stems from the desire to protect our collective egos. Deming himself identified this problem when he speculated on why the Japanese had been more receptive to his ideas than the Americans were: "The Japanese businessman is never too old or successful to learn. . . . The American businessman feels that if he asks for help, he will be considered unqualified for the job."

Doubtless it is threatening to one's self-esteem to be asked to defend a decision made in the past that one now realizes was a costly error. So I was willing to let the matter drop there. But when

Deming died in early 1994 (at age ninety-three), I decided to revisit the issue one last time with a few managers who had actually dealt with the man. Several common themes ran through their replies to my questions. First, they all respected Deming's genius. Second, they all volunteered that he had been right all along and that America had paid a high price for resisting the changes he advocated. Third, none of their companies used his methods today. Why? One manager explained, "Deming insisted on doing things his way. If managers made a slight change in Deming's way to tailor it to their needs, he dismissed everything they did as unworthy. It was always his ideas, and never ours." Said another: "It wasn't simply that he was insulting and impolitic; I think we were big enough to discount that. The problem was that he had 'the truth.' He didn't listen to us, to our needs, to our concerns. He was a nonstop lecturer, a little like Peter Drucker in that regard. Worse, it felt like he was always trying to shove his ideas down your throat. After a while of being ignored, you just turned him off."

Listening to these managers, I finally started to see a pattern. Was it that Drucker, Deming, the famous author described in the Chapter Seven—indeed, all of us who had been "right" for so long—had failed to get our message across to managers because it was *our* agenda and not *theirs*? Then it hit me: when Deming first dealt with the Japanese, he listened to them, showed them respect, and couched his ideas in terms of their needs. But later, when he came to deal with Americans, he was imperious and arrogantly demanded that they swallow his philosophy whole (doubtless because he was bitter at having been ignored for so long in his own country). Because I had so admired Deming, it took his death to open my eyes. Then I finally started to hear what managers had no doubt been telling me for twenty years. Talk about powers of resistance!

A variety of factors cause us to be myopic: defensiveness, ego, self-delusion, and everything else on that list of thirty-three reasons why we resist change. Indeed, the reason why it is so hard to answer the questions raised in this book is rooted in the very same phenomena that cause us to resist change: people avoid looking too closely at themselves. Worse, when they are in mutually reinforcing groups, inbred values and shared assumptions magnify this resistance exponentially.

Here's reality: if it was hard for me to understand the Deming phenomenon because I had met and admired the man, imagine how hard it was for the people who rejected Deming to analyze objectively why they did so. Thus it behooves the prudent change agent to choose as a heuristic example something as far away and as long ago as possible. Attempting to gain that needed perspective, we will move backward to a time before anyone alive today was born.

Our subjects in Chapter Ten will be the scores of men and women who rejected the ideas of Robert Owen, the early-nineteenth-century entrepreneur. We revisit the resistance to change through the example of Owen not simply because he lived long ago but also because society's rejection of his ideas concerned an issue—the abolition of child labor—that is sufficiently noncontroversial today. Hence we can examine the motives of the people who rejected Owenism without unconscious defensiveness stemming from contemporary beliefs or, as in the case with the managers who resisted Deming's way, without the need to defend past errors.

Like Deming, Owen was a man ahead of his time whose ideas were ultimately vindicated by the court of public opinion (however, the social knowledge that Owen advanced would not be accepted until well over a century after his death). The rejection of Owen, like that of Deming, has often been explained with reference to the man's flaws of character. And as with Deming, we find that the critics of Owen's character say as much about themselves as they say about Owen.

Yet we also learn from our study of Owen that there are indeed two sides implicated in failures to bring about necessary change. In addition to the ever-present sources of social resistance, there is also the issue of the change agent's skill in overcoming those forces. The absence of this skill is no more a character flaw than the lack of skill at hitting a golf ball or the inability to sing on key. But the possession of the skill of overcoming resistance to change is what separates the mass of individuals with good ideas from the few leaders who are able to implement them.

10

· ·

Owen Unrecognized
The Early Promise of the New Management

Peter Drucker, W. Edwards Deming, and other twentieth-century thinkers who have a claim to paternity of the New Management were in fact all Johnnies-come-lately. Robert Owen (1771–1858) was ahead of them all by a century and a half in the corporate arena—he was the Thomas Edison of social invention. He was the first to devise or advocate numerous practices in industrial relations, education, and social policy that are still considered progressive today, more than 130 years after his death. Owen's most successful social laboratory was the Scottish mill town of New Lanark, where he owned and managed a large and profitable textile factory between 1800 and 1824. Creating a model business there, he was the first employer to introduce relatively short working hours, a grievance procedure, guaranteed employment during times of economic downturn, and contributory health, disability, and retirement plans.

Owen was the first capitalist to practice what is now disparagingly called paternalism, then a marked improvement over the Dickensian norms of the Industrial Revolution. A century before such paternalistic American managers as Henry Ford and George Eastman introduced enlightened industrial practices, Owen provided clean, decent housing for his workers and their families in a community free of controllable disease, crime, and gin shops. Most singularly, he took young children out of his factory and put them in a school he founded. There he invented preschool, day care, and the brand of progressive education that stresses learning as a pleasurable experience (along with the first adult night school).

Not content with what he had accomplished in his own enterprise, Owen tried to gain passage of national factory reform legislation and, in his declining years, agitated for the eight-hour workday. He sought legislation to create public service jobs during the too-frequent depressions of that era of laissez-faire, and he lobbied for free public education for all British children and the creation of state-supported teachers' colleges. He failed miserably in all these efforts to amend public policy.

Owen established both the consumer and producer cooperative movements, and in his old age, turning to organized labor after a half century of failure to convert his fellow capitalists, he reluctantly chaired the first national trade union movement in Great Britain. Owen's contributions before age forty-seven are among the most remarkable in history; nearly all his many ideas ultimately became accepted practices in Europe and America. Yet Owen's career stands as a classic example of resistance to change. Although some twenty thousand visitors witnessed Owen's successful experiments at New Lanark, not a single capitalist of his day followed his lead, only one school copied his educational system during his lifetime, and no government adopted his proposed social legislation. Tragically, business and political leaders' failure to embrace his benign prescriptions allowed social conditions to fester, causing untold human suffering and fostering the growth of a far more dangerous medicine, Marxism.

Owen Resisted

Owen then is the quintessential historical embodiment of the phenomenon we are discussing. In hindsight, he was clearly right, and the reforms he proposed were in the self-interest of the people who opposed them. We can thus ask again—this time with the benefit of the distancing effect of history—why the changes he proposed were resisted, and if there were something he might have done differently as a leader that might have caused his ideas to have gained acceptance.

Born to a lower-middle-class family in Wales in 1771, by his late twenties Owen had gained, through hard work and entrepreneurial vision, the kind of reputation that computer prodigy Bill Gates enjoys in America today. He exploited the latest technology of his time—Arkwright's spinning mill—and amassed great wealth before he was thirty. Having begun as a typical Industrial Revolution businessman seeking his fortune, he was soon confronted with the maimed bodies, demoralized spirits, and shortened lives of factory workers. Yet unlike many other entrepreneurs then seeking to exploit the new technologies of the era, Owen apparently never felt that he had to choose between his own welfare and that of others. We do not know what prompted Owen, alone among industrialists of the era, to ask himself, in effect, "How can I make manufacturing pay without dooming my employees to misery and moral degradation?" Before reaching midlife he had disproved his friend David Ricardo's gloomy economic theories by demonstrating that a company could make enormous profits *and* treat its employees well. Indeed, he would argue that it was by the very act of *breaking* Ricardo's "iron law of wages" that he had made his workers more productive.

In 1799, when Owen and a group of partners purchased the New Lanark mill, this vision had not yet begun to form in his mind. The former owner of the mill, his father-in-law, Robert Dale, was widely respected as a progressive employer, even though his workforce of two to three thousand souls labored, often standing the entire time, from thirteen to fifteen hours a day in extremely unhealthy conditions. Worse, there were children in the factory, some as young as five or six, who had been indentured by contract with local workhouses. Soon after his arrival, Owen concluded that the entire system was "wretchedly bad." Much later, he wrote in his autobiography, "I determined therefore that the engagements made by Mr. Dale with the parishes should run out; that no more pauper children should be received; that the village houses and streets should be improved; and new and better houses erected to receive new families to replace the pauper children; and that the interior of the mills should be rearranged, and the old machinery replaced by new."

Owen was a practical businessman, not a social worker; he proceeded with due economic deliberation. "These changes were to be made gradually and to be effected by the profits of the establishment," he wrote. "I found it necessary, as the foundation of all future success, to make the establishment not only self-supporting, but also productive of sufficient surplus profit to enable me to effect the changes of the improved conditions which I contemplated. My partners were all commercial men, and expected a profit in addition to interest for their capital. I had therefore to readjust the whole business arrangements, and to make great alterations in the building and gradually to change the whole machinery in the mills."

Understandably, the workers saw these alterations as nothing more than an old-fashioned speedup and "were systematically opposed to every change which I proposed, and did whatever they could to frustrate my object." At this point Owen proved his genius as a leader of change: "I therefore sought out the individuals who had the most influence among them from their natural powers or position, and to these I took pains to explain what were my intentions for the changes I wished to effect."

A hundred years ahead of the pack, Owen perceived instinctively that effective leadership is a matter of communicating a vision, not barking orders: "By these means I began slowly to make an impression upon the least prejudiced and most reasonable among them; but the suspicions of the majority, that I only wanted, as they said, to squeeze as much gain out of them as possible, were long continued."

As is increasingly recognized today, building trust is a long-term process, and it ultimately rests on what the leader does, not what he or she says. After seven years of patient effort, Owen was able to win the full trust of his employees by responding with admirable creativity to an event beyond his control. When the United States imposed a trade embargo on all British goods, leading to the clos-

ing of mills throughout the country and consequent mass unemployment, Owen did not close his mill: "I therefore concluded to
stop all the machinery, retain the people, and continue to pay them
their full wages for only keeping the machinery clean and in good
working condition . . . and during that period the population of
New Lanark received more than seven thousand pounds sterling for
their unemployed time, without a penny being deducted from the
full wages of anyone."

According to a contemporary observer at New Lanark, "It has
been the great object of Robert Owen to extinguish the government
by fear"; by all accounts, he achieved his aim. Ironically, just as
Owen had succeeded in winning his workers' trust and productivity at New Lanark had started to soar, his co-owners began to question his practices, expressing "disapproval of the mixture of
philanthropy and business." Their complaint was not that the mill
was unprofitable—by all accounts it was a fantastic moneymaker—
but that it could be made more profitable still if Owen would quit
mollycoddling the workforce. In the end, unable to convince his
partners that the profits resulted from the workers' unusual productivity, he decided to buy them out.

In 1815, in firm control of his own enterprise and in firm possession of a clear theory of enlightened capitalism, Owen acted
swiftly to put his beliefs into practice at New Lanark. He reduced
the workday from thirteen to ten and three-quarters hours (the lowest in the industrialized world at the time), ended the practice of
summary dismissal (except for persistent drunkenness), and established the right of appeal (to himself, if necessary) for workers who
were dissatisfied with their supervisors' ratings of their performance.
Along the way he established a contributory sickness and retirement plan, a precursor to a modern credit union, and a company-
controlled food store that offered products at a 25 percent discount
over prices charged by local competitors (while still producing profits that were used to support the company school). He even provided parks and a second story for each worker's house.

Some of this was out-and-out paternalism, intolerable to both modern trade unionists and libertarians. We must remember, though, that what he did was unprecedented. The conditions that workers faced in his competitors' factories were grotesque. The entire business world was shocked when he prohibited corporal punishment in his factory and dumbfounded when he retrained his supervisors in humane disciplinary practices. He reluctantly discharged supervisors who would not give up brutal and authoritarian ways and, somewhat paradoxically, commanded that all discipline at New Lanark was to be accomplished through moral suasion, education, and peer pressure. Recalcitrant workers were not to be dismissed even if they publicly disagreed with his liberal system. While giving his workers an extremely high standard of living compared to other workers of the era, Owen was making a fortune at New Lanark. This conundrum drew twenty thousand visitors to Lanarkshire between 1815 and 1825. Among those who signed the mill's guest book were leading industrialists from America and the Continent, two princes of Austria, and Nicholas of Russia, soon to be czar.

Owen then turned to government to legislate the reforms he thought necessary to avert class warfare, making his first foray into the public arena in response to the massive unemployment that followed the Peace of 1815. He advocated, in modern terms, public works employment at less than private sector wages, the program to remain in effect only as long as depression conditions existed. The proposal was derided. One critic wrote that it "turns the whole country into a workhouse," and Parliament summarily dismissed it on the grounds that it failed to address the two underlying causes of depression—high taxes and Malthusian overpopulation. Owen would soon address the issue of taxation. First, he argued that there was sufficient food, but the poor lacked the wherewithal to buy it. This argument fell on deaf ears. In the memorable words of one of his finest biographers, G.D.H. Cole, the decision was made "to depress the poor out of existence."

Game to try again, Owen was soon before a parliamentary committee as Sir Robert Peel's star witness in behalf of the First Factory Reform Act. (Peel, son of a wealthy cotton manufacturer, founder of the Conservative Party, and later prime minister, was an early admirer of Owen's.) This bill would have banned the employment of children under ten, provided thirty minutes of education per day for children under eighteen, abolished night shifts for all children, shortened their workday to ten and a half hours, and been enforced by government inspectors in factories. The quid pro quo would have been a repeal of the import tax on cotton. Owen, a strong believer in free trade, argued as vigorously for the repeal as he did for the reform, but he would not accept the one without the other. His early allies in this venture were the aristocracy, led by Owen's close friend, the duke of Kent (King George III's brother and father of Queen Victoria). The peers of the realm were disposed favorably to the idea of reform; if nothing else, as landowners they rather relished the idea of taking the uppity manufacturers down a peg or two.

From the introduction of the bill in 1815 to its passage in unrecognizably whittled-down form in 1819, things went from promising to disappointing for the British working class and for Robert Owen. His problems started when a member of Parliament questioned him about testimony he had given in support of the bill. Pressed on an irrelevant fact about an investigatory tour of British mills that he had just completed, "Owen," writes his first biographer, Frank Podmore, "relying as he apparently did on his memory . . . , attached the incident to the wrong place and person—a thing which might easily happen in the course of a tour of some weeks. But the episode no doubt had a damaging effect."

Resistance Sets In

As parliamentary debate on the bill proceeded, its opponents argued that it would be both bad for business and bad for workers. They argued that no prima facie case had been established for the need of legislation; that the majority of manufacturers were, of their own free will, doing most of what the bill would require; that the appointment of inspectors—an unconscionable violation of privacy—would expose business secrets; that paying higher wages to attract adult workers would threaten British preeminence in world markets; that reduced working hours would necessitate reduced pay, thus increasing poverty; that the government would intervene in family matters, subverting parents' authority; that the number of families on the dole would increase; and that large families would be unable to support themselves by "virtue of their joint industry," reducing their "independence and comforts." In sum, it was in the interest of the poor that the bill not pass: "All experience proves that in the lower orders the deterioration of morals increases with the quantity of unemployed time of which they have the command."

Owen considered these arguments mere rationalizations, both disingenuous and immoral. Most immoral, he thought, were the medical doctors who testified that there was "no scientific evidence" that it was injurious for children to work night shifts, to stand for twelve hours a day at their tasks, to eat their meals while standing and working, to go out thinly clad into the cold night after working twelve hours in a hot factory, or constantly to breathe air heavy with cotton fluff. This was one of the first of what would become common instances when the "lack of scientific evidence" was used to block a change whose proponents based their arguments on morality, fairness, and common sense.

When the bill finally passed, it was reform in name only. This defeat, coupled with his new business partners' decision to introduce orthodox religious training at the New Lanark school, led Owen to give up on his homeland. He then turned his boundless energies to the task of creating a just society in the still-verdant pastures of the New World.

The Robert Owen who embarked for America in 1823 was the father of social democracy. Had he died then (at about age forty-seven), he would have gone down in history as a uniquely farsighted entrepreneur, a genius before his time. Up to that point, everything he had said and done was in the belief that people of all classes could work together to solve their problems in a flawed but workable capitalist system. Unlike the Luddites of the day, he was not against technology, and unlike the radicals (soon to become Marxists), he was not against profit or private property. And unlike the Tories, who opposed universal suffrage, he had faith in the ability of all people—men and women of all classes and races—to participate in government. It is not terribly surprising, then, that he was attacked from left to right across the political spectrum. What is more puzzling is that he found no true support in any corner. And what is inexplicable is that no faction was willing to draw even the simplest lessons from his successful workplace and educational experiments at New Lanark. In essence, society wanted nothing of Owen or Owenism.

One can guess what an uplift for Owen's spirit it must have been to be received in America by President Andrew Jackson and former presidents John Quincy Adams, James Madison, and, especially, Thomas Jefferson, in whom he found a fellow child of the Enlightenment. The two men shared a fundamental faith in the efficacy of education, and most happily for Owen, Jefferson, too, was a deist. We do not know what transpired at Monticello, but we can picture Owen talking the ear off of the Sage, then in his early eighties, sound of mind but infirm of body. After engaging Jefferson's interest in his schemes, Owen moved to Indiana, where he spent most of his accumulated fortune founding the ill-fated cooperative community of New Harmony. He lived to see that and many subsequent utopian dreams dissolve amid bad planning and internal dissension. He ultimately returned to England, where he died in 1858 at age eighty-seven, having spent his dotage in spiritualist communication with Jefferson's shade!

Meanwhile, Owen had accomplished many other innovations: the creation of garden cities, greenbelts, and other ideas that influenced modern community planning; the formation of old-age homes owned by pensioners; the creation of cooperatives for producers, consumers, and farmers that have their descendants in such varied modern institutions as Mondragon in Spain and employee stock option plans in America. At sixty-three, he launched and briefly chaired the Grand National Consolidated Trades Union, now recognized as the forerunner of the modern British national trade union movement. There, "he seems to have found a more congenial environment amongst the working classes. For the rest of his life his appeal was mainly to them; and if the response which it evoked was not always the precise kind at which he aimed, the effects at any rate were more enduring."

Rejection by His Fellow Capitalists

Whether the effects among the working class were enduring is open to question, but there is no doubt that for nearly the next century, Owen's ideas had no great influence among British intellectuals, industrialists, or any middle-class group with political power. Yet history has judged Owen's ideas better than the accepted practices of his day. Today, leading capitalists, educators, and politicians safely assert Owenisms without apology—generally without knowing the source. Many of the ideas and schemes he advanced after 1825 did not deserve to survive; one needn't be antiromantic to conclude that his utopian communities were disasters, historical curiosities at best. Of concern to us, though, are the reasons why his successes and rational ideas were rejected, in particular the enlightened capitalism he practiced at New Lanark and his call for the abolition of child labor. We must focus on the fact that though he had succeeded brilliantly at leading internal change at his mill, he failed totally when it came to leading change among his fellow entrepreneurs.

It is understandable that the capitalists of the early 1800s were initially skeptical about the reports emanating from New Lanark: an individual who insists on "sleeping on" a new notion displays admirable prudence, and new ideas must be tried in the court of public opinion. Moreover, Owenism was a flawed philosophy that did not deserve to be embraced in the unadulterated manner that Owen prescribed. Owenism was nonetheless better than the prevailing industrial system. Even if one is inclined to argue that the industrialists of the day did not understand that it is harmful to place children five to eleven years of age in factories, it was common knowledge that child labor generated virulent class conflict and anticapitalist sentiment. Thus the question is not the validity of the particulars of Owenism but rather why proposals for even elementary reform were resisted for the better part of a century. Why did moral, decent, and rational people tolerate for so long conditions that were, by their own stated Christian standards, immoral, indecent, and irrational? Had they wished, nineteenth-century capitalists could have experimented here and there with a few of Owen's laborsaving ideas—ideas that would have lengthened, if not saved, the lives of millions of laborers—and could have acted alone or as a group to improve selectively some of the worst industrial conditions. In fact, for generations most capitalists rejected reform in toto.

Owen's arguments to his entrepreneurial peers were invariably cast in practical terms. He appealed not to the goodness of their hearts but to the content of their purses and argued for their enlightened pursuit of self-interest. He was careful to pay obeisance to Adam Smith's invisible hand, their reigning deity: "The natural course of trade, manufactures, and commerce should not be disturbed," he told them in 1816, "except when it interferes with measures affecting the well-being of the whole community." He advocated measures to alleviate workers' misery in terms of the long-run interest of the entrepreneurial class. "No evil ought to be more dreaded by a master manufacturer than low wages of labour. . . . These [workers] in consequence of their numbers, are the greatest consumers of all articles, and it will always be found that when wages are high the country prospers; when they are low, all classes suffer from the highest to the lowest, but more particularly the manufacturing interest. . . . The real prosperity of any nation may be at all times ascertained by the amount of wages, or the extent of the comforts which the productive classes can obtain in return for their labour." This insight was prescient: Marx drew on it when he predicted that capitalism would self-destruct because of manufacturers' shortsighted refusal to pay their workers enough to buy their products, and Henry Ford used it in 1914 in his famous demand-side justification for paying his auto workers the unheard-of sum of five dollars a day. In the Great Depression, Keynes convinced Franklin Roosevelt to revive the economy by stimulating demand (yet one suspects that the idealistic Owen would have preferred his fellow capitalists to have had the sense to follow Ford's private efforts).

Even more remarkable, Owen anticipated the University of Chicago's concept of "human capital," calling for scientific calculations of returns on investment in education and of the overall savings to society of a workforce that was productively employed, as opposed to being on the dole or engaged in crime.

> Will you then continue to expend large sums of money to procure the best devised mechanism of wood, brass, or iron; to retain it in perfect repair; to provide the best substance for the prevention of unnecessary friction, and to save it from falling into premature decay? Will you also devote years of intense application to understand the connection of the various parts of these lifeless machines, to improve their effective powers, and to calculate with mathematical precision all their minute and combined movements? And when in these transactions you estimate time by minutes, and the money expended for the chance of increased gain by fractions, will you not afford some of your attention to consider whether a portion of your time and capital would not be more advantageously applied to improving your living machines?

But his fellow industrialists did not appreciate the concept of human capital, and nothing Owen said engaged them.

By 1830, Owen's fears of revolution were being realized on the Continent; having failed to convince capitalists to avoid class warfare, he turned his efforts to changing the objectives of the increasingly restive and radicalized British working class. He appealed to them to ignore the advocates of a proletarian revolution, offering a remarkably foresighted prediction of its outcome:

> But, suppose [that] you triumphed over every obstacle, and that you had wrested political power from your opponents, who now possess it. The victory must have been achieved by political force, and some individuals must thereby attain the political power now possessed by the aristocracy of this country. Who the parties acquiring this power, after such a revolution, might be, no man can know, probably some more fortunate military chiefs. . . . You will have succeeded in giving political power to a new set of men, who have been trained from their birth in as much error as those you would have displaced. . . . It is true, the error may be different in character, but it is doubtful which class of errors, when in power, will produce the most misery to the mass of the people.

Only Tocqueville among Owen's contemporaries so clearly anticipated the totalitarianism that would follow the violent revolutions of the nineteenth and twentieth centuries. Owen felt that a proletarian revolution was not only morally wrong but also politically unnecessary—much as he felt that the worst practices of the industrial revolution were not only morally wrong but also economically unnecessary. He believed that society's choices were never either-or: no zero-sum game existed between labor and capital. Instead, the issue was to use one's moral imagination to create a system that was good for all. In spite of such manifestly moderate ideas, Owen was often portrayed as a wild-eyed radical and an enemy of freedom, lumped in with the dogmatic socialists who set the stage for modern-day totalitarianism. Such judgments are not supported by Owen's writings. In 1848, he urged the French masses, then preparing to take to the barricades, to adopt a democratic government: "beneficial employment, universal education, freedom of speech and thought, graduated property tax, 'rational association, local self-government,' 'non-interference by any power except as a mediator to stay hostilities,' and an armed force for self-defence; for practical purposes 'the American Government in principle with some essential modifications in their practice.'"

Admittedly, Owen was never a great believer in the power of the ballot. Frustrated throughout his life by the way Britain's limited suffrage thwarted reform, he misread this experience. Putting his faith instead in the process of education and the conversion of the powerful, he did not foresee the reformist tendencies that modern democracies would assume with full suffrage. Even late in his life, though, when he was said to have grown muddled and dogmatic in his thinking, Owen remained an opponent of tyranny and a champion of a free society. "Truth must ultimately prevail over error" was his guiding principle, and he never lost his faith in the persuasive power of good ideas to change the thinking and behavior of individuals and society.

Owen wrote of his successful system at New Lanark, "What then remains to prevent such a system from being immediately adopted into national practice? Nothing, surely, but a general distribution of the knowledge of the practice." When he wrote those words in his forties, everything seemed to be going right in his life, but his optimism was soon to be proved dead wrong. Instead of the general diffusion of the social knowledge he created, everywhere he turned he was met with a barrage of criticism and, ultimately, total rejection. By the end of his life, it was clear that he had been a prophet well before his time.

In the following chapter we explore several alternative explanations of why Owen's ideas were rejected during his lifetime—explanations that offer clues to the general puzzle before us: Why do people resist change that is in their best interest?

Owen Rejected

Valid Reasons or Rationalizations?

Why were the changes that Owen advocated rejected by his contemporaries? The facile answer is for all the thirty-three reasons listed in Chapter Seven (and more)! Because that answer is insufficiently precise to allow us to explore what Owen might have done differently to gain possible acceptance of his ideas, we must attempt to focus on the major sources of resistance. Luckily for us, seemingly everyone who ever met Owen or heard about New Lanark was quick to record why he or she thought Owenism was a peculiarly unattractive philosophy.

Critics on the Right

Owen's critics on the right were, and still are, his harshest. Their first charge has been that he was not enough of a profit maximizer to warrant emulation. One critic of his day wrote that Owen "hardly cared a rap whether he made money or not." In fact, evidence points to the conclusion shared by several biographers that "Owen was an extraordinary good organiser and businessman; and he made of his mills a model of business efficiency." Owen went through three sets of partners at New Lanark. The first partnership, from 1800 to 1809, was fabulously profitable even by the high standards of that boom era. After the purchase of the mill from Dale for the sum of £60,000 and payment of 5 percent interest to the partners on their capital contributions, the profit on the mill amounted to about £60,000 over the ten-year period. The second partnership, which lasted until 1813 and benefited more fully from Owen's unique managerial system, was even more profitable. After an initial investment of £84,000 in the mill, and again allowing for 5 percent interest payments, this partnership realized a profit of some £160,000 in four years, including capital gains.

The third partnership was not a great moneymaker, but it was never intended to be. Having made himself rich, Owen had turned his interests in other directions, and his third group of partners were more interested in saving souls than accumulating capital. This collection of noted Quakers, Nonconformists, and pillars of the Church of England invested with the understanding that, after Owen's habitual 5 percent interest payments, all profits would be reinvested in worker welfare and education. Perhaps Owen should have foreseen that such a partnership would fall apart over his refusal to permit religious education—but it was not a business failure. In fact, the most famous of the partners, the Libertarian hero Jeremy Bentham, called it his "only successful investment."

Owen was a successful capitalist, then, but he was not a classic profit maximizer. Although the mills were always profitable, his early investors—and other business sorts watching from the sidelines—thought that he invested too much in peripheral activities, which they believed reduced profit. As G.D.H. Cole reminds us, these "were men who wanted not merely a moderate return on their money, but the largest return that could be extracted in those halcyon days of low wages, high profits, and rapid accumulation of capital."

Owen's critics were especially indignant to learn that his enlightened practices extended not just to employees but to other constituencies as well: "It was Owen's habitual practice that when he foresaw a fall in the price of yarn to ask his customers whether they would not wish any orders which might be in hand to be deferred so that they might take advantage of the lower prices; and in the same way, he would write to his correspondents before a rise, and urge them to buy."

Increasing numbers of business leaders today advocate a similarly enlightened capitalism, arguing that firms must build long-term relationships with all their constituencies—employees, suppliers, customers, and local communities, in addition to shareowners— because the way to serve owners' interests effectively in the long run is to create conditions of mutual benefit in the marketplace. But today's critics, like Owen's, object to this sacrifice of immediate profit to build long-term loyalties and dismiss these practices as philanthropic and not businesslike. Milton Friedman has argued that such practices are tantamount to stealing from investors.

Owen got much the same treatment from Friedman's ideological forebears. At best, he was considered naive not to extract every farthing of short-term gain. At worst, he was accused of breaking the laws of economics newly minted by Smith and Ricardo, laws thought to be as immutable as Newton's new physical laws. These economic laws had been particularly well received, of course; because they justified the capitalists' single-minded pursuit of profit, but their major effect was more to snow-blind manufacturers than to turn them into ideologues in the modern Friedmanite sense. Most were simply unable to connect Owen's treatment of his workers and customers with the financial success of the New Lanark mills. Instead, his fellow capitalists saw the success as the by-product of a kind of industrial witchcraft, searching for Owen's black magic in such enigmas as the unique air of New Lanark, the unusual work ethic of the Scots, the irreplicable configuration of the plant site— in everything and anything but Owen's managerial practices. Amazed as they were that he got away with breaking the laws of economics, and curious as they were about how he accomplished the trick, they had no interest in imitating it.

Did Owen operate on an intellectual plane different from that of his peers? While he sought to create a system even the least privileged members would see as legitimate, his fellow capitalists could not imagine any issue of moral welfare that was their particular concern. Perhaps some, in the manner of Adam Smith, philosophized that all society would benefit in the long term from unalloyed laissez-faire, but Cole suggests otherwise: "Each entrepreneur was too busy with the abundant tasks and opportunities that lay ready to his hand to be disposed to give much thought to the wider problems of the new order."

Almost all of Owen's critics, from his day to ours, have also faulted him for wanting to move too far too fast. A modern observer writes: "Owen's obsessive and imaginative conscience would not allow him to accept social reforms in stages, and this unwillingness colours many of his writings and certainly affected his actions. He impressed a diverse group of individuals with his sincerity, but for most, his refusal to accept modest and slow changes in existing practices proved an embarrassment if not an overpowering disadvantage."

One must ask, though, how Owen's insistent, uncompromising desire to take five-year-olds out of factories could be called obsessive impatience. He rightly suspected that in the mouths of gradualists, *go slow* meant "no" and *not yet* meant "never."

Owen's opponents found reason to despise him for a further transgression: after his well-publicized investigatory tour of British factories, he broke the eleventh commandment and made his peers look bad by publishing his findings: "For a master manufacturer, however pure his motives, to play the spy on the conditions of working in other factories was an invidious business."

Critics on the Left

Paradoxically, the left also found Owen untrustworthy, accusing him of being not only a manipulative capitalist but also "in the government's pay." They claimed that his intent was to "divert the working classes from even the peaceable achievement of reasonable political aims." His attempts to persuade the bourgeoisie to mend their own ways, his hobnobbing with royalty (even though he was trying to win their help for the working class), his repeated calls for class harmony and the repudiation of violence, and, most of all, his own considerable wealth were all suspect. While he waged his one-person war in 1815 to establish public works programs for the chronically unemployed, radicals called his proposed worksites "a community of slaves." Working-class leaders continued such attacks for the next half century, dismissing New Lanark as "really a capitalist enterprise with an infusion of business ethics and paternalism"—in fact, an accurate description. The imagination of the left, like that of the right, was unable to accommodate the thought of a socially responsible capitalist. Owen could not win. While leftist journals described him as "a consistent upholder of the status quo in politics, hostile to all reforms," for generations, tradition-minded working-class leaders attacked Owenites for their championship of feminism, divorce, and birth control.

No attackers left as permanent a smudge on Owen's reputation as Marx and Engels. Marx harbored a conventional hatred for the bourgeoisie, but he reserved his most inimical vitriol for progressives, reformers, and socialists who failed to embrace Marxist communism. In private, Engels and Marx were patronizing about Owen: after hearing an address by Owen at age eighty, Marx wrote to Engels that "in spite of fixed ideas, the old man was ironical and lovable." In print, they were unmerciful: in *Condition of the Working Class*, Engels wrote, "English Socialism arose with Owen, a manufacturer, and proceeds therefore with great consideration towards the bourgeoisie and great injustice towards the proletariat in its methods."

Engels accused Owen of expropriating the profits at New Lanark that were rightly due to labor, a profit that Engels claimed amounted to "more than £300,000 sterling" (equivalent to perhaps $6 million in current U.S. dollars) during his quarter century at New Lanark. To people who believed that property is theft, that amounted to larceny on a grand scale, and they damned him for doing what the capitalists damned him for not doing: getting filthy rich.

Marx and Engels also singled out Owen for special scorn in *The Communist Manifesto* as one of a half dozen socialist enemies of the people who did not appreciate the necessity and inevitability of the class struggle: Owen and his ilk "by degrees sink into the category of the reactionary conservative socialists . . . differing from these only by more systematic pedantry and by their fanatical and superstitious belief in the miraculous effects of their social science."

According to a modern German scholar, Erwin Hasselman, Marx and Engels's characterization of Owen "did not derive from honest motives, but from the intention to kill off intellectual competition." They succeeded; the disparaging epithet *utopian* they gave Owen in the *Manifesto* has remained associated with his name like a scarlet letter ever since. The ultimate sign of their success is that conservative economists today—who would rather advocate tax increases than quote from the *Manifesto*—unquestioningly accept Marx's trivializing label. Worse for Owen's reputation, such contemporary intellectuals as Isaiah Berlin and Michael Oakshott have also used the label to relegate Owen to the netherworld outside serious thought.

Personal Criticism

Much of the criticism of Owen over the years has been directed against his character. The literature is rife with personal criticism of the man, most of it based on the fact that in his old age he pressed his ideas on all who would listen—including Napoleon, Santa Anna, and seven sitting or former U.S. presidents—and that in his final years he became indisputably loony. Admittedly, that's a difficult bill of particulars to ignore; yet it fails to explain the resistance to his leadership. Admittedly, this is not self-evident; please read on.

Even the embarrassments of his dotage, his irritating unflappability in the face of great obstacles, and his unrelenting advocacy of such then-unpopular notions as deism, feminism, and divorce do not account for his contemporaries' total rejection of his numerous farsighted ideas. There are gaping lacunae in the logic of such critiques. Why, for example, did industrialists reject Owen's ideas in the early 1800s when he would not become batty until forty years later? Accounts of his character during the first eight decades of his life leave the impression of a kind, gentle, patient, and privately charming person (who was, however, didactic, bland, and long-winded as a public speaker). He may have been quirky, but he was never cruel or obnoxious.

Most of Owen's biographers have been overwhelmed by his complexities: he was an outspoken egalitarian whose earliest allies were the aristocracy, a business magnate whose only reliable followers were of the working class, an outspoken advocate of feminism and divorce who endured a conventional and loveless marriage, and a leading light of the Enlightenment who seldom bothered to read or to refine his intellectual arguments. As R. H. Tawney noted, "A career so disjointed lends itself to caricature."

Such a man seems deserving of dismissal as an eccentric, had he not been—by the standards of the twentieth century, at least—among the most farsighted thinkers of his time (along with Thomas Jefferson, James Madison and Thomas Paine). And even if he were slightly eccentric, the finest minds of Owen's era were nothing if not dotty in the endearing British manner: Adam Smith's famous perambulations in a state of reverie caused him to be caricatured as the quintessential absentminded professor; Samuel Johnson had more quirks, tics, and compulsive mannerisms than Robert De Niro in the film Awakenings; and John Stuart Mill was a depressed social isolate who flaunted Victorian decorum.

Even if we admit that Owen was absolutely insufferable, we would nonetheless search in vain for historical instances of great ideas being rejected because obnoxious creators advanced them. The world did not reject Marxism in justifiable recoil from the overbearing person of Karl Marx, so it seems highly improbable that it rejected Owenism in abhorrence of the gentle quirkiness of Robert Owen. The actual source of resistance must be found elsewhere.

When the New Lanark entrepreneur first began to challenge the worldview of his peers, Cole reports that "respectable people began to shake their heads, and dismiss Owen as a philanthropic visionary, whose good intentions had run away with his judgment." The more he pushed, the more intemperate became the criticisms: he was called "a bit mad," "rigid," and "doctrinaire." Macaulay condescended that Owen was "always a gentle bore." William Corbett, Owen's earliest critic, found him wildly impractical and overly optimistic in his beliefs about the education of the working class. He dismissed Owen's view of human nature: "How the little matters of black eyes, bloody noses and the pulling of caps are to be settled, I do not exactly see." Corbett was merely the first in a long line of critics to discover how easy it was to make Owen look the fool by nudging him into the utopian camp.

Madison, according to his recent biographer, Drew McCoy, thought Owen failed to understand that many of the difficulties he proposed to cure were rooted not in deficient and corrupting institutions but rather in the "natural proclivities of man." It is not surprising that the father of pluralism believed that the best a government can do is to offset those ugly "natural proclivities" by the shifting balances of factions in mass society. In that day, as in ours, nothing more damning could be said of one's intellect than that one failed to understand human nature. To argue against hardheaded realism—to say, as Owen did, that all human beings are inherently equal as well as capable of altruism—was (and is) to identify oneself as naive and impractical.

The essayist William Hazlitt wrote Owen off as "a man of one idea," a grossly inappropriate charge that shows how far Owen's contemporaries went to avoid facing the issues he raised. Hazlitt also accused Owen of being a clever manipulator who managed to trick his workers into greater productivity. Nothing gives as much social delight as the uncloaking of hypocrisy: true capitalists need not apologize for the pursuit of profit, but to disguise the aim was dishonest! Hence the great glee in certain London circles when disgruntled

New Lanark employees were found willing to state publicly that Owen was a tyrant in the guise of a benefactor. One widely quoted former worker said of the managers of New Lanark that "they had got a number of dancing-masters, a fiddler, a band of music; that there were drills and exercises, and that [employees] were dancing together till they were more fatigued than if they were working." On hearing this shocking news, fashionable men and women emerged from their salons to attack the evil genius who dared to abuse the working class by the inhumane means of excessive dance.

Owen's character was sufficiently flawed to allow the charges of his critics to adhere with the force of superglue. Even his friends say he was inflexible and politically naive. Yet had he been a spokesman for the Tory establishment with the same traits, would he have found himself so discredited? Would British manufacturers have abandoned child labor if the chief advocate of that practice had been exposed as a deist? It is difficult to sort out rationalization from rational criticism, but it would seem that the personal attacks on Owen were the former.

In general, the intellectual arguments advanced by Owen's critics on the left and the right appear to modern readers to have been spurious, shortsighted, or self-serving. The Owenism of New Lanark was neither disguised collectivism, as rightists claimed, nor disguised laissez-faire, as collectivists were wont to assume. In hindsight, we can see that it was in fact the most reasonable alternative to the horrors of the Industrial Revolution. Setting aside the rationalizations they offered, the puzzle remains for us to discover why, in fact, industrialists and working-class leaders resisted an alternative that would have benefited them both.

Owen's Shortcoming as a Leader

Should the failure to embrace reform and, perhaps, to avoid the worst excesses of the Industrial Revolution thus be laid entirely at the feet of Owen's nineteenth-century critics? Not entirely. Those who criticized his paternalism, impatience, naïveté, hypocrisy, and business philosophy certainly revealed more about themselves than about Owen, but the charge that he wouldn't listen to others is more serious, for if true, it would say more about him than about them. Many critics (and more than one friend) have written that Owen was "deaf to the opinions of others." An admirer, Harriet Martineau, wrote that Owen's greatest failing was that he was so certain that he alone was possessed of truth that he would not listen to other views. She once quipped that Owen "is not a man to think differently of a book for having read it." Not only is such bullheadedness unattractive, but it can prove ruinous for a leader, as the tragedies of Creon and Lear remind us. It is particularly damning that Tawney, who shared Owen's values, described the man as "an exacting, and at times, imperious chief. Modest in manner and intransigent in beliefs, he claimed with a mild, impersonal arrogance, regardless of such trifles as majority votes, the obedience due to the voice of the inspired—or, as he would have termed it, rational truth."

The tragedy of Owen's life was that he left no converts to his vision of a "new moral order." In Owen's old age, Emerson reputedly asked him, "Who is your disciple? How many men possessed of your views, who will remain after you, are going to put them into practice?" Owen answered, sadly and truthfully, "Not one."

In short, Owen created no followers. By the sheer force of powerful ideas, he had attempted to impose on others his vision of the good society. The more he forced, the more they resisted. The causes of the resistance to Owen's ideas, then, were not simply the weaknesses of his potential followers, nor were they simply shortcomings of leadership. Resistance arose from the complex of interactions between would-be leader and would-be followers.

Owen never learned how to overcome the deeply rooted resistance to change, a skill that is a prime characteristic of great moral leadership. That Owen suffered from this flaw is not a tragedy in itself, for few people have the ability to change the minds and behavior of others. The tragic aspect to Owen's story is that humanity suffered for nearly a century from that singularly consequential flaw of one of history's gentlest souls.

We thus cannot learn the art of leading change from Owen's story. What we must take from it is greater understanding of why others resisted his ideas. We may now ask which, among the list of thirty-three hypotheses about the resistance to change, are the major sources of that rejection? In the next chapter we see that John Stuart Mill's hypothesis comes closest to being a useful explanation.

12

Mill Interpreted

The Despotism of Custom

From Owen's final written words, we can assume that he went to his grave not quite as confident as he had once been that "truth must ultimately prevail over error": "I thought previous to experience, that the simple, plain, honest enunciation of truth, and of its beautiful application to all the real business of life, would attract the attention and engage the warm interest of all parties; and that the reformation of the population of the world would be comparatively an easy task. But, promising as many things appeared at first, as I advanced I found superstitions and mistaken self-interest . . . deeply rooted and ramified throughout society." Based on the numerous frustrations of his life, he had come to conclude that "superstitions" and "mistaken self-interest" were at the root of what he had experienced as impenetrable resistance to social knowledge and change. By superstition, Owen meant not only his personal bête noire, organized religion, but other traditional values and beliefs as well. In this he predates by two years John Stuart Mill's hypothesis that the force behind the resistance to change is "the despotism of custom."

In *On Liberty*, Mill argued that society views individuality as an "affront to custom." The individual who advocates change will not be seen as offering the prospect of progress, but as giving reproach to the duly constituted social order. Hence the "eccentric" individual will be squelched by the "collective tyranny" of society. Mill argued that this "despotism of custom" gripped England in the nineteenth century. During this era of remarkable material progress, it was not resistance to technological or scientific knowledge that alarmed Mill. Rather, he rued the fact that rational arguments advanced in support of the emancipation of women, religious tolerance, the cessation of prosecution of victimless crimes, and, in general, the rights of freedom of expression and action were being rejected by Victorian society. Indeed, these civil libertarian ideas—Mill's *own* ideas, for goodness sake—were rejected much as Owen's reforms had been resisted or ignored.

Like Owen, Mill thought he knew the cause of the rejection. To him, the chief obstacle to social progress was *tradition* in the form of such social institutions as conventional marriage, religious orthodoxy, and, especially, the unwillingness to sanction social experiments (the very constraints of tradition, which were also Owen's bugbears). Even as Mill acknowledged the necessity of tradition—and was personally hostile to anarchism and revolutionary extremism—he felt nonetheless that society errs too much on the side of conformity: "Society has now fairly got the better of individuality; and the danger which threatens human nature is not the excess, but the deficiency, of personal impulses and preferences. . . . In our times, from the highest class of society down to the lowest, every one lives as under the eye of a hostile and dreaded censorship."

By censorship, Mill did not have in mind some Victorian prototype of the Soviet bureaucrat excising officially disapproved sentiments from "radical" periodicals. He was not so much worried about the totalitarian power of the state (Victorian England was, after all, the most laissez-faire of modern societies) as he was about the "tyranny of the majority"—the stifling power of middle-class convention that he believed was the mother of mediocrity. To Mill, the source of human excellence and social progress could be found only in the ideas of people who dared to challenge the status quo. Mill's hero was the nonconformist, the eccentric—not the eccentric in mannerisms and behavior but the eccentric in *ideas:* "Precisely because the tyranny of opinion is such as to make eccentricity a reproach, it is desirable, in order to break through that tyranny, that people should be eccentric. Eccentricity has always abounded when and where strength of character has abounded; and the amount of eccentricity in a society has generally been proportional to the amount of genius, mental vigor, and moral courage which it contained. That so few now dare to be eccentric, marks the chief danger of the time."

Society will tolerate eccentricity in taste and fashion, which, like Samuel Johnson's tics and Adam Smith's odd public reveries, are not threatening to social custom. Mill was concerned, instead, with society's rejection of the advocates of change: "The man, and still more the woman, who can be accused either of doing 'what nobody does,' or of not doing 'what everybody does,' is the subject of as much depreciatory remark as if he or she had committed some grave moral delinquency."

In Mill's eyes, eccentric innovators and entrepreneurs—the true sources of progress and change—didn't stand a chance. He likened the prevailing social sentiment in Victorian England to the doctrine of the ancient Locrians, which required that "the propounder of a new truth" or "the proposer of a new law" should stand "with a halter round his neck, to be instantly tightened if the public assembly did not, on hearing his reasons, then and there adopt his proposition." The great irony was that the power of tradition in laissez-faire England overcame the very spirit of individualism that the free market was said to honor and inspire. "The greatness of England is now all collective," Mill wrote of the most powerful industrial nation in the world. At the time, there were only seventy-nine thousand government employees in England (as opposed to nearly a million in France); hence if progress was being stifled, it was not being done so by the bureaucratic power of the state but by the "despotism of custom": "The despotism of custom is everywhere the standing hindrance to human advancement, being in unceasing antagonism to that disposition to aim at something better than customary, which is called, according to circumstances, the spirit of liberty, or that of progress or improvement."

Mill tells us that progress had come to a complete halt in China, where "the despotism of custom is complete." But why is tradition so tyrannically opposed to change? He suggests a reason why progress comes to be resisted: "The majority, being satisfied with the ways of mankind as they now are (for it is they who make them what they are), cannot comprehend why those ways should not be good enough for everybody." The source of this innate conservatism is straightforward in Mill's mind: "The general average of mankind are not only moderate in intellect, but also moderate in inclinations: they have no tastes or wishes strong enough to incline them to do anything unusual, and they consequently do not understand those who have, and class all such with the wild and intemperate whom they are accustomed to look down upon." This is the same conclusion to which Einstein would be drawn a century later: "Great souls have always met with violent opposition from mediocre minds."

Mill posited that societies such as China may for a time enjoy periods of spectacular advancement, but their people will ultimately grow self-satisfied and turn from encouraging change to defending custom: "A people, it appears, may be progressive for a certain length of time, and then stop: when does it stop? When it ceases to possess individuality."

Here, then, is a reasonable hypothesis for why Owen's ideas were rejected: the source of resistance was "custom" or the "collective despotism" of the status quo. Because individuality—eccentricity, in Mill's eyes—is universally viewed not as a source of progress but as an affront to custom, the eccentric ideas of an Owen (or a Deming or a Mill) will invariably be seen as a reproach to society and consequently rejected as such.

Like Occam's razor, Mill's argument cuts through an entangled mass of complexity and supposition, and presents a simple philosophical explanation of the phenomenon before us. In particular,

Mill's hypothesis appears to be a causal explanation, as opposed to Drucker's alternative argument based on "ripeness," which, in contrast, seems to be more of a historical description (though it may be accurate to say that "the time was not ripe for change," this does explain why the era was unpropitious). Moreover, the facts of the rejection of Owenism fit rather nicely with Mill's hypothesis: in fact, Owen's call for change was perceived as an affront to bourgeois social order, and the collective despotism of society effectively crushed both Owen and his ideas. Hence Mill's hypothesis withstands the first test of validity that all arguments must pass: it "squares with the facts."

Mill's hypothesis seems so reasonable both because it equates with common sense and because it is argued brilliantly by one of the great essayists in the language. Indeed, Mill effortlessly whisks the reader of *On Liberty* through a digest of the essential historical and philosophical thinking on the subject of resistance to change. This is as easy as pie for Mill, who was, after all, the champion whiz kid of all times (he knew Greek when he was three and had mastered the calculus before he was out of knee breeches). But *we* need to slow down. Mill may be raising more questions than he answers. Is the process he describes inevitable? That a people will turn from progress to embrace custom seems undeniable, but that the cause is the cessation of individuality is not quite so self-evident. Could not the loss of individuality be a symptom rather than, or in addition to, a cause? And what role do the factors of power, social class, ideology, and ordinary fear play in the rejection of social knowledge?

Mill was clearly on target when he described the "despotism of custom," but he did not score a bull's-eye. His hypothesis, as we shall see, is valid as far as it goes, but it is not a complete analysis. Even Owen's casual explanation of the resistance to his own ideas goes a step further than Mill's more formal theorizing about "custom" and "superstition." Owen suggests a factor not mentioned by Mill: "mistaken self-interest." By this Owen meant the proclivity to consider only the short term and only the welfare of one's immediate social group. Although this additional factor is not a contradiction of Mill's hypothesis, it is certainly a broadening of the analysis.

Moreover, there is no reason to limit this expansion of Mill to the one additional factor suggested by Owen. Indeed, the facts concerning the resistance to Owenism suggest that many factors were at play in addition to those considered by either Mill or Owen. Neither Mill's construct nor Owen's addendum goes far enough in explaining the what, who, when, where, how, or why of resistance to change.

What Was Being Resisted?

According to Mill, in cases such as Owen's, what society was resisting was "individual eccentricity." To Mill, all the world behaves like the Japanese adage: The nail that sticks up gets pounded down. Yet Victorian England admired people who stood out, who excelled, who were individualistic. For example, the four notables profiled by Lytton Strachey in *Eminent Victorians* were eminently eccentric, yet the "despotism of custom" was not evoked by polite society to hammer them down. Quite the opposite: Cardinal Manning, Florence Nightingale, Thomas Arnold, and General Charles George "Chinese" Gordon were revered as pillars of Victorianism.

Comparing these four individuals to Owen, it would seem that society makes a distinction between the "harmless" eccentric and the "dangerous" one. Society tolerates people who choose to wear fluorescent socks or proselytize for the Flat Earth Society; but that same society mobilizes against those who challenge its basic premises or belief structure. Consider a modern example: in the 1960s, American society rejected the dangerous eccentricity of Linus Pauling, the opponent of nuclear weapons; yet in the 1980s it tolerated the harmless eccentricity of the same Linus Pauling, who had by then become known as an advocate of daily megadoses of vitamin C. As the reactions to Pauling and Owen demonstrate, society has a sixth sense about what is safe and what is threatening. It is more probable that what the eccentric stands for—ideology, ideas—is more important than mere eccentricity per se as the source of resistance to knowledge and change. Of the four individuals profiled by Strachey, only Nightingale was an advocate of fundamental change. Although the changes she advocated were successfully resisted, she herself was not ostracized. She was not viewed as a threat, presumably because as a woman she possessed insufficient power to bring about change.

Who Is Doing the Resisting?

To Mill, the monolith that he called society was doing the resisting. But as we see with Owen, not all groups resist change in the same way or with the same fervor. Owen was not rejected by the aristocracy as long as his target was clearly and solely the manufacturing class. And although Owen's workers were initially skeptical of his efforts, he eventually won them over. In general, beneficiaries of proposed reforms are seldom opposed to them (often they are unaware of the potential benefits, and they may doubt the motives of their purported friends; as with Owen and the working class, the potential beneficiaries are often disfranchised participants in the process of reform).

Yet it is not simply that those whose oxen stand to be gored are the only ones opposed to change. If that were the case, there would be no mystery for us to explore. The puzzle is that people resist things that are clearly in their self-interest. Moreover, that resistance is neither predictable nor invariable. In some cases, the resistance may be a question of individual choice: some members of a group may resist and others not. In other instances, entire populations may divide (or coalesce) along such established fault lines as social class, race, profession, level of education, gender, religion, or special-interest grouping. And as Madison posited in his theory of pluralism, these alliances are ever shifting in democratic societies:

middle-class women may stand with middle-class men on some issues, then join with poor women on others; trade unionists and environmentalists are united on some issues, but divided on others. What are we to conclude? The obvious: the people with the most to lose are the most likely to resist change. But we quickly lose confidence when it comes to adding even a smidgen more specificity about the matter of who resists.

When Does Resistance Occur?

Mill hypothesized that society begins by being open to individuality; later it will close and become tradition-bound. He guessed wrong on this. Anthropological research conducted since Mill's death is relatively consistent in finding that the most tradition-bound societies are those in the earliest stages of development (as opposed to the later stages we call civilization). As with all questions associated with human behavior, the actual facts are complicated: among the modern (or literate) societies about which we have the longest historical record—in China, Greece, Egypt, the Fertile Crescent—the pattern has been one of alternating receptivity and resistance to change. To confuse matters further, comparative studies find nothing universal or predictable about this pattern of freezing and unfreezing. To add additional complexity, within any given society we may find receptivity to change in one domain and resistance in another (as we have seen, Victorian England was receptive to technological change but resistant to social reform). This raises another intriguing question: Why is there a difference in the intensity of resistance to social knowledge and to scientific knowledge? Could the difference lie in the fact that the former compels action but the latter does not? For example, accepting the law of gravity requires nothing of the individual or the group; in contrast, accepting the equality of women requires a major shift not only in attitude but also in behavior.

Further, any theory about change must account for the most important fact we have before us: ultimately, Owen's ideas *were* accepted. Even a die-hard pessimist must admit that change occurred and that the outcome was in the direction of progress: there are no more children working in factories in the Western world. The issue then becomes one of identifying the factors that led to change (rather than bemoaning, as Mill did, the innate conservatism of society in certain stages of development).

Where Does Resistance Occur?

Is resistance more untractable in democracies than in benevolent dictatorships? (This, like other questions being raised, can be turned around and profitably asked in a positive form: Where does change occur?) Consider three practical manifestations of this question: Was it not harder for Franklin Roosevelt to change democratic America than for Hitler to change totalitarian Germany? More recently, Mikhail Gorbachev asked for dictatorial powers to bring about perestroika in the Soviet Union, arguing that the process of democracy would create insuperable obstacles to change—a position that later gained Boris Yeltsin's sympathy. And corporate leaders in modern America frequently voice the opinion that only a "strong hand at the helm" can turn a business organization around. Yet in contrast to such common wisdom, was it not the process of democracy that ultimately led to the acceptance of Owen's reforms in Britain? Was the "spirit of democracy" the reason that Owenism originally fared better in America than in Britain? Perhaps the key variable in the tug-of-war between resistance and receptivity is not democracy at all but rather the age of the society or organization in question—or perhaps it is a matter of the size of the institution or society. Mill's hypothesis offers no guidance on such issues.

How Is Change Resisted?

To Mill, the answer is simple: society treats the change agent as an outcast, a position from which the person is powerless to affect the system. The facts surrounding the rejection of Owen lend considerable weight to this line of reasoning. Yet society clearly has many other means at its disposal to block change. For example, it can co-opt the advocate, smothering the person with crippling praise and prestige. This possibility raises an even broader question: Does fundamental change ever occur from inside the established order? Perhaps being an outcast is the price anyone must pay to achieve change. Turning the question around, must one be a revolutionary to effect change? In answering that question, we must decide if, in the final analysis, the most successful change agent was Robert Owen or Karl Marx.

Assuming that Mill is correct that the "despotism of custom" inhibits change, how can that knowledge be used by individuals trying to bring about change? Ultimately, Owen's efforts to abolish child labor bore fruit—but during that slow process, the life prospects of several generations of children were irretrievably lost. Might Owen have done something to accelerate the process? And today, how would an individual go about overcoming the despotism of custom in a work organization? Mill pessimistically throws up his hands on such practical matters.

Why Do People Resist Change?

What makes people in groups seek to preserve the status quo? On this, the most important question before us, we find Mill's hypothesis at its bleakest. Recall that, in proper Einsteinian fashion, he tells us that "the general average of mankind are not only moderate in intellect, but also moderate in inclination." In other words, people tend to be satisfied with their unsatisfactory lot. Admittedly, there is a certain elegance to Mill's point. Yet cognitive dissonance arises immediately when we consider evidence from Owen's case: change was resisted by the best and the brightest—by the intelligentsia of both left and right. And given the realities of power, was it unrealistic for the disfranchised masses to lack hope that the system within which they found themselves could be changed? At the risk of putting words in Mill's mouth, would it not be equally accurate to say that the problem is a lack of imagination? That is, could it be that people embrace the status quo because they cannot imagine anything better? But even this little restatement may not rescue Mill's proposition. People who resisted change were not required to supply much in the way of imagination: Owen had demonstrated before their very eyes a manifestly more desirable alternative. Why, then, did both the masses and the most educated people of the day balk at following Owen to a better society? Mill's explanation boils down to an unhelpful bemoaning of the "natural conservatism" of humankind.

Does the problem rest solely with the followers, as Mill suggests, or is it the role of the leader to give vision to those who lack imagination and hope to the dejected? Mill places the entire burden of resistance at the feet of the followers and releases the advocate of change from all leadership responsibility. Whereas most theorists of change have erred by focusing almost entirely on the personality of the leader, Mill seems to go to the other extreme with his fixation on the shortsightedness of the followers. In fact, as James MacGregor Burns was the first to note, the reality is almost always found in the dynamic process of interaction between the two parties.

· · · · · · · ·

In sum, Mill's hypothesis is useful as far as it goes; it just does not go far enough. To explain more fully the rejection of Owenism—and the common pattern of resistance to all social knowledge and progress—we must create a more robust theory. The foundation for such a theory comes from a complaint about Owen, advanced in 1817, that may be the most straightforward (and most self-aware) criticism the establishment ever leveled against him: "Everybody, I believe, is convinced of Mr. Owen's benevolence, and that he purposes to do us much good," wrote a beleaguered industrialist. "I ask him to *let us alone*, lest he do us much mischief."

This is more than an appeal to laissez-faire; it is a *cri de coeur* from a member of a class whose intellectual and material comfort is threatened by a meddling reformer. Owen was attempting to impose his values on a group who had neither asked for his counsel nor felt any need for it. Worse, he was attacking the very values that the upper classes most cherished—values that made them feel superior to the "lower orders." As Mill posited, Owen's call for change was perceived as an affront to the established social order, and the collective despotism of society effectively crushed both Owen and his ideas. But to explain the virulence of the attacks on Owen, and the power of the resistance to his ideas, we must go beyond Mill's focus on custom's dead hand on the mediocre masses. Owenism was rejected by the most exceptional individuals of his era. Those who resisted were not as concerned with defending custom—or even with defending their social and economic privileges—as they were with defending the basic assumptions that provided social cohesion. Like the Azande of the Sudan, Victorians were primarily concerned with preserving their collective worldview. Owen was rightfully seen as a dangerous threat to everything they believed, particularly because they had no rational responses to his challenge. And nothing is more certain to stir up resistance to change than a challenge to the psychological comfort of the powerful.

The Ideology of Comfort

A "Good Enough" Explanation
of Resistance to Change

Who would have predicted it? After the great thinkers have offered their explanations of the sources of resistance to change, along comes Chrysler's supersalesman, Lee Iacocca, to top them all with three pithy sentences capturing the essence of the phenomenon: "From Wall Street to Washington, from boardrooms to union halls, what anybody with power is most scared of is change. Any kind of change. Especially change that's forced on them." As we shall see, evidence abounds to support Iacocca's contention that the key dimensions of resistance are power, fear, and imposition of the will of others. Iacocca's hypothesis is the most useful explanation of why changes proposed by Drucker, Deming, and Owen were rejected. Anthropological research supports his conclusion that groups resist "any kind of change," and sociological and psychological theories underscore that groups particularly abhor "change that's forced on them." If valid, this insight is of singular usefulness, for it would follow that leaders can succeed in overcoming resistance to change only when followers feel that they are not being forced to act against their will. We shall flesh out that argument by way of review and analysis of over a half century of research that bears on the issue before us.

Anthropologists on Change

The heyday of social anthropology lasted roughly fifty years. The first of the classical participant-observers was a Polish-born British subject named Bronislaw Malinowski, who began his fieldwork in Melanesia in 1915; the last of the breed were packing up their tape recorders at about the time of the death of Margaret Mead in 1979—their work largely done, with no "tribes" unsullied by civilization left to study. During this brief period, anthropologists had moved (uninvited) into tropical villages in Pago Pago, into rough log huts of the Kwakiutl in the verdant Pacific Northwest, and into the lean-tos in the barren lands of our earlier acquaintances, the Azande, in sub-Saharan Africa. In hundreds of ethnographies produced during nearly three generations of fieldwork, the anthropologists discovered countless variations in the structure of kinship, marriage, religion, and political authority—all to the delight of lovers of the diverse and the exotic.

What they did *not* find anywhere was *change*. Traditional, small-scale societies—it has become politically incorrect to call them "primitive tribes"—were everywhere discovered to be paradigms of stasis. Even though humankind in its myriad "natural" states was found capable of the most advanced forms of ratiocination and imaginative solutions to social problems, nowhere did preliterate peoples display a capacity for the kind of behavior that civilized folk call progress.

In the middle of the twentieth century, anthropologists advanced a general theory of social change. Because they had observed resistance to change in all groups they had studied, they assumed that the behavior must fulfill a necessary function. They concluded that collective resistance to change is not only rational but also *necessary* for the continuity of social order and cohesion.

Moreover, it was found that wherever and whenever small-scale societies came into contact with civilization, the result was disastrous for the former: American Indian cultures were destroyed by European settlers and homesteaders; Aboriginal culture was destroyed by land-hungry Australian farmers, shepherds, and prospectors; African cultures were destroyed by French, Belgian, Portuguese, and British colonials; and the traditional cultures of Latin America were destroyed by Spanish clerics and gold-crazed conquistadors. Small-scale cultures were nowhere a match for the depth and breadth of change wrought by the powerful West. For the overpowered primitives, the result of contact with civilization was—inevitably and invariably—chaos and alienation. To anthropologists, the process of social change was a history of disintegration of traditional societies. No wonder they concluded that change was "nonfunctional."

One of the last major studies of change conducted in the classic tradition—Colin Turnbull's heartrending portrait of the Ik of Uganda—graphically traced the transformation of a once well-ordered society into a state of anarchy and savagery. Though some critics argued that Turnbull's account was sensationalized, many scholarly works published earlier had linked the same pattern of disintegration of the family, the breakdown of norms and values, and the introduction of such social problems as alcoholism, crime, and prostitution to the inability of small-scale societies to cope with changes wrought by Christianity, science, and a market economy. Depending on one's ideological predilections, there were alternative ways of interpreting this pattern of destruction: most anthropologists tended to see it as a villainous crime perpetrated by imperialists; most economists saw it as an unfortunate side effect of the process of development by which millions of primitive peoples had been brought the advantages of modern science, commerce, medicine, and law. Observers in the first camp saw a loss of innocence; those in the second, a loss of ignorance.

Regardless of ideology, however, modern civilization has been seen by all trained observers as a powerful force of change. In study after study, gemeinschaft has been equated with stasis and gesellschaft with change—to do only a slight injustice to the German sociologist Tönnies's misleading turn-of-the-century dichotomizing of the world into the categories of change-resistant small-scale communities and dynamic large-scale societies. This is misleading because, on closer examination, modern societies were found to be nearly as change-resistant as traditional communities (and the "primitives," on closer study, were not as primitive or as change-resistant as the pioneering social scientists had assumed). Doubtless the process of resistance differs between modern and traditional societies, but, ironically, the main advantage that modern society was supposed to enjoy over traditional societies, a predisposition to change, exists mainly as a matter of degree—and then only conclusively so with regard to scientific progress.

In truth, as the noted scholar L. Iacocca notes, change is resisted by all human groups: modern nations, business corporations, religious institutions, political bodies, voluntary societies, government agencies, university faculties, labor unions, and even scientific entities. These groups, like the tribes from which they long ago evolved, resist change with much the same persistence, if not effect, as their social precursors. It is easy to conclude, as most social scientists have, that resistance must be rooted in human nature, which, by definition, is common to all men and women everywhere and at all times. Yet certain facts do not support this contention. One of the most important legacies of anthropological research is that it revealed the human animal in all its variety: it was discovered that no two societies have ever been organized in identical ways. Presumably, if we all had exactly the same nature (whatever that might mean), we would not display such a variety of behaviors. That we are all members of the same reasoning species, *Homo sapiens*, does not mean we all think the same thoughts.

Moreover, to say that it is human nature to resist change is to deny the many obvious exceptions to that rule found in our own culture and experience. We all know or know of people who thrive on change: explorers become restless when they stay in one place too long; inventors seek the new and unseen; entrepreneurs innovate; people who divorce and remarry desire change—it would seem defensible to claim that boredom is as much a part of human nature as the resistance to change! At any rate, arguments beginning with definitions about human nature seldom progress beyond the definitions.

Today social scientists are increasingly careful not to generalize about the behavior of the entire human race. That is why a useful theory of resistance to change needs to be limited to *us*—modern, Western men and women living in postindustrial democratic societies. Even then we must recognize possible differences between demographic subgroups: in some instances, Italians may respond to the pressures for change differently from Swedes; in the United States, Catholic Hispanic culture may differ from that of Protestant northern Europeans in its receptivity to change. In addition, there is the complicating issue of where one stands in the social system. The German sociologist Karl Mannheim argued that how we think is determined by our social status (an idea related to the anthropological insight that how we think is determined by who we are culturally).

But modern society is not just a collection of tribes or social classes. Democratic capitalism is predicated as much on individualism as it is on such traditional collectivities. Hence how we respond to pressures for change is determined not just by who we are but also by what we want, that is, by our personal objectives, goals, and values. Of course, where we stand in the pecking order, who we are culturally, and what we want personally are all so complexly interrelated that it is impossible to show which of these factors are causes and which are effects. To complicate this immense social puzzle further, there are different forms or processes of change in modern society (to cite just three: unstructured change in the beliefs of populations at large, structured change by way of democratic processes, and structured micro-organizational change), and there may well be different patterns of resistance to each of these.

Given such complexities, caveats, and distinctions, the absence of a scientifically valid general theory about the resistance to change is not surprising. In fact, the state of the art of what rightly should be called the social studies is such that, in general, no complex aspect of human behavior is scientifically explicable. We can no more prove why some people resist change than we can prove why others pursue power. All we can seek, realistically, is a "good enough" understanding of the phenomenon to allow leaders to respond purposefully and effectively when resistance is encountered.

Though not enough is known to state scientifically why change is resisted, there is enough knowledge to draw some rough but useful conclusions (social knowledge differs from scientific fact, but it is instructive nevertheless). The various hypotheses and historical examples examined in this book have allowed us to identify certain potentially useful patterns of behavior. For instance, in the cases of Drucker, Deming, and Owen, the concept of power has been present—implicitly or explicitly—as a kind of leitmotif. It might be said that, in all three of these examples, the would-be leaders lacked power to effect change. This commonly observed link between change and power has led countless observers to jump to the conclusion that the exercise of authority in a hierarchical system is the essential ingredient needed to bring about change. Such reasoning underlies the dominant "strongman" theories of leadership. Indeed, when we have finished constructing our "good enough" theory, we shall have discovered that power is a necessary ingredient. Although power-based theories are valid in part, we shall nonetheless find that the forms of exercise of power that are acceptable—and effective— in modern democratic society are changing. We will eventually conclude that the traditional strongman assumptions about leadership are in many ways anachronistic—or at least obsolescent. But we are not there yet.

A Practical Theory

First we must construct our "good enough" theory from several specific instances we have explored: General Motors, postwar U.S. industry, Victorian England. In these examples, as in all modern nations and organizations, it is evident that some individuals have more power than others. Here power means influence, authority, and access to resources, as opposed to the blatant and blind wielding of force found in some small-scale traditional (and modern nondemo- cratic) societies. Moreover, in democratic societies, differences in the possession of power are increasingly matters of degree rather than kind. For example, in the past, women could not vote and workers followed orders; today women have less power than men and work- ers less power than managers, but in both cases these differences are questions of degree—and such differences are shrinking.

In modern social systems, most of the people with the most power are more content with the status quo than those who have less power. Indeed, when it comes to power, all societies are com- posed of haves and have-nots, and the haves are divided into have- mores and have-lesses.

Dramatis Personae of Change

The Players	Their Roles	Attitude Toward Dominant Ideology
Haves		
Have-mores	To lead resistance	Subscribe and defend
Have-lesses	To support resistance	Subscribe and defend
Progressives	To advocate reform	Subscribe with reservations
Have-nots		
Uninvolved	To resist passively	Accept passively
Working-class Tories	To support resistance	Subscribe and defend
Revolutionaries	To advocate a new system	Reject entirely

Though the have-lesses may want more power, more influence, and better conditions for themselves relative to the have-mores, they are unlikely to question the legitimacy or basic operating rules of a social system. The have-lesses, like the have-mores, partake fully in the culture of that system, accepting its norms, values, and assumptions as their own. They subscribe to the dominant canon of beliefs, buttressed by a common reading of history, and accept the culture's heroes and myths. All dominant groups embrace such a shared culture because it is necessary for the defense of the system—without shared beliefs, no group can function effectively. That was a fundamental finding of anthropologists with regard to primitive societies, and it is equally true for advanced societies and for all their constituent organizational parts.

The Haves and the Prevailing Ideology

In a complex society, the belief system that functions to protect the existing order may be called an ideology. The term was first used in this fashion by Karl Mannheim, who in *Ideology and Utopia* explained that ideologies are the myths that groups create to justify their behavior and distinguish them from other groups: "There is implicit in the word 'ideology' the insight that in certain situations the collective unconscious of certain groups obscures the real condition of society both to itself and to others and thereby stabilizes it." It is this ideology that allows groups to have "somnambulistic certainty" about the rectitude of the existing order. "Ideology is a phenomenon intermediate between a simple lie at one pole, and an error, which is the result of a distorted and faulty conceptual apparatus, at the other." Mannheim's use of *ideology* in this fashion derives from Francis Bacon's sixteenth-century theory of *idola*. Bacon's idols (of the tribe, the cave, the market, and the theater) are "preconceptions" derived from human nature, society, and tradition that lead to "a wonderful obstruction of the mind." Once a social proposition has been established, Bacon wrote, every fact adds "fresh support and confirmation: and although most cogent and abundant instances exist to the contrary, [the collective mind of society] either does not observe or despises them or gets rid of and rejects them by some distinction, with violent and injurious prejudice, rather than sacrifice the authority of its first conclusion."

This is the same phenomenon that Evans-Pritchard observed three hundred years later among the Azande; Mannheim, too, "discovered" it on a massive scale in Mitteleuropa. In the early 1930s, the many ethnic tribes of Europe could not see beyond "their narrow and particularized positions," and Mannheim feared—with good reason, as it turned out—that the dictators of the era would seize on this ethnocentric blindness and use it as a pretext for great mischief. Ideology leads to dangerous collective myopia because, in the words of Bacon, "human understanding resembles not a dry light, but admits a tincture of the will and passions, which generate their own system accordingly, for man always believes more readily that which he prefers."

As we have seen in the chapters on Drucker, Deming, and Owen, the most powerful members of a society are those most comfortable with its ideology. Not all who share the ideology must be comfortable *materially*—in fact, some may be economically impoverished—but they all must be *socially* and *psychologically* comfortable with the established order. That is, they must have something to lose if the status quo were to be overturned, even if they have no wealth at risk. It is because they have something invested in the system in terms of status, beliefs, or values that the vast majority of haves—be they have-mores or have-lesses—embrace the dominant ideology.

Still, there may be a minority of haves who are not content with aspects of the system. Though they do not question its underlying legitimacy, they nonetheless advocate change or reform. Their reasons and motivations may be moral or practical (or both). Often these progressives fear that the system is losing its vitality and must either restore its former vigor or face decay from within. But when progressives call for renewal, they may be either ignored or condemned by their fellow haves. They may be called revolutionaries, utopians, malcontents, radicals, impractical fools, or—if they advocate fundamental change—traitors or dangerous agents of whatever enemies the group may have. By calling the prevailing ideology into

question, progressives thus attack the system at its strongest link—
at the bond that holds the group together. Consequently, progressives
almost never prevail during their lifetimes—witness Robert Owen.

Hence resistance to change arises when a would-be leader challenges the comfort of the group, the members' satisfaction with the
established level of their power, prestige, privileges, position, and
satisfaction with who they are, what they believe, and what they
cherish. Invariably, this agent of change—the reformer or would-
be leader—is perceived as trying to impose his or her will on the
group. In almost all instances, the majority of haves resist the progressives' call to reform, not so much because they fear change, but
more because they bristle at having the will of others imposed on
them. They resent having the ideology with which they are comfortable called into question, and they resent even more being
forced to question that ideology themselves. Because the proposed
change disturbs the carefully constructed psychological world of the
powerful elite, they strike back with considerable venom. Though
they appear to attack the loyalty, sanity, or propriety of the progressives, what the haves are really saying is, "Who do they think
they are, telling us to change, telling us what to think and do?"
Thus a major factor in our resistance to change is the desire not to
have the will of others forced on us.

Indeed, the overpowering desire to be left alone—that common
wish not to be bothered by progressives, reformers, and change
junkies—seems to be an integral component of nearly every culture, and is at the root of the rejection of the Demings and Owens
of this world. A recent example is the near-unanimous rejection by
the legal profession of efforts by a California judge to use innovative sentencing as an alternative to jailing. Nearly everyone who
has studied the current system concludes that it is unjust and ineffective. Yet according to *Time* magazine, California's attorneys and
judges reacted nearly as one in dismissing the ideas of the reformist
judge on the grounds, in the words of one law professor, that "he
thinks he's smarter than everybody else."

Over the past quarter century, opponents of strip-mining in Appalachia have argued that the practice destroys the viability of the land and endangers the health and welfare of future generations. In the Pacific Northwest and British Columbia, opponents of clear-cutting have advanced similar arguments. In both locales, the struggles that ensued have not revolved around the validity of arguments advanced by the reformers. Instead, both situations degenerated into tests of will, with the defenders of the status quo resisting change for the reason that it was being imposed on them. I witnessed this firsthand in British Columbia in 1970 when clear-cutting loggers gave in to Sierra Club pressures and agreed to leave a single row of trees standing alongside a river to provide shade for spawning trout. The day after press photographers came to the forest to photograph the trees, the loggers angrily cut them all down. When I asked them why, one explained, "Nobody tells us what to do."

On the level of individual psychology, one can readily reproduce this phenomenon: Simply tell someone you know to change a fundamental aspect of his or her behavior. Whether you say, "You talk too much; try listening more" or "Quit smoking; it's in your own interest," the response is not likely to be acquiescence or gratitude. Predictably, the person will flush with anger and, if a blunt and uninhibited type, will say, "Who the hell do you think you are, telling me what to do?" If you want to end a relationship, try this experiment in front of others! In modern democratic societies, no person is seen as having the right to impose his or her will on another.

The same is true with groups. All groups resist challenges to their unquestioned ease with the moral rectitude of established practices and values. The roots of this confrontational reaction are part survival mechanism and part deep-seated human need for power, dominance, and control. The relationship of resistance to power— why it is so difficult to achieve social change—now becomes clearer: to succeed, a minority of progressives must force their will (their visions, beliefs, and values) on a larger group of haves who are deeply invested in the status quo and in the ideology on which it is predicated. Thus even though progressives may argue that change will not affect the power, prestige, and positions of the haves, the haves understand intuitively that in fact change must undermine their ideology, upset their belief system, and discomfit them greatly. It is an unacceptable affront to be forced to change one's mind. Individuals are what they believe, and groups are their cultures; hence to require a group to change its shared beliefs is to threaten its very existence.

In the minds of the haves, progressives have no *right* to demand change; in practice, they also lack *might*. Therefore, for any system to change peacefully, the majority must willingly admit the position of the minority. Peaceful change thus requires acquiescence in upsetting the dominant worldview—in effect, the collective eating of crow by those who have the most power to resist change. But realistically, why would any group be willing to do this? Why would thousands of lawyers be willing to accept the ideas of one dissenter? Why would strip miners listen to outside agitators and traitors? Why would clear-cutters listen to tree huggers?

Reaction to the imposition of the will of others can also be seen as a major source of resistance to the abolition of slavery. Why would slaveholders in pre–Civil War Virginia be willing to listen to the abolitionist minority, such as Thomas Jefferson, among their peers? Could the slaveholders have simply said to progressives, "Well, we admit you are right. Slavery is evil. Everything that we have stood for all our lives is wrong"? As brilliant as Jefferson was at engineering social change, it is no wonder that he died frustrated in his attempts to make inroads into the ideology of comfort that buttressed the will of his fellow Virginian slaveholders. Jefferson was not asking his fellow haves simply to give up their slaves—arguments were easily enough advanced that slaveholding was uneconomical and not in the self-interest of plantation owners or white society in the long term. He was asking a powerful group to bow to a minority position. To accept the will of even one as manifestly great as Jefferson was simply too much for the proud and powerful slaveholders to swallow, even though Jefferson was clearly one of their own. (Still, we might wonder if Jefferson might have overcome some of this resistance with a bit more Rushmorean leadership. Was he not a bit like General Motors' Robert Stempel in that he was opposed to slavery in his head, but insufficiently so in his gut to be an effective change agent?)

We now see why it was improbable that nineteenth-century industrialists would accept Owen's reforms, even when it was in their own interest to do so. How could they say, "We've been wrong about the natural inferiority of the working class and wrong about the rectitude of our ruling position in society"? Similarly, how could the heads of American industry admit to Drucker and Deming, "You're right—adversarial labor relations are self-defeating; we should involve workers in decisions that we have always defended as solely our prerogatives." The absurdity of such mea culpas is self-evident. To accept the rightness of the arguments of others is to give up our beliefs, our essence. No individual is programmed to do so willingly; no group with the power to resist can be expected to do so.

That is why, in most systems, force or compulsion must come from outside for change to occur. Ironically, if the force is great enough to compel change among the haves—but not great enough to overthrow them—the ideas of progressives may become incorporated subtly into the revised prevailing ideology. Perhaps the progressives will then be remembered as prophets before their time. But history shows that before such recognition occurs, the vindicated progressive is most likely to be dead (Owen), or safely superannuated (Deming).

The Lot of the Have-Nots

The only recognition that progressives can count on during their lives is the begrudging acknowledgment of their ideas among certain categories of have-nots. Despite a trend in democracies toward more evenly and equitably distributed power, the majority of individuals in most social systems remain relatively powerless. Most societies and organizations are hierarchical, with the majority of power concentrated at the tip of the social pyramid. People with little or no power—the have-nots—can be broken down into three subgroups based on their attitudes toward change: revolutionaries, the uninvolved, and working-class Tories.

Revolutionaries are always few in number and seldom effective. Chronically disaffected, they harbor deep anger and resentment. They see only one way to overcome the shortcomings of the system: take power from the haves. Whereas revolutionaries would resort to violence in previous eras, in today's democratic societies they are more likely to reject the legitimacy of the entire system and to form countercultures and antiestablishmentarian movements (for example, the Greens). Often revolutionaries offer the same criticisms put forward by progressives and, to a lesser extent, may embrace some of the same reforms offered by them. But they will not, in the final analysis, make common cause with the progressives because they do not trust them; they recognize that the goal of the progressives is the reform of the existing system, not its overthrow. In recent times, radical trade unionists and leaders of extreme minority groups have been revolutionary in this way. Revolutionaries are typically expelled from work organizations (with the exception of educational systems and public agencies).

The vast majority of the relatively powerless are uninvolved in questions of governance or management. While a large percentage of the uninvolved may agree with the revolutionary critique, and may admire the brilliance and courage of progressive leaders, they see the social situation as either unchangeable or insufficiently objectionable to merit joining the revolutionaries in its overthrow. The uninvolved, too, have their own ideology of comfort. Though this belief system is different from the prevailing ideology of the haves, it is complementary to the extent that it, too, serves as a bulwark against change.

Finally, the people whom the British would call working-class Tories form a small minority of the powerless who firmly believe in the rectitude of the status quo and, particularly, in the legitimacy of the rule of the haves. These "Archie Bunkers" accept the prevailing ideology book, chapter, and verse—even concurring in the haves' assumption of their own inferiority.

In a democratic society, the haves typically garner the support of working-class Tories, and the acquiescence of enough of the uninvolved, to win elections. Progressives occasionally prevail during times of crisis when they are able to mobilize the support of the uninvolved. In voluntary organizations, the process is similar, but the power of the haves is far greater because progressives and revolutionaries tire and opt out of such systems. In private work organizations, the struggle is almost entirely between haves and progressives because, typically, ruling groups need not worry about building a popular majority.

Some Conclusions

This analysis refocuses attention on the central problem of leading change. The current focus of leadership studies in business has a misplaced emphasis on helping haves (corporate leaders) overcome resistance among the have-lesses and have-nots in their organizations. As we see from the foregoing analysis—and from the examples of Drucker, Deming, and Owen—the far greater problem is overcoming resistance among the haves. In fact, it is progressives inside and outside corporations who face resistance from the people who have the most power to resist: the established leaders.

In all instances in modern society, then, change is exceptional. When it comes about, it does so primarily as a response to outside forces. It may also occasionally occur through shifts in values—say, as a result of social learning "when the time is ripe." And most rarely, it may come about as the result of leadership. But in no case does it come about readily. Indeed, if the anthropologists' conclusions about traditional societies can be extended to complex ones, a world in which change is the rule would be characterized by chaos leading to social collapse. Therefore, a society must have one foot permanently on the brake; it must have a predisposition to tradition and conservatism.

Herein lies the rub: the source of resistance to "bad," frivolous, and dangerous change is the same as the resistance to "good," necessary, and positive change. The ideology of comfort draws no distinction between resisting the calls of a Hitler to change society, on the one hand, and resisting the calls of a Churchill to resist Hitler, on the other. Advanced societies thus become as resistant to progress as small-scale, tradition-bound communities.

In essence, then, the challenge in a modern nation or organization is for leaders to distinguish for their fellow haves the differences between moral and immoral, virtuous and evil, and true and false change. We saw in the first part of this book that the natural conservatism of groups can only be overcome by a leader's appeal to a manifestly moral necessity. The leader must convince the people with power of the rectitude of the proposed change. Even more, the leader must be able to show that the proposed change is a necessary step toward progress *as defined by the haves.*

This is the most difficult challenge of leadership. Bringing about change without imposing one's will on others is a paradoxical, but not impossible, art to master. In both statecraft and the craft of business, there are numerous examples of men and women who have overcome the resistance to change by virtue of their moral leadership. This values-based leadership may not be for everyone, but it is the only course open to leaders who wish to be effective agents of change.

Georges Comes to the Park

Creating Order Through Design, Composition, Tension, Balance, and Harmony

"Putting it together, bit by bit. . . ."

—Stephen Sondheim

"Bring order to the whole through design, composition, tension, balance, . . . and harmony." With that stirring mandate, the late nineteenth century painter Georges Seurat began work on his masterpiece *Sunday Afternoon on the Island of La Grande Jatte*. At least, those are the words composer and lyricist Stephen Sondheim puts in the mouth of the character Georges Seurat in the modern musical "Sunday in the Park with George." What the real Seurat actually said is lost to us. Nonetheless, Sondheim/Seurat's words ring true. Isn't all art the creation of order through design, composition, tension, balance, and harmony?

And what is true for painting, sculpture, architecture, music, poetry, fiction, drama—and Sondheim's own metier, popular opera—is true as well for the liberal arts of philosophy and history, the social sciences, and even for the sciences themselves. Consider Einstein' bringing order to our understanding of the physical universe with his equation "energy equals mass times the speed of light squared." There it is: design, composition, tension, balance, and harmony.

As we began with leadership lessons found in a painting by James Ensor, balance and composition dictate that we end with leadership lessons found in Seurat's "Sunday," which he finished about two years before Ensor began work on *Christ's Entry into Brussels in 1889*. The question Seurat's painting raises for us is this: Isn't leadership like all purposeful human activity (art, science, education, religion, politics, family, and community life) in that it involves the processes of design, composition, tension, balance, and harmony? Isn't the leadership of a great company an integrated whole much like a great work of art? Aren't the strategies, structures, policies, programs, objectives, behavior, and values of a great company—of *each* great company—all of a piece?

If so, this means that each company is different and unique with an order or culture all its own. For example, Pepsi-Cola and Coca-Cola are both great companies, even though their cultures are almost antithetical. Thus, there are no universal laws or rules of management, and in this regard, contingency theory is accurate. Yet, those two companies are alike in the way the two great paintings of Seurat and Ensor are alike. That is, both manifest the common qualities of design, composition, tension, balance, and harmony. These two paintings—completely different in form, style, subject, and substance—are at the same time similar in that they are each so well composed, so well integrated.

Like the task of the painter, it is the role of leadership to make a company composed and integrated, to make certain it does all the things that must be done in ways that are coherent and mutually consistent. When the late Thornton Bradshaw was president of ARCO, he saw the role of corporate leadership as balancing conflicting tensions. As early as 1970, he argued that managers must create a consistent set of principles to guide the corporation in dealing with the conflicting values and needs of its stakeholders. When a young manager once asked Bradshaw about ARCO's culture, Bradshaw's reply paralleled the artistic integration sought by Seurat, "The culture must all be of a single fabric. From the company's social posture, through the way it treats its employees, to the care it takes in the artistic decor and style of its buildings—everything must manifest a commitment to quality, to excellence, to service, and to meeting the aspirations of our owners, workers, customers, and the broader society."

The problem, of course, is that such strategic unity is elusive exactly because corporate stakeholders have different aspirations, that is, different values. In fact, the challenge of reconciling conflicting values is common to all leaders. Consider a political leader who wishes to introduce a system of health care that would be widely perceived as fair by the many competing constituencies of her country. Those citizens whose highest value is *liberty* will demand a system free of government interference in the individual's choice of doctors and hospitals. Those who value *equality* will call for universal coverage on the grounds that each citizen has a right to health care. Those who value *economic ends*—for example, a high standard of living—will demand a system, the financing of which does not jeopardize the ability of the nation's key industries to compete efficiently in world markets. And those who value *quality of life* issues will demand a system that encourages personal responsibility for maintaining health—for example, by not smoking, not eating animal fats, and the like.

What is such a leader to do? By pandering to just one of those vocal constituencies, she would alienate the others. If she tries to strike a wishy-washy compromise among them, she would achieve no better than deadlock. But she must act. She must decide. After all, leaders must lead. But how?

Great leaders recognize that the perpetual lot of institutions in modern, democratic societies is flux and spirited disagreement among those with conflicting values. Conflict, tension, and turmoil are the order of the day—today and tomorrow. Thus, great leaders recognize that there is no single truth, no final answer, and that the process of leadership is a never-ending struggle to balance the constant and never-abating demands of those with different objectives. Utopia is simply impossible to achieve in a society in which there are different values. In pluralistic societies, the process of leadership is for now and forever a dynamic process—each person or group sometimes gaining, sometimes losing. But if leadership is to be seen as legitimate, every member of the system will expect at all times to be treated fairly and with respect. Because it is not possible to ignore, nor to completely satisfy, the conflicting demands of all constituencies, leaders live in a state of perpetual tension. Poor leaders cannot tolerate this discomfiting posture, and they attempt to resolve the tension by either giving in to the demands of those who are most powerful, or by issuing a command that represents their own will.

There is another way: the values-based leadership described in this book. At its core, the process of values-based leadership is the creation of moral symmetry among those with competing values. Significantly, that entails something far more difficult to achieve than mere compromise. While values-based leadership requires listening to all sides, it equally demands being dictated to by no one side. Instead, values-based leadership brings order to the whole by creating transcendent values that provide a tent large enough to hold all the different aspirations, and in which all can find satisfaction. It is possible therefore for the political leader to create a health care system that will appeal to common, higher-order values that transcend the narrow self-interest of her conflicting constituencies. Hence, the task is to lead through the processes of design, composition, tension, balance, and harmony. It might be argued that such leadership is so rare as not to exist. But it *has* existed in this country: witness the Rushmoreans.

Such leadership exists today in the Czech Republic. President Vaclav Havel not only has declared the need for a system of transcendent values to "bring order to the whole" world, he has demonstrated by his own actions how such leadership can be practiced. What is his secret? Havel's leadership is not based on specialized knowledge: he is not an expert in finance, not an experienced administrator, not a trained lawyer, and has never served in Parliament. Yet he is both a moral and effective leader of the Czechs whose legitimacy is accepted by his supporters and political rivals alike. That legitimacy was not won by pandering to the wants of the least-common denominator, nor was it won by command. Most of all, Havel is not an indecisive, touchy-feely leader. He made tough decisions throughout his career and went to jail rather than compromise his principles.

Havel's example shows us that leaders must decide. What separates effective and moral leaders from the ineffective and immoral is *how* they make those decisions. When Havel chooses a course of action, the decision process always is based on the principle of what he calls "civility," which is the collective practice of respect for people. The most difficult decision he has made—presiding over the dissolution of Czechoslovakia—was an exercise in such civility. Rather than imposing his will (or the will of the stronger Czechs) on the misguided Slovaks, he stood aside while half his nation chose independence. After numerous appeals to common sense failed, Havel reluctantly bid Godspeed and farewell to his Slovak cousins rather than engaging them in a costly war, which would have wasted in destruction the resources both countries needed to recover from the mismanagement of their former communist masters. Few leaders in history have chosen peace over war under these circumstances. Havel practiced civility. Havel respected the Slovaks.

On July 4, 1994, Havel received the Philadelphia Liberty Medal at Independence Hall. There, in a widely quoted address, he explained the practical leadership function of transcendent values. In a world rent by ethnic discord and ideological diversity,

> [t]he central political task of the final years of this century . . . is the creation of a new model of coexistence among the various cultures, peoples, races, and religious spheres within a single interconnected civilization. Many people believe that this can be accomplished through technical means—the invention of new organizational, political, and diplomatic instruments.
>
> Yes, it is clearly necessary to invent organizational structures appropriate to the multicultural age. But such efforts are

doomed to failure if they do not grow out of something deeper, out of generally held values.

In searching for the most natural source for the creation of a new world order, we usually look to an area that is the traditional foundation of modern justice and a great achievement of the modern age: to a set of values that were first declared in this building. I am referring to respect for the unique human being and his or her liberties and inalienable rights, and the principle that all power derives from the people. I am referring to the fundamental ideas of modern democracy.

Havel admitted that even building on those necessary fundamental values would be insufficient to create a large-enough tent under which all of humankind's warring ethnic factions could find comfort and repose. But those values are more than sufficient for the narrower leadership tasks men and women face in modern Western nations and organizations. We can see that his own leadership in the Czech Republic is based on those values of democratic pluralism: decency, reason, responsibility, tolerance, and human rights. What is of singular importance is that Havel does not attempt to micromanage the Czech polity or economy. He is a leader who trusts the quotidian affairs of the nation to a group of other leaders who share his values. And those values should be the starting place for corporate leaders who wish to apply Havel's approach to the task of leading business organizations—a far simpler task than leading a nation out from under communist tyranny, let alone leading the world to ethnic harmony.

Are there corporate Havels? The examples given in this book offer positive encouragement to those who believe there are, or can be, such leaders. As *Christ's Entry into Brussels in 1889* illustrates, there is no longer a need to lead by command, manipulation, or paternalism. The alternative is Havel's values-based leadership, which is an art that can be learned. In Stephen Sondheim's words, one begins acquiring this art much as one does any art, by "putting it together, bit by bit, piece by piece." If one wishes to learn this particular art, the first piece that must be put into place is personal acknowledgment that no other form of leadership can be both moral and effective. Once a leader makes that difficult commitment, all the other pieces will eventually fall into place, bit by bit.

Notes and References

· ·

Christ Comes to Brussels

There is no single source to turn to for an adequate elucidation of James Ensor's *Christ's Entry into Brussels in 1889* (as the Getty Museum now officially titles the painting). Indeed, it is hard even to find a decent reproduction of the painting. I picked up a book with a fair reproduction in a remainders bin: Jacques Janssens's *James Ensor* (Bonfini Press, Switzerland, 1978). The Getty Museum circulates informal "notes on the collection," and I found a brief one on Ensor written by Jennifer Helvey to be useful. Here and there, passing references to Ensor in texts on art history all pretty much agree that the theme of the painting is the "isolation of the artist," and that Ensor personally suffered from "alienation" based on the fact that nobody noticed him. Well, somebody did: when the painting was finally displayed publicly in 1927, the King of Belgium granted Ensor a barony!

p. 9, *James MacGregor Burns explains:* J. M. Burns, *Leadership,* Harper Torchbooks, 1978, p. 4.

p. 10, *Madison wrote that the effective democratic leader:* J. Madison, "The Federalist," paper number 10.

p. 14, *In the words of John Kenneth Galbraith:* J. K. Galbraith, *The New Industrial State, Second Edition,* Mentor, 1971, p. 38.

Chapter One

In this chapter, my primary sources are (in general and on Washington in particular) James MacGregor Burns's *The Vineyard of Liberty*

(Knopf, 1981) and Alf J. Mapp's two volume biography of Jefferson: *Thomas Jefferson: A Strange Case of Mistaken Identity* (Madison, 1987) and *Thomas Jefferson: Passionate Pilgrim* (Madison, 1991). For TR, I have drawn on David McCullough's *Mornings on Horseback* (Simon & Schuster, 1980) and Edmund Morris's *The Rise of Theodore Roosevelt* (Coward, McCann & Geoghegan, 1979). On Lincoln, my sources are Gary Willis's *Lincoln at Gettysburg* (Simon & Schuster, 1993) and Gore Vidal's *Lincoln* (Random House, 1984). Some may find the latter to be "cheating" on my part. Actually, it was the only source I could find that dealt with Lincoln's leadership as other than hagiography.

p. 19, *readers who resisted the changes:* T. J. Peters and R. H. Waterman, *In Search of Excellence*, Harper & Row, 1982.

p. 22, *the socialist Eugene V. Debs:* B. Miroff, *Icons of Democracy*, Basic Books, 1993, pp. 159–160.

p. 25, *abolitionist William Lloyd Garrison castigated:* J. MacGregor Burns, *Leadership*, Basic Books, 1993, pp. 191–192.

p. 25, *leading James Russell Lowell to observe:* J. MacGregor Burns, 1993, pp. 191–192.

p. 27, *"It's good to be the king,":* Mel Brooks, "History of the World, Part I."

p. 29, *Historian David M. Kennedy points out:* D. M. Kennedy, "Hollow to the Core: Leaders Appear Morally Bankrupt," *Los Angeles Times*, May 10, 1992.

p. 29, *Madison argued that the role of leadership:* J. Madison, "The Federalist," paper number 10.

p. 30, *His vice president, John Adams, wrote:* A. J. Mapp, 1991, p. 257.

p. 30, *According to Alf Mapp:* A. J. Mapp, 1991, p. 266.

p. 31, *Jefferson's grandson wrote:* A. J. Mapp, 1991, p. 257.

p. 31, *Roosevelt had it right when he said:* R. V. Friedenberg, *Theodore Roosevelt and the Rhetoric of Militant Decency*, Greenwood Press, 1990.

p. 31, *Jefferson offered the following retort:* A. J. Mapp, 1991, p. 266.

p. 32, *John Stuart Mill, perhaps the finest explicator:* J. S. Mill, *Autobiography*, Bobbs-Merrill, 1957, p. 126.

p. 32, *Far from being as poetic as Lincoln:* D. McCullough, 1980.

p. 32, *Even the cerebral and publicly shy Jefferson:* A. J. Mapp, 1991.

p. 33, *eloquent refutation of Henry Kissinger's:* H. Kissinger, *Diplomacy*, Simon & Schuster, 1994.

p. 34, *James MacGregor Burns, reminds us:* J. MacGregor Burns, 1978, pp. 106–112.

p. 36, *In a State of the Union address, he sought:* G. Will, "Rhetorical Presidency," *Newsweek*, Feb. 8, 1993.

Chapter Two

Much of what I report in this chapter I learned at the source. Unless otherwise indicated, all facts, data, and quotes are derived from corporate publications and unpublished corporate documents, from interviews with the leaders cited or with employees of their organizations.

p. 38, *After the settlement, he told Solomon:* S. D. Solomon, "The Bully of the Skies Cries Uncle," *New York Times Magazine,* September 5, 1993, p. 12.

pp. 38–41, For more on the amazing Frances Hesselbein, see Laura Sharper Walters's "A Leader Redefines Management," *The Christian Science Monitor,* September 22, 1992; Patricia O'Toole's "Thrifty, Kind—and Smart as Hell," *Lear's,* October 1990, p. 26; and R. Todd Erkel's "One Tough Cookie," *Pitt Magazine,* October 1990.

p. 40, *In a 1990 Business Week cover story:* "Profiting from the Nonprofits," *Business Week,* March 26, 1990.

pp. 42–49, All Max De Pree quotes are from De Pree's *Leadership Is an Art* (Doubleday, 1989). Much of what is here appears in different form in my Foreword to that book.

pp. 46–49, I draw heavily on Warren Bennis's *On Becoming a Leader* (Addison-Wesley, 1989).

p. 47, *Ralph Waldo Emerson's "inner voice":* W. Bennis, 1989.

p. 50, *The company's fine new CEO, J. Kermit Campbell:* R. Rosen, *Healthy Companies Newsletter,* No. 4, Jossey-Bass.

p. 50, *When Campbell first took the job of CEO:* R. Rosen (as above).

pp. 51–53, I draw here on interviews with Forrest Behm. Houghton speaks articulately for himself in his speech "Leadership's Challenge: The New Agenda for the '90s," reprinted in *Planning Review,* September/October 1992, p. 8, and in "World-Class Quality," *The TQM Magazine,* 1991, 3(1), p. 27.

p. 53, The description of Erwin Ceramics is taken from Robert Levering's and Milton Moskowitz's *The 100 Best Companies to Work for in America* (Doubleday, 1993), pp. 75–77.

p. 54, *in the words of Horace Mann:* H. Mann, "The Importance of Universal, Free, Public Education," In M. Mann (ed.), *Lectures and Annual Reports on Education,* Vol. 3, 1867.

pp. 54–57, I draw here on lengthy profiles of Galvin and Motorola in my book *Vanguard Management* (Doubleday, 1985).

p. 56, *"Our challenge is to continually evidence:* R. Galvin, *The Idea of Ideas,* Motorola University Press, 1991, p. 12.

p. 57, *His Moments of Truth offers a quintessential overview:* J. Carlzon, *Moments of Truth,* Harper & Row, 1987.

p. 61, Simler profile can be found in "Diary of an Anarchist," *The Economist,* June 26, 1993, p. 66.

pp. 63–64, I draw on an interview with Ernie Savoie and on R. T. Pascale's *Managing on the Edge* (Simon & Schuster, 1990).

pp. 66–68, Profiles are adapted from my article, "Do Good, Do Well: The Business Enterprise Trust Awards," *California Management Review*, 1991, 33(3).

p. 69, *but as described in Joline Godfrey's*: J. Godfrey, *Our Wildest Dreams*, Harper-Business, 1992.

pp. 69–70, Larry Lewis used to be in the same law firm where my wife is a partner. But I got the anecdote about the press conference from an article by Steve Lowery in the *Long Beach Press-Telegram*.

pp. 71–76, Information—including the De Pree, Morland, and Reeves quotes—is recycled from my book *Vanguard Management*.

Chapter Three

All references to Plato's *The Republic* can be found in Books II and VII.

p. 81, Time *magazine's Jay Branegan reports*: J. Branegan, "Is Singapore a Model for the West?" *Time*, January 18, 1993, p. 36.

p. 81, *in the wake of Marxism's demise*: J. Branegan, 1993, p. 36 (in which Fukuyama is quoted).

pp. 82–83, Lee quotes are from a widely reported speech he gave in the Philippines in late 1992.

pp. 83–84, *Here's how Doug Allen, a management professor*: T. Mulligan, "It's All a Matter of How to Crack Whip," *Los Angeles Times*, April 3, 1993, Business Section.

pp. 84–85, For experiment results, see Robert R. Blake's and Jane S. Mouton's "Effective Crisis Management," *New Management*, 1985, 3(1), p. 14.

p. 90, *In June 1994, syndicated columnist Cal Thomas*: From Cal Thomas's syndicated column, which appeared on the op-ed page of the *Los Angeles Times* on June 9, 1994.

pp. 93–94, Information about Kazarian is from Adam Bryant's "Behind the Mutiny at Sunbeam-Oster," *New York Times*, January 16, 1993, Business Section.

Chapter Four

p. 102, *what philosopher Mary Midgley terms "moral isolationism."*: M. Midgley, *Heart and Mind*, St. Martin's Press, 1981, pp. 69–74. I thank Kenneth Goodpaster for calling my attention to this piece.

p. 102, *Midgley illustrates this latter point*: M. Midgley, 1981, pp. 69–74.

p. 105, *in the words of contemporary philosopher Mario Bunge:* M. Bunge, "A Critical Examination of the New Sociology of Science," *Philosophy of the Social Sciences*, 1991, 21(4), p. 524.

p. 107, *even Gary Wills, whose adherence to contingency theory:* G. Wills, *Certain Trumpets*, Simon & Schuster, 1994.

pp. 109–122, I draw here on a variety of sources: all of the positive information about Welch can be found in Noel Tichy's and Stratford Sherman's *Control Your Own Destiny or Someone Else Will* (Doubleday, 1993). Sherman's 1989 cover story "Inside the Mind of Jack Welch" (March 27, 1989) and the January 25, 1993, cover "Jack Welch's Lesson for Success" bracket *Fortune's* one-sided reporting of the rise of Welch. Not until September 5, 1994, did *Fortune* find fault with their unflawed CEO: Terence Paré's "Jack Welch's Nightmare on Wall Street" (pp. 40–48) concluded that it was Welch's leadership that had created the environment in which the Kidder scandal could occur ("Like it or not, the scandals at Kidder Peabody were brought on by GE's management").

pp. 113–114, It is instructive to view Warren Bennis's interviews with Welch and De Pree. I have spent many fruitful hours with the uncut tapes. The edited versions are available from Video Publishing House of Schaumburg, Illinois.

p. 121, Data on GE from Terence Paré's *Fortune* article (cited above).

p. 122, *my former colleague Morgan McCall calls attention:* McCall showed a transparency with these two quotes at a seminar for the Dwight D. Eisenhower Leadership Development Program at the University of Southern California on December 7, 1993.

p. 124, *It was first expressed by the Chinese philosopher Lao-tzu:* W. Bynner (trans.), *The Way of Life According to Laotzu*, Berkley, 1986.

Chapter Five

p. 129, *He was one of the first U.S. managers to observe:* The Haggerty quote is from an old TI training film.

pp. 138–140, *In a controversial article in the* Harvard Business Review: J. B. Rosener, "Ways Women Lead," *Harvard Business Review*, November 1990.

Chapter Six

pp. 143–144, A much abbreviated version of Drucker's description can be found in P. Drucker, *The Ecological Vision*, Transaction, 1993, Chapter 24.

p. 144, *In Leadership Jazz:* M. De Pree, *Leadership Jazz*, Doubleday, 1992.

p. 145, "As a conductor I am utterly: M. Swed, "From Protégé to Mentor," Los Angeles Times, May 29, 1994.

p. 145, in a May 1994 interview: M. Swed, 1994.

p. 147, "I have no doubt: R. Dahl, Democracy and Its Critics, Yale University Press, 1989.

p. 147, Though he admits: R. Dahl, 1989.

p. 148, As Max De Pree explains: M. De Pree, 1989, pp. 22–23.

p. 148, As the statesman Harlan Cleveland writes: H. Cleveland, Birth of a New World, Jossey-Bass, 1993.

p. 148, In the words of Vaclav Havel: V. Havel, Summer Meditations, Knopf, 1992.

pp. 148–149, "Each of us, no matter: M. De Pree, 1989, p. 24.

Chapter Seven

pp. 155–159, Source for quotes from Stempel is John Simmons's "Robert Stempel: Turning Around 75 Years of GM's Culture," New Management, 1988, 5(4), p. 28.

p. 160, E. F. Schumacher may have been: E. F. Schumacher, Small Is Beautiful, Harper & Row, 1973, p. 38.

p. 167, He showed that outmoded: T. J. Kuhn, The Structure of Scientific Revolutions, New American Library, 1962.

pp. 168–169, The discussion of Evans-Pritchard and Polanyi is a variation on the same theme found in my Vanguard Management, pp. 59–60.

Chapter Eight

This chapter draws on the three best books about General Motors: Peter Drucker's Concept of the Corporation (Mentor Executive Library, 1972), Alfred P. Sloan Jr.'s My Years with General Motors (Doubleday, 1963), and J. Patrick Wright's On a Clear Day You Can See General Motors: John Z. De Lorean's Look Inside the Automotive Giant (Wright Enterprises, 1979). But, even more, I draw on Peter Drucker's autobiography, Adventures of a Bystander (Harper & Row, 1978), for his chapter on "The Professional: Alfred Sloan."

p. 171, Drucker's reply to Bennis's: P. Drucker, 1972, p. 246.

p. 172, The word was first leaked: P. Drucker, 1972, p. 82.

p. 173, "G.M. is an organization of managers: P. Drucker, 1972, p. 249.

p. 174, He answered Drucker in a book: A. P. Sloan, 1963, pp. 52–54.

p. 176, He writes, "And since: A. P. Sloan, 1963, p. xvi.

p. 176, *He writes that GM's great strength:* A. P. Sloan, 1963, p. xvi.

p. 177, *what Daniel Bell calls:* D. Bell, *The Coming of Post-Industrial Society,* Basic Books, 1973.

p. 177, *Sloan writes, "Mr. Durant:* A. P. Sloan, 1963, p. 4.

p. 177, *Sloan concludes that:* A. P. Sloan, 1963, p. 72.

p. 180, *De Lorean contributed:* J. P. Wright, 1979, p. 39.

p. 183, *Galbraith calls this:* J. K. Galbraith, *The Culture of Contentment,* Houghton Mifflin, 1992.

Chapter Nine

This chapter draws on telephone conversations and correspondence with Deming and on Myron Tribus's "Deming's Way" in *New Management,* 1983, *1*(1), p. 22.

p. 189, *In the words of MIT's Myron Tribus:* M. Tribus, 1983, p. 22.

p. 191, *Deming would recall:* "Dr. W. Edwards Deming," interview in *Military Science & Technology,* 1(3). From Deming's personal files; no date or pages.

pp. 191–192, *According to one authoritative account:* M. Tribus, 1983, p. 22.

p. 195, *He recalled that managers:* "Dr. W. Edwards Deming" (as above).

p. 197, *"Special mention must be made:* K. Koyanagi, *The Deming Prize,* Union of Japanese Scientists and Engineers, 1960, p. 8.

p. 197, *Deming himself identified this problem:* "Dr. W. Edwards Deming" (as above).

Chapter Ten

Here are the main sources I mined for the two chapters on Owen: Butt, J. (ed.), *Robert Owen: Prince of Spinners* (David and Charles, 1971) (especially four chapters: Butt, J., "Robert Owen as a Businessman" [study of profitability of New Lanark], pp. 169–214; Fraser, W. H., "Robert Owen and the Workers," pp. 76–98; Browning, M., "Owen as an Educator," pp. 52–78; Ward, J. T., "Owen as a Factory Reformer," pp. 99–134); Cole, G.D.H., *The Life of Robert Owen,* Third Edition (Archon, 1966); Engles, F., *Anti-Dühring* (1878); Engles, F., *Conditions of the Working Class* (1844); Garnett, R. G., *Cooperation and the Owenite Socialist Communities in Britain 1825–1845* (Manchester University Press, 1972); Marx, K., and Engles, F., *The Communist Manifesto* (1848); McCoy, D. R., *The Last of the Fathers*

(Cambridge University Press, 1989); Morton, A. L., *The Life and Ideas of Robert Owen* (International Publishers, 1969); Owen, R. D., *The Life of Robert Owen by Himself* (1857); Owen, R. D., *A New View of Society* (1817); Owen, R. D., *Threading My Way* (1874); Podmore, F., *Robert Owen* (Appleton, 1906); Pollard, S., and Salt, J. (eds.), *Robert Owen: Prophet of the Poor* (Bucknell University Press, 1971) (especially four chapters: Tsuzuki, C., "Robert Owen and Revolutionary Politics," pp. 13–38; Garnett, R. G., "Robert Owen and the Community of Experts," pp. 39–64; Silver, H., "Owen's Reputation as an Educationist," pp. 65–83; Hasselmann, E., "The Impact of Owen's Ideas on German Social and Cooperative Thought During the Nineteenth Century," pp. 285–305); Tawney, R. H., *The Radical Tradition* (Minerva Press, 1964).

p. 206, *One critic wrote that:* G.D.H. Cole, 1966, p. 187.

p. 206, *In the memorable words of one:* G.D.H. Cole, 1966, p. 187.

p. 207, *"Owen," writes his first biographer:* F. Podmore, 1906, p. 196.

p. 208, *"All experience proves:* F. Podmore, 1906, p. 22.

p. 210, *There, "he seems to have found:* F. Podmore, 1906, p. 284.

p. 214, *In 1848, he urged the French masses:* G.D.H. Cole, 1966, p. 63.

Chapter Eleven

p. 215, *One critic of his day wrote:* G.D.H. Cole, 1966, p. 167.

p. 215, *the conclusion shared by several biographers:* G.D.H. Cole, 1966, p. 12.

p. 216, *As G.D.H. Cole reminds us:* G.D.H. Cole, 1966, pp. 166–167.

pp. 216–217, *"It was Owen's habitual practice:* G.D.H. Cole, 1966, p. 215.

p. 218, *but Cole suggests otherwise:* G.D.H. Cole, 1966, p. 6.

p. 218, *A modern observer writes:* J. Butt (ed.), 1971, p. 13.

p. 218, *"For a master manufacturer:* F. Podmore, 1906, p. 193.

p. 219, *While leftist journals described him:* W. H. Fraser, "Robert Owen and the Workers." In J. Butt (ed.), 1971, p. 77.

p. 219, *Marx wrote to Engels:* C. Tsuzuki, "Robert Owen and Revolutionary Politics." In S. Pollard and J. Salt (eds.), 1971, p. 32.

p. 220, *Marx and Engels's characterization of Owen:* E. Hasselmann, "The Impact of Owen's Ideas on German Social and Cooperative Thought During the Nineteenth Century." In S. Pollard and J. Salt (eds.), 1971, p. 287.

p. 221, *As R. H. Tawney noted:* R. H. Tawney, 1964, p. 32.

p. 222, *Cole reports that:* G.D.H. Cole, 1966, p. 21.

p. 222, *Madison, according to his recent biographer:* D. R. McCoy, 1989, p. 206.

p. 223, *One widely quoted former worker said:* J. T. Ward, "Owen as a Factory Reformer." In J. Butt (ed.), 1971, p. 110.

p. 224, *Tawney, who shared Owen's values, described:* R. H. Tawney, 1964, pp. 37–38.

p. 224, *In Owen's old age, Emerson reputedly asked:* Anecdote about Emerson in *Encyclopaedia Britannica* biography of Owen.

Chapter Twelve

All references to John Stuart Mill are from *On Liberty*, which was published in 1859, just two years after Owen's autobiography, *The Life of Robert Owen by Himself*, reached the public. Despite the similarities of the two authors' opinions on the subject of this chapter, there is no evidence that either influenced the other's thinking. Thus, we should not believe that Mill had Owen in mind as his model of the brilliant eccentric whose ideas are rejected by the despotic tyranny of majority opinion. In fact, Mill's exemplar was his own socially misunderstood self! Still, I suggest that Owen is a better example of the phenomenon that Mill described than was Mill himself.

p. 232, *the four notables profiled by Lytton Strachey:* L. Strachey, *Eminent Victorians*, Wiedenfeld and Nicolson, 1988.

Chapter Thirteen

The works referenced in this chapter are Karl Mannheim's *Ideology and Utopia, Harvest Fourth Edition* (Harcourt Brace & Co., 1965), Colin Turnbull's *The Mountain People* (Simon & Schuster, 1972), and Francis Bacon's 1620 classic, the *Novum Organum*.

Georges Comes to the Park

This chapter raises the question of how leaders create moral symmetry among competing values. I address this question in a book that in many ways is a companion piece to this volume: *The Executive's Compass: Business and the Good Society* (Oxford University Press, 1993).

pp. 256–257, *Bradshaw's reply paralleled:* This quote is from my *Vanguard Management*, p. 46.

General Bibliography of Books Not Cited Above

Helen S. Astin and Carole Leland, *Women of Influence, Women of Vision*. San Francisco: Jossey-Bass, 1991.

Warren Bennis, *Why Leaders Can't Lead: The Unconscious Conspiracy Continues*. San Francisco: Jossey-Bass, 1989.

Warren Bennis and Burt Nanus, *Leaders: The Strategies for Taking Charge*. New York: Harper & Row, 1985.

Dorothy W. Cantor and Toni Bernay, *Women in Power*. Boston: Houghton Mifflin, 1992.

John Kenneth Galbraith, *The Culture of Contentment*. Boston: Houghton Mifflin, 1992.

John Gardner, *On Leadership*. New York: Free Press, 1989.

Charles Handy, *The Age of Paradox*. Cambridge, Mass.: Harvard Business School Press, 1994.

Rosabeth M. Kanter, *The Change Masters*. New York: Simon & Schuster, 1983.

Edward E. Lawler III, *High-Involvement Management*. San Francisco: Jossey-Bass, 1986.

Edward E. Lawler III, *The Ultimate Advantage*. San Francisco: Jossey-Bass, 1992.

Morgan McCall, Michael M. Lombardo, and Anne M. Morrison, *The Lessons of Experience*. New York: Lexington Books, 1988.

Douglas McGregor, *The Human Side of Enterprise*. New York: McGraw-Hill, 1985.

Will McWhinney, *Paths of Change*. Newbury Park, Calif.: Sage, 1992.

Richard Mason and Ian Mitroff, *Challenging Strategic Assumptions*. New York: Wiley-Interscience, 1981.

Burt Nanus, *The Leader's Edge*. Chicago: Contemporary Books, 1989.

Burt Nanus, *Visionary Leadership*. San Francisco: Jossey-Bass, 1992.

George Odiorne, *The Change Resisters*. Englewood Cliffs, N.J.: Prentice-Hall, 1981.

Tom Peters, *Thriving on Chaos*. New York: Knopf, 1987.

Robert H. Waterman, *The Renewal Factor*. New York: Bantam, 1989.

Index